SRT
DIVER

by
Mark V. Lonsdale

Additional Books by
Mark V. Lonsdale

Raids
CBQ (Close Quarter Battle)
Sniper Countersniper
Sniper II
Advanced Weapons Training
Bodyguard

Check out our website at

www.sttu.com

SRT DIVER

DIVER

A GUIDE FOR
SPECIAL RESPONSE TEAMS

by

Mark V. Lonsdale

S.T.T.U.

DISCLAIMER

The author, STTU and those who contributed to this book take no responsibility for the use or misuse of material herein.

SRT DIVER was written as a guide for qualified and experienced law enforcement and military personnel, with no intention of contradicting their current agencies' policies.

SRT diving and training is a potentially dangerous activity that could lead to serious injury and death if not properly organized and supervised. The training methods and techniques indicated in this book should be undertaken by selected and trained personnel only, under the strict supervision of qualified instructors and diving supervisors. Each and every individual involved in SRT diving operations should act as a safety officer, and be constantly alert for any potential safety violations.

Although this book covers many aspects of diving it is not a basic diving manual and does not cover the physics, physiology or mechanics of diving. It is intended for use by divers and administrators with an already advanced knowledge of basic SCUBA diving. SRT DIVER is an overview of police diving and should be used only as a guide and not a training manual.

SRT DIVER
First Printing October 1989
Second Printing February 1993
Revised Edition July 1999

ISBN 0-939235-02-1

Library of Congress Catalog Card Number 89-92319

PRINTED IN THE UNITED STATES OF AMERICA

Dedicated
to the memory of
Dean Westgaard

ACKNOWLEDGEMENTS

Throughout my diving career, and especially while doing the research for SRT DIVER, I have had the pleasure of meeting many fine individuals involved in this specialized field. The following is just a brief list of those individuals and agencies that contributed, sometimes unknowingly, to the material in this book. To all of you, and those I may have forgotten, my sincerest thanks and I look forward to diving with you again in the near future.

Dr. Glen Egstrom, UCLA/SEB Marine Company 218
Bill Angioni, Los Angeles County Sheriff's SEB/ESD
Lt. Mike Quinn, Los Angeles County Sheriff's Office
Tony Rouhotas, Imperial County Sheriff's URT
Thomas M. Riley, USFWS, Division of Law Enforcement
Mike Von Alvensleben, SBCC Marine Technology
Lt. Leo Robichaud, Kodiak ASAP/Fire Department
Lt. Rick Neal, Charlotte County Sheriff's Office
Julius Wiggins, Miami Police Department/A.I.R. Specialties
Mike Gast, Metro-Dade Police Underwater Recovery Unit
Det. Robert Foley, Broward County Sheriff's Office
James Billberry, Miami PD Bomb Squad
Captain Dale Riedel, NYPD Harbor Unit
Sgt. Paul Stiso, NYPD SCUBA Unit
James A. Corry, US Secret Service/NASAR
Jim Joiner, College of Oceaneering
Steven J. Linton, Dive Rescue International
Mike Pelissier, Ocean Technology Systems
Jeff Bozanic, NSS-CDS Cave Rescue Team
Capt. Dan Tomlinson, Three Rivers Dive Rescue Team
Jarrod Jablonski, GUE/WKPP

Artwork by William Abell (pages xviii, 115, 202, 238, 324) and available from Sports Ink, P.O. Box 943, Monroe, WA 98272

PHOTOGRAPHIC CREDITS

Special thanks must go to all the divers, agencies and photographers who submitted photographs during the research for SRT DIVER. The photos used have added greatly to the quality and value of this text, and those not utilized will be kept on file at STTU for future reference.

Those photos not listed are the work of the author or STTU staff. Those contributed by other photographers are listed below by page number and location.

KEY — If there is more than one photo to a page they will be identified as follows:

T=top;   B=bottom;   C=center;   R=right;   L=left

Cover: Mark V. Lonsdale
Back Cover: Shelly Rouhotas

Karen K. Lewis — 161, 245, 250, 251, 255, 256, 262B, 263T, 264T, 292, 293, 305T, 323B.

Tony & Shelly Rouhotas — 6, 15, 66T, 74, 75, 78, 79, 80, 81, 82, 83, 162, 164, 206T, 220T, 221B.

Mike Gast/Metro-Dade — 177T, 207B, 212, 215, 216, 217L, 220B, 222B, 225, 226, 227.

Steve M. Barsky, Courtesy Viking America, Inc, — 44, 49, 71T, 267, 278, 319.

Walt Johnson — 165, 166, 167, 168, 169.

Lt. Leo Robichaud — 4, 19T, 34L, 35L, 136, 137T, 144, 145.

RAIDS — 313.

Eric Micheletti — 272, 284.

Yves Debay — 300B.

SIRPA — 286, 290, 300T, 321.

Glen Egstrom — 232, 233.

Jens Rubschlager — 124T.

GUE/Halcyon – 200,201T, 202, 330, 336.

Alan Brosnan — 270, 277, 282, 320.

Jeff Bozanic — 196B, 198T, 199, 200B, 200C, 201.

OTS/Oceanic — 276T, 309B, 322, 323T.

Sillinger— 126, 127T, 138B, 317, 318.

USAF — 3, 34R, 142, 147, 148.

D.S.I. — 55B, 56.

NYPD — 173.

ABOUT THE AUTHOR

Mark Lonsdale is the Director of Training & Studies for STTU with experience in most aspects of police and military special operations training. This includes, but is not limited to, program development and training of public safety diving teams, primarily in the areas of search, rescue, recovery, dignitary protection, EOD identification, narcotics interdiction and maritime tactical operations.

Mark is a former deep saturation commercial diver, and in addition to his duties at STTU, is a Diver, Diving Supervisor and Training Officer for LA Sheriff's SEB Marine Company Dive Team.

Related qualifications include:
- ◆ LA Sheriff's Dive Team & Diving Control Board
- ◆ GUE Technical Diving Instructor
- ◆ NAUI / UCLA Instructor Trainer & Course Director
- ◆ Full Cave & Tri-Mix Certifications
- ◆ Surface Supplied Diving Instructor
- ◆ Former NASAR Spec-Ops Diving Coordinator
- ◆ Oilfield Saturation & Commercial Mixed Gas Diver
- ◆ Top Graduate College of Oceaneering (1977)
- ◆ Special Operations & Maritime Counter Terrorism Instructor

AUTHOR'S NOTE

It is only in recent years that police and public service diving has begun to expand and change for the better. New equipment, new techniques and improved policies and procedures are appearing almost on a weekly basis. Until now, individuals and agencies have adapted sport and commercial diving procedures to suit their individual needs. No longer is this necessary. Books, training groups, instructors and national associations have become available exclusively for the law enforcement diver.

But since SRT diving is in its infancy, these procedures, policies and techniques will continue to be improved, changed, modified and adapted for several years to come. I have attempted to give the reader an overview of U.S. police diving as it stands today. I have drawn on personal experience, the experience of several very qualified individuals and the experiences of several agencies. Even with all this work and research, I feel sure that much has been lost in the shuffle or overlooked.

Agencies and individuals are invited to submit their experiences, procedures, team structure, training programs, photographs, videos or newspaper clippings for inclusion in future editions of this book. SRT DIVER will be updated and revised with each new edition.

Although the photographs in this book show a wide variety of diving equipment being used, it is not my intention to recommend one piece of gear over another. There are several manufacturers of quality equipment that are not represented in this book — it is only unfortunate that we did not happen to have pictures suitable for publication. Manufacturers are invited to submit photos, specifications, or actual equipment for testing, to STTU for possible inclusion in future books.

It must be understood that this book reflects only the views of the author and not those of the agencies that he may be formally or informally associated with. Similarly, many agencies are depicted in the photographs and text in this book, but they had no input or control over the final product, and are not officially associated with STTU or the author.

It is my sincere hope that this book will be of some value to all the dedicated divers and individuals involved in the dirty and dangerous work of rescue/recovery, and are seldom acknowledged for their efforts.

INTRODUCTION

SRT DIVER is the third in a series of books based on the training methods of the SPECIALIZED TACTICAL TRAINING UNIT. The two previous titles, SNIPER COUNTER SNIPER and ADVANCED WEAPONS TRAINING are in use by hundreds of U.S. and overseas law enforcement and military teams, and are considered essential reading for anyone involved in special operations.

It is hoped that SRT DIVER will become an equally valuable text to all law enforcement personnel involved in aquatic rescues, recoveries and investigations.

The material in SRT DIVER is not drawn from the experiences of one team or one instructor but from the experiences of several teams in quite diverse locations. For this text to be of value to all dive teams, the contents must reflect the needs of teams all the way from the frozen north to the tropical south. The hazards of ice diving are unknown to the police divers of Southern California and Florida, just as the ASAP teams of Alaska probably have very little exposure to the toxic wastes that flow from Mexico into the waterways of San Diego and Calexico.

To give the reader a balanced perspective of law enforcement diving in the U.S., the author travelled to several states to dive with different teams, interview the divers and administrators, or simply to observe the teams in training and on operations. Additional material was obtained through telephone interviews, newspaper clippings and photos forwarded by various teams.

Time and space do not allow for an in-depth review of each team's policies and procedures, so the author has attempted to take the best from each. Although procedures are suggested in this text, they will need to be modified to suit local conditions and operational requirements. SRT DIVER is not intended as an A to Z diving manual but more as an overview of police diving that an experienced instructor or team leader can use as a reference. The actual mechanics of diving are left to the certifying agencies, the in-house instructors and books like the U.S. Navy Diving Manual and the NOAA Manual.

No book can stand as a substitute for quality instruction and hands-on experience. For knowledge to be of value, it must be practiced, integrated into existing procedures and then applied at the right time. Although SRT DIVER may give team members several new ideas for training and operations, these techniques must be first practiced to see if they work under local conditions, and then perfected before being applied to an actual operation. There is no substitute for "time in the water."

Several chapters in this book assume that the reader has read previous chapters. It is recommended that the book be read from start to finish, then the reader is free to use individual chapters for reference. For example, Underwater Investigation (Chapter 16) is also touched on in the chapters on Search, Photography, Penetration and Recovery.

STTU training programs place maximum emphasis on tried and proven methods and continuous hard work. For a team to have a high degree of success in diving operations, their priorities must include highly trained and physically fit individuals, regular training days and ruggedly simple equipment. A team that places undue emphasis on high-tech gear and "gadgets" is doomed to fail in the face of adversity.

A law enforcement diving team will often have more applicants than they have available slots. A selection process must be initiated to eliminate all but the fittest and most motivated team players. The fact that an individual may really like diving and have his own gear does not automatically qualify him for the rigors of an SRT team. If STTU has noted one thing over the last few years, that is the number of overweight, unfit individuals that enjoy "playing" on an SRT team. The team, the individual divers and the agency cannot afford the liability of weak personnel involved in hazardous operations.

With the intense pressure placed on an SRT team by the ever-present news media and a concerned public, it is essential that teams constantly strive to expand their knowledge and hone their skills. Hopefully SRT DIVER will help in the first instance and STTU can help in the second.

Mark V. Lonsdale

CONTENTS

I PREPARATION

II DEPLOYMENT

III SAR OPERATIONS

IV TACTICAL OPERATIONS

PART I

PREPARATION

1
ROLE OF THE SRT DIVER

The use of divers by law enforcement and emergency service agencies is not new. Since the fifties and sixties Police, Sheriff's and Fire Departments have called on local divers to recover bodies, evidence and lost property. Since many agencies had keen sport divers or ex-military divers within their own ranks, it was not long before these men formed loose knit diving teams. With time, and a few successful recovery operations, the team finally received official status, but rarely a budget or equipment.

As the recreational use of our public waterways, rivers, lakes and beaches increased so did the number of accidents, fatalities and body recoveries. With increased population densities and the accompanying increased violent crime, more evidence, weapons and murder victims were being dumped into canals, rivers and from piers or boats.

With the influx of drug trafficking and law enforcement's coverage of land routes, the drug runners soon began using the less patrolled swamps, beaches and everglades to move their valuable contraband. Again, planes, boats and evidence were disappearing below the surface of these new drug lanes into the U.S.

Shipboard terrorism, hijacking and drug trafficking meant a need for trained personnel in maritime tactical operations, assault swimming and EOD/bomb search.

Thus the fully equipped, specially trained SRT Diver came to be. Whether it be rescue, recovery, tactical or investigative, the law enforcement community has a very real need for skilled personnel who can operate safely and effectively in an aquatic environment.

OVERVIEW OF U.S. TEAMS

Police/Sheriff: Most municipal, county and state law enforcement agencies with an aquatic environment, be it lakes, rivers, beaches or man-made, have developed a dive capability. It may be as little as two officers with their own SCUBA gear or up to a 36 man team like the NYPD SCUBA Unit, or LA Sheriff's 17-man ESD team supported by a 24 man Reserve Marine Unit. The bulk of their work being body recoveries and evidence searches.

Only the police dive teams of the colder northern States have a realistic chance of rescuing and reviving a near-drowned victim — usually one that has fallen through the ice on a frozen lake or river.

Fire Departments: Along with volunteer Search and Rescue teams, firemen and paramedics have long been the primary responders to non-crime related emergencies. Over the years many fire departments developed dive teams to handle rescues, fires and natural disasters that occurred on or near water. These divers are often requested to assist in all manner of recoveries, especially in areas that have no diving law enforcement agencies.

Coast Guard: The Coast Guard would be most people's first thought when it comes to locating a dive rescue team, but in actual fact, diving is a very limited part of the Coast Guard's capability. Some regions have no in-house divers at all. When the need arises, the Coast Guard will call on, or work in conjunction with, local police and fire dive rescue teams. The Coast Guard resources, ships, helicopters and planes can be of great assistance in a maritime disaster, but the divers that they deploy may well be from another agency.

The Coast Guard does have a number of highly trained divers and rescue swimmers, especially the USCG Atlantic Strike Force Team. This team is airmobile and can respond to any natural or man-made disaster (e.g., ruptured oil tankers), in or near U.S. waters.

Federal Agencies: FBI, US Customs, DEA and other similar investigative and enforcement agencies have long had a use for divers, employed primarily in an investigative mode. In field offices where in-house divers are not available, the federal agency may call on local law enforcement for an assist with underwater investigations.

U.S. Fish and Wildlife Service (USFWS) along with State Fish and Game utilize divers in a wide range of tasks including: wildlife study, investigation of trapping and fishing violations, endangered species relocation, and recovery operations.

N.A.S.A.: The Kennedy Space Center and NASA maintain a 31 man diving team as part of their Off-Site Contingency Operation Team. They are a fully equipped, helicopter mobile team that is responsible for astronaut rescue, should the space shuttle abort into the ocean.

In training, these divers have pulled several full-size dummies from a training orbiter, in 30 feet of water, with extremely limited visibility, within eight minutes — the duration of the astronauts' underwater air supply. It was only bad luck that the 1986 Challenger exploded and did not stay intact long enough for a rescue of the astronauts to be effected.

Military: Apart from the U.S. military's combat divers (SEALS, Special Forces, Rangers, Marine Force Recon) there is also a sizable rescue capability. The U.S. Navy has their Aviation Rescue Swimmer program and the Air Force has the Pararescue team (PJs) that specializes in the rescue and recovery of downed pilots, both in and out of combat zones.

Public Utilities: Many cities and counties that have parks, lakes and reservoirs will support public utilities dive teams. A good example is the City of San Diego Water Utilities team, who serve as combination Park Ranger/Divers. This 30 man team is responsible for toxic weed eradication from the reservoirs, limited law enforcement for the recreational use of the parks and waters, and recovery of vehicles, bodies and lost property that may end up in the lakes.

USAF Pararescue divers (PJs) assist in the recovery of early space capsule.

FUNDING A DIVE TEAM

The old adage of "if something is worth doing it is worth doing well" is a good maxim to live by when establishing a dive team. Good diving equipment is not cheap, and when it comes to equipping a whole team it can get quite expensive. Teams often begin with individuals supplying

3

their own personal SCUBA gear, occasionally with minimal support from their administration or community.

This group of dedicated individuals will only become a team when the agency, state or city gets behind them and allocates the funds for a full set of dive gear for each man, a distinctive team uniform and an adequate training budget.

A cold water rescue team, with a few well publicized "saves" will have no problem getting the civic leaders to dip into the city coffers for financial support. Two divers in Kodiak, Alaska went to the State with their request and were allocated $24,500.00 to establish the ASAP (Arctic Sub-arctic Aquatic Pararescue) team. Large counties and cities realize the need for a dive rescue/recovery team and will hopefully budget for them. Whatever the situation, a little publicity of successful operations, and some quiet PR, can go a long way toward making the community proud of their public service dive team.

Once the Special Response Team is established and equipped there is still the problem of training time. Only limited value can be drawn from classroom training and there is no substitute for hands-on experience and diving under realistic conditions. The dive team should take advantage of every opportunity to get wet, learn new skills and hone old ones. Members should be sent to outside schools for specialty training, or independent instructors can be brought in so that the entire team can benefit from the experience.

Kodiak Alaska ASAP team.

Local swimming pools can be used for basic training, swim conditioning and the testing of new techniques, but the bulk of training must be in an environment similar to that expected on actual operations. Work with specialized equipment like boats, surface-supplied gear, closed-circuit rebreathers, communications systems and helicpoters must be incorporated into the training schedule, on a regular basis, so that all team members can maintain their skills and confidence.

Oftentimes the divers must be prepared to train on weekends, evenings and days off to reach the required professional standard. When the team looks good, performs well in the water and becomes a political asset to the agency, the brass will be more inclined to allocate additional time for training.

*LASD diver recovers drugs/evidence
in a maritime law enforcement exercise.*

MUTUAL AID AGREEMENTS

Inter-agency cooperation and mutual aid for an SRT team could be either diving or non-diving in nature. Many police dive teams depend on local Harbor Patrol or Coast Guard for non-diving aid in the form of diving support vessels. Others may have their own boats but depend on civilian volunteers or commercial charter operators to skipper them.

Smaller municipal agencies, without the funds for their own helicopter, will have to turn to the Coast Guard, Air/Sea Rescue, National Guard or County Aero Bureau for training and support in helicopter operations.

A search and recovery operation can drag on for several hours or several days, and it does not take long to burn up a team's bottom time if the dives are cold, arduous or deep. Mutual aid and training, with the next county or city, will greatly extend a search operation's range and intensity. The aid may be limited to equipment, e.g., extra tanks, communication gear, sonar, boats, helicopters, surface-supplied gear, etc., or extend to divers and support personnel. Whatever the level of assistance, it will require similar standards and procedures, pre-planning, familiarity with signals and adequate rehearsal time.

If local divers are to be deployed in a tactical mode, in support of U.S. Customs drug interdictions, FBI surveillance or Secret Service advance team EOD searches, there should be pre-arranged written procedures detailing the parameters of the specific assistance.

Imperial County Sheriff's Underwater Recovery Team act as safety divers during military testing of amphibious vehicles.

6

2
THE DIVING TEAM

Most public service diving teams are part of a larger agency, and therefore already fall into a particular command structure. For example: Sheriff's Department, Fire Department, Coast Guard, State Police, etc. But a diving team must also have its own unique structure within the parent agency. Even though the dive team ultimately answers to the Chief or Director of the agency, the immediate command element must be part of the team, or at least have an in-depth working knowledge of SRT diving and standard dive procedures.

The following is a break-down of the various elements of a diving operation. On smaller teams one man may serve in several roles, but many teams in the U.S. have over 20 members, requiring a clearly written guideline to each member's role and responsibilities.

TEAM STRUCTURE
Diving Control Board:
All dive teams should have an active Diving Control Board that is essentially an administrative group of select personnel whose expertise can greatly assist the team. The board is responsible for:

- Establishing the team's role within the parent agency
- Establishing policies and procedures
- Setting team standards for fitness, selection and operations
- Selecting/testing new equipment
- Handling the team budget
- Maintaining dive team, equipment and maintenance records
- Liaison with outside agency dive teams
- Disciplinary diving review board
- Selection of the Diving Officer

7

The Diving Control Board could consist of senior agency personnel, a medical officer, highly qualified members of the dive team and definitely the senior Diving Officer.

Diving Officer:

The Diving Officer (DO) can be the most important member of the dive team, since the team's performance will be a reflection of his own personal and professional standards. At a minimum, the Diving Officer should be a certified Divemaster with experience in all aspects of the team's diving responsibilities. The position of DO is definitely a demanding hands-on job for only the most qualified person. His responsibilities include, but are not limited to:

- Interface with the Control Board
- Selection and training of new personnel
- Enforcement of team standards and procedures
- Supervision of equipment repair and maintenance
- Documentation of all training and operations
- Maintenance of team logs, medical records and incident reports
- Supervision of all major diving operations

One of the Diving Officer's primary roles is to insure the safety of the dive team and the safe conduct of all training and diving operations. It is the Diving Officer who has the final say as to whether divers are committed to the water or not, and if and when an operation will be terminated because of hazardous conditions. His word is FINAL!!!

On a large team, with a wide area of responsibility, the Diving Officer may come to depend on a select number of Diving Supervisors and Safety Officers. These men will also need to be dedicated and proficient SRT divers with all the necessary certifications to run an operation in the Diving Officer's absence.

Diving Supervisor:

The Diving Supervisor (DS) is like the Platoon Sergeant in the military — the heart and soul of the operation. Apart from the obvious dive qualifications he must also show good leadership qualities and sound judgment under stressful conditions. The DS will control individual dive teams of 4-10 men involved in a specific task, e.g., a rescue, evidence search or body recovery. Diving Supervisors will be responsible for:

- Supervision of training
- Mobilization of the dive team and equipment
- Site surveys and dive planning
- Pre-dive checks
- Diver selection and rotation for individual operations
- Maintenance of diving and decompression records
- Coordination of on-site personnel

- Termination of operations that become hazardous to the team
- Direction of post-dive equipment maintenance, transportation, storage, etc.

With all the Diving Supervisor's responsibilities he must be careful not to let non-diving related problems distract him from his primary role — **the safety of his divers in and out of the water.**

Divers:

The SRT Diver has responsibilities to both himself and the team. He is ultimately responsible for his own safety and has the option, without recrimination, of refusing to dive if he believes the conditions to be hazardous to his health or beyond his personal capabilities. There will be days when it is his turn to dive but he is feeling under the weather — he must know his own limitations, not let ego get in the way and pass the dive to another team member. To continue with the dive against his own better judgment is to endanger his own life, the life of the diver who will have to recover him and the reputation of the team.

The individual diver's responsibility to the team is to stay in shape for the stresses of diving, maintain his equipment, maintain his diving and rescue skills, and strive to become a more valuable member of the unit.

SRT divers should be certified Advanced and Rescue Divers with strong watermanship skills and thorough training in all aspects of their assignment, be it rescue, recovery, tactical or investigative. All divers should work towards becoming certified Divemasters and be willing to shoulder the responsibilities of supervision. More experienced members of the team may be designated as **Team Leaders** or **Lead Divers** to assist with safety and operations.

Trainee Divers:

Most dive teams have a very low turn-over of personnel due to individual dedication and pride that one draws from being part of a special unit. Nevertheless, there always comes a time to select and train new personnel. Since the selection and training of **competent** divers is quite a long process, it should be done well before the actual need arises.

Potential team members will generally be drawn from the ranks of patrol personnel or from the list of applicants that have shown an interest in the team. The selection and training process is covered in a later section of this book so for now we will restrict ourselves to the trainee diver's role on the team.

The trainee SRT diver should have come to the team as a certified Basic Openwater SCUBA Diver or better. He should have also demonstrated a sound knowledge of the principles of diving, good basic SCUBA skills and strong watermanship. The trainee should be put through a 90-120 day probationary period in which he is taught the fundamentals of Special Response Diving operations, standards and procedures and gets an opportunity to dive with the team to find out if he is suited to this cold, wet and dirty job. The team will also have the opportunity to evaluate the new candidate and decide if he meets their professional standards.

Instructors:
It is an asset if at least one member of the team is a certified SCUBA Instructor and can handle the initial training of new personnel, or work with team members who wish to up-grade their certifications to Master Diver, Divemaster or Assistant Instructor. Be aware that individuals certified to teach SCUBA diving are not necessarily qualified to train SRT divers. Many of the hazardous operations of a rescue/recovery team are far removed from the pleasures of sport diving under ideal conditions. The tactical operations are a whole different ball game again; silent swimming with a full weapons load, possibly a closed-circuit breathing system, in the middle of the night, on a compass bearing is a far cry from Open Water I.

Smaller teams will often have to look to larger agencies, or qualified contract instructors, for the more specialized aspects of SRT diving. Larger teams will have the experience and resources to develop good in-house programs for the training of new divers in their particular job requirements. The Diving Officer may assign a team member as Training Officer even if he is not a certified Instructor. But at a minimum, he should be a very experienced Divemaster or Assistant Instructor with good organizational and communication skills and several years of SRT experience.

Support Personnel:
Many of the non-diving related tasks of the dive team can be handled by support personnel from within the agency, or in cooperation with other agencies. This would include drivers, boat handlers, helicopter pilots, EMT/Paramedics, hoist and crane operators, equipment maintenance and repairmen, crowd control officers, etc.

Boats can often be supplied by Harbor Patrol or County Life Guards, helicopters by Coast Guard or Aero Bureau, equipment maintenance by a local dive shop and heavy lift by local contractors. Even though these are outside support, they must come under complete and total control of the Diving Supervisor when divers are involved or in the water.

TEAM SELECTION

A carefully selected team that maintains the highest standards can be a credit to any agency, but a totally volunteer team with no regard to standards is a very real liability. Although all SRT divers should be volunteers there must still be a selection and screening process.

The prerequisites for a dive team member should be a specific amount of time (1-2 years) on conventional duties to learn the routine agency procedures, basic SCUBA certifications like Open Water I and Rescue Diver, essential first aid/CPR/EMT skills and good physical condition.

From here the individual must submit a full written application, medical history form and a resume of dive related skills and training. Add to this copies of all certifications and log books. The candidate must then submit to:

- A complete dive medical examination by a doctor familiar with the stresses of diving
- An interview by the Diving Control Board
- A written examination on diving and related subjects
- A stress/swim test
- An evaluation of basic SCUBA skills

Apart from any medical limitations the review board should be trying to establish other reasons that would prevent an individual from becoming an asset to the team. These could be:

- A fear of water or height
- A fear of dark or confined spaces
- Lack of mature judgment
- An inability to handle stress
- A dangerous "Hero Complex"
- An inability to function as part of a team
- A lack of practical or mechanical aptitude
- A drinking problem
- A disregard for authority or procedure

The ideal diver is a strong, well adjusted young individual with an affinity for the water, a keen sense of duty and a mature outlook on life. He/she should be able to think for himself, know his limitations, but still function as a part of a team.

Once an individual is accepted onto the team, there should be a probationary period where the diver receives the basic training essential to SRT operations. This 90-120 day period will give the Diving Officer the opportunity to evaluate the trainee as a team member and make the final cut if there are several candidates for only one slot.

Diving Supervisors and Team Leaders should have a minimum certification of SCUBA Divemaster and considerable time and experience with the team. They should be natural leaders with the respect of the dive team and the ability to lead by example.

Pieces of paper and certificates, although necessary, mean very little when it comes to getting in the water and getting the job done. Rank should not automatically give an individual control over a diving operation.

Members of any Special Operations Team, whether it be SWAT, HRT, SAR or Dive Rescue must be subjected to periodic evaluation and recertification. Individuals that do not maintain their health, physical fitness and diving skills must be cut from the team or put on the warning board and given the opportunity to shape up.

FITNESS FOR DIVING

All law enforcement and emergency services personnel should enjoy an above-average level of general fitness. Unfortunately many fall far short of this mark. The fitness levels for SRT divers should be higher than most. Heavy smokers, alcoholics, the grossly over-weight and the non-athletic need not apply.

Diving, by nature, imposes high demands on the human body and unless the diver has conditioned himself to these rigors he could well end up a statistic. General fitness is not sufficient for SRT diving — the diver must condition himself with a dive/swim training program, and all team training and selection should have a stress/exercise factor built into it.

What we are talking about is S.A.I.D. — Specific Adaptation to Imposed Demands. In other words, the training program must develop the **specific** muscles and skills that will better **adapt** the diver to the **imposed demands** of rescue/recovery work.

Whether it be heavy surf, rough seas, extreme cold, extreme heat, strong currents, restrictive gear or mental stress the diver must be fit enough to handle the local conditions. This conditioning, or **specific adaptation,** must be done in training with an anticipation of the future rescue conditions — the **imposed demands.**

One of the unique features of the human body is that the more one increases the work load, the stronger the body becomes. By gradually increasing the duration and intensity of the training dives and swims, the individual will become a fitter, more confident diver. Ample rest and a sensible diet are also essential contributing factors.

This conditioning process is far more than just physical fitness. The diver must also develop the mental fitness to handle the very real stresses of black water diving, deep diving, penetration diving — not to mention the often imaginary stresses of dangerous marine life and "monsters" from the deep. Searching for a decomposing body in sixty feet of cold, murky water, in the middle of winter is not considered a stress-free existence. Nor is having to recover the body of a small child from a sewage pipe as the family grieves topside. Recovering accident victims from a mangled car, after it has crashed through a bridge railing and fallen thirty feet into a fast flowing river, can tax a diver to the limits of physical and mental endurance. There is not the satisfaction of saving a life — only the knowledge and pride that comes with succeeding at a difficult task that others would not even consider.

The SRT diver must be able to make calm, rational decisions under less than ideal, and often stressful conditions. His emergency procedures must be learned and **over-learned** so that he will react correctly in the face of adversity. The Diving Supervisor/Instructor must be ever watchful for the diver that is prone to stress and anxiety. A small amount of stress can be beneficial to the diver but uncontrolled, it will lead to increased heart and respiratory rates, muscle tension and perspiration. This increased energy expenditure can lead to additional problems of involuntary hyperventilation, hypoxia, fatigue, muscle cramps, and panic. With panic comes the loss of a logical thought process, exhaustion and, without help, death.

Stress is either **diver induced** or **situation induced,** but peer pressure is also a significant contributing factor. Humans by nature seek approval and recognition from their peers, and this is compounded when those peers are an elite, competitive group like an SRT team. The peer pressure can be self-imposed by the individual that is striving for acceptance, or team imposed by the group that sets high standards and then watches the new diver with a critical eye. Some people function well under these conditions while others make small mistakes, become stressed and ultimately fail the set task. Trainees being subjected to new skills and diving conditions must be given encouragement and support during the first few training sessions. Only once the skill is learned should they be subjected to the stresses of testing and evaluation.

Even seasoned divers can be stressed when confronted with difficult tasks, but it is more common in the newer team members. A good Diving Supervisor or Team Leader must be aware of the pre-indicators of stress. Before the dive the diver may exhibit some of the following behavioral responses:

- Slow in responding to the dive site
- Forgetting essential equipment
- Excessively slow dressing-in
- Fussing with small equipment adjustments
- Quiet and withdrawn/introverted
- Procrastinating
- Rapid breathing and apprehension
- Making simple mistakes in equipment donning
- Extreme cockiness and macho comments
- A disregard for the apparent dangers of the dive
- Irritability, loss of patience or short temper

In the water there are several good indicators of stress that the dive buddy or stand-by safety diver should be aware of:

- Inefficient swim stroke
- Rapid, shallow breathing
- Excessively heavy breathing

- Wide-eyed expression
- Clinging to objects, lines or boats for security
- Ditching mask and regulator immediately upon breaking surface
- Tunnel vision or object fixation
- Constantly fussing with, or continually readjusting equipment
- Loss of coordination
- Making small procedural mistakes

All of these indicators can lead to increased stress, and if unchecked, panic and death. The Diving Supervisor must be willing to pull a diver from the rotation if he exhibits more than the normal amounts of stress associated with rescue/recovery operations. Continued stress/anxiety related problems are grounds for dismissal from the team, and/or professional counselling in stress reduction.

There are some techniques that can be used by a supervisor to combat stress and anxiety within the team, or when confronted by difficult situations.

- Buddy up the weaker divers with strong, experienced team members (but not arrogant types)
- Be consoling and friendly when necessary
- Answer the diver's questions by accenting the positive
- Fight negative distractors with positive distractors
- Praise and encourage good work and initiative
- Occupy the divers with physical tasks that will take their minds off of the stressors
- Be informative and reinforcing

On a personal level, stress and panic can be controlled by careful self-evaluation, breaking a situation down into manageable components and then systematically solving them one at a time. STOP — THINK — ACT.

LA Sheriff's ESD logo incorporates all facets of SRT operations: special weapons, emergency medicine, mountain and dive rescue.

SRT divers must often dive in heavily contaminated waters.

For a more complete study of this subject, the reader is strongly advised to find and read a book titled: **STRESS AND PERFORMANCE IN DIVING** by **Glen Egstrom** and **Arthur Bachrach.** These gentlemen pass on a lifetime of experience in the fields of stress, stress indicators, anxiety and panic control as it relates to diving, physical conditioning, skill and behavioral development and the principles of learning and over-learning emergency procedures.

LASD SEB Marine Company 218

B. Abell ©92

3
TEAM TRAINING

The nature of the training given to an SRT diver will be dependent on the type of agency employing the divers and their geographic location. The needs of a New York Police diver are very different from a West Coast Search and Rescue team. Just as the Alaskan ASAP teams have much harsher weather conditions than a Florida Sheriff's Department. Agencies with high altitude lakes, cave systems and fast flowing rivers may have no use for the contaminated water diving skills of a Mid-Western, industrial city Fire Department's recovery team.

Nevertheless there are training and skills that are common to almost all dive teams. These will be covered first, followed by some of the more specialized areas of training. Training is broken into two parts: firstly, the initial training a probationary team member receives to bring him up to speed. Secondly, the on-going training that should be a part of every team's training program. The greatest amount of time must be spent on the skills most often called upon by the particular team, be they public safety or law enforcement.

SAFETY, PROCEDURES AND POLICIES

Every dive team member, from the newest recruit to the senior administrator, must be intimately familiar with the written and unwritten Standards, Procedures and Policies of the team. To avoid confusion and possible legal problems, it is best that the policy manual be as complete as practicable, read and signed by every new arrival to the unit and periodically reviewed.

A team that does not currently have a set of standards and procedures should consider adopting the NASAR "Guidelines for Public Safety Divers" authored by Jim Corry, chairman of the Diving and Water Rescue Committee.

Since diving operations have a greater potential for death or injury than most occupations it is imperative that trainees have a firm grasp of the team's top-side and underwater safety and accident management procedures. These should include:

17

- Conscious and unconscious diver rescue
- Emergency line-pull signals
- Identification & handling of diving related injuries
- Victim transportation
- Recompression and treatment procedures (if applicable)

This should be done before the trainee accompanies the team on any training or field operations where someone else's life may depend on his reactions. The trainee will also need a thorough briefing on the hazards unique to his particular region; e.g., strong currents, bottom debris, parasitic infections, heavy surf action, hypothermia, etc.

Once all these areas have been covered the probationary diver is ready for a 2-4 week basic training cycle.

BASIC TEAM SKILLS

The basic skills taught will make the new arrival a reliable member of the surface support team and better prepare him for underwater operations. Some recruits will bring these skills with them to the team, but they must still be reviewed to make sure their methods are compatible with the rest of the team's.

Emergency Medical Training:

Most dive teams have a search and rescue role within their community, so advanced first aid skills are essential. Even if the team does not have a public safety responsibility, they must be at least capable of rescuing and ministering to their own personnel. Diving operations are seldom within close proximity to hospitals and medical assistance can be slow coming.

Los Angeles County Sheriffs send all their Emergency Services Detail divers through a five-month Paramedic program, after completing basic SWAT and EMT schools.

If not all, at least some members of the team should be EMT qualified with additional training in **oxygen administration** and **dive related** injuries. The NASAR oxygen administration program is an excellent course that will be of value to any rescue diver. Other areas of medical training would be:

- Management of decompression sickness (DCS) and embolisms
- Identification & treatment of gas related problems
- Application of back-boards, C collars and spinal support
- Transportation of injured divers
- Recompression chamber familiarization
- Cold-water near-drowning, where applicable
- Trauma care and the treatment of shock
- Hypothermia and exposure treatment

ASAP divers practice diver rescue and CPR as a regular part of their training program.

Florida police divers receive instruction in oxygen administration.

Pararescue personnel undergoing emergency medical training.

Knots and Rigging:
Whether it be SAR, rappelling, maritime operations, securing loads or doing heavy lifts, a practical working knowledge of both knots and rigging is essential. Team members with a maritime, rigging or mountaineering background will probably be the best suited to teach this part of the program. A more complete look at this subject is covered in Chapter 9.

Basic Seamanship:
The team member does not necessarily have to be capable of skippering a large boat but he should be comfortable handling smaller patrol boats and inflatable Zodiacs. At a minimum he should be a useful member of the crew and be able to handle lines, stow gear, operate the radio and depth finder, set the anchors and assist in docking procedures. A knowledge of nautical charts, navigational aids, Loran and maritime protocol would also be useful.

Surface Support and Communications:
Before a new diver can be committed to the water he must have a working knowledge of all surface support operations. This would include chain of command, diver tending, organizing the dive site, radio communications, hand and line signals, equipment operation, emergency procedures and public relations.

Emergency Vehicle and Equipment Operation:
The diver must be able to drive all vehicles, operate all winches and compressors, set up extraction tools, handle the EMT Datacom units, and know the location of any piece of equipment on the trucks or in the Go-bags.

First Responder:
First responder training refers to the first patrol officer or dive team member to arrive at the dive site. This is especially important if the team is going into Rescue Mode. He/she will have to evaluate the scene, establish contact with the witnesses, call the appropriate emergency services personnel, prevent key witnesses from leaving and protect any possible evidence from damage or loss. These are all areas that need to be covered in basic training.

Witness Interview:
Whether it be a crime scene, rescue operation or recovery, the initial contact and interview of the witnesses could be critical. The trainee must be taught what questions to ask, what details to record, how to evaluate a witness's credibility and how to handle friends or family members of a missing victim. The witnesses will be critical to establishing a "last-seen-point" (LSP) of any plane, person, vehicle or object that has disappeared below the surface.

Site Survey and Mapping:
Search patterns are far more effective when a plan is used to cover a given area. This will prevent researching areas that have already been covered and allow the logging of areas of high probability. Sketches, diagrams, and reports with time, dates, locations, names and descriptions will also be required for evidentiary purposes, insurance claims and agency records.

Crowd and Scene Control:
Diving operations, especially at the scene of an accident or crime, will always draw crowds, reporters and camera crews. Every dive team member should receive some training on how to secure the dive site, handle crowds, respond to the press and comfort the victim's relatives. The divers will also need to shield the body, during a body recovery operation, from unnecessary photography and filming.

Divers should have no contact with the news media and reporters except to refer them to the Press Relations or Information Officer. If a homicide, suicide or foul play is suspected, the entire dive site will need to be secured to preserve evidence and keep unwanted spectators at a distance.

Evidence Preservation:
Although law enforcement divers will have had ample training in the documentation and handling of evidence, there are some unique techniques for handling weapons, bodies and paper documents under water. It is also not uncommon that the responding dive team is from a fire department or volunteer group that has very little, if any, experience in the preservation of evidence. Non-police dive teams should request special training from agencies experienced in underwater crime scene preservation and evidence handling.

INITIAL DIVER TRAINING

Because of considerable inconsistencies in the standards set by certifying sport SCUBA diving agencies, all SRT diver training should begin with a thorough review of the physics and physiology of diving. This can be followed by decompression theory, dive tables and a review of local tidal conditions, water hazards and dangerous marine life.

The classroom is also a good place to address fitness for diving, physical conditioning, stress and panic management and safe diving procedures.

From the classroom it is into the pool for a review of basic SCUBA skills, additional swim/stress tests, diver rescue techniques and equipment donning and doffing.

Diver Rescue Techniques: The first responsibility of a diver is to his own safety and that of his dive partner. The key to a successful rescue is

Julius Wiggins of Miami Police Department lecturing on Scuba equipment maintenance at Broward Community College/Criminal Justice Institute.

Police divers receive hands-on experience in regulator repair and maintenance.

that the rescue divers must become the **solution** and **not part of the problem.** Any time a diver enters a somewhat hazardous situation he must have confidence in his buddy's ability to render assistance, if necessary. Diver rescue techniques, oxygen administration, first aid and CPR training are all intended to make the new diver a dependable and safe member of any team.

Zero Visibility Diving: Since the problems that require the attention of SRT divers are seldom found in the crystal clear waters of popular dive sites, one of the first orders of business is to get all team members comfortable in black water diving. Diving in murky swamps, polluted rivers and even raw sewage is one of the skills that separates the professionals from the weekend sport divers.

This type of training should be first simulated in confined water with blacked-out masks so that the training staff can evaluate the new diver's ability to handle the claustrophobic effects of zero-vis diving. The trainee should then progress to the ponds, rivers and sites that they are likely to get called to. **Squeeze signals** may have to be substituted for conventional hand signals:

One for OK!?
Two for "Continue!"
Three for "Stop!"
Four for "Surface!"

These will vary from team to team and for various operations.

Reserve SEB divers receive introductory training in the use of the EXO-26 full face mask.

Underwater Navigation: Most public safety diving requires searches for evidence, bodies or vehicles so a thorough understanding of both natural and compass navigational techniques is essential. Compass bearings are also commonly used to relocate sites and for documenting the location of evidence or body recoveries.

Underwater Photography: The evidentiary value of crime scene or accident scene photographs is invaluable in court room testimony. A case may not go to court for two to three years and the photographs can be a great aid to the diver's memory. Also, many volunteer dive teams are not trained in crime scene preservation so the photographs will be of great value to the non-diving investigators or Coroner.

Pictures should be taken before the divers disturb anything. Label the film with time, date, location and diver's name.

Night Diving: The need for divers invariably comes just as one sits down to dinner, enters a movie theater or falls asleep. Night diving should be as natural to the recovery diver as night patrol is to the police officer. Although many operations can be suspended until first light — rescues and major crime scenes may require immediate response.

Night diving requires a little more preparation, a closer control of dive personnel and some extra equipment like dive lights, surface lights, buddy lines, back-up lights and an illuminated entry/exit point.

Deep Diving: There are documented cases of body recoveries and plane wrecks in water in excess of 150 feet. Since sport divers are discouraged from venturing below 100 feet, SRT divers will need special training in deep diving techniques, the hazards, the necessary preparations and the principles of in-water decompression. NASAR suggests the certification of public service divers to various depths, based on training, experience and logged dives. Certifications could be 0'-60', 60'-100', 100'-150' and 150'-190' (in extreme circumstances).

Underwater Search Procedures: This should include line searches, drift searches, tow-bar searches and navigational searches (all covered in a later chapter). Training searches for small and large objects are a regular feature of all dive programs. Special attention should be given to line handling and line signals.

Cold-water Near-drowning Rescues: The documented cases of drowning victims being revived after over 40 minutes under water has given us the "Golden Hour" — that first 60 minutes of a dive rescue operation when there is a reasonable chance of saving a life. Other operations also fall into the Rescue Mode:

- Drowning victims falling through ice
- Victims swept down river
- Flooded cave rescues
- Bridge jumpers and attempted suicides
- Water-skiers or swimmers hit by power boats
- Victims that accidentally fell from boats, wharves or cliffs
- Light aircraft and vehicle crashes into the water

The team that has a rescue capability must drill constantly to reduce their response time and improve the chances of a "save". On any rescue operation where time is of the essence, there must always be a careful weighing of the risk to the dive team as opposed to the possible benefit to the victim. One does not throw good life after bad. This is known as the **Risk/Benefit Factor** that must be attached to all operations.

Body Recovery: When that Golden Hour has passed and the chances of saving a life are lost, the operation slows down into a methodical, systematic search. No one particularly likes to be the diver who finds the body, especially in the murky waters of most accident scenes. But nevertheless, the SRT diver must develop the ability to take his turn in the water with the very real chance of bumping into the body while swimming a search pattern. A new diver should be buddied with a more experienced diver on his first body recovery, just to add moral support. Even the recovery of a dead body should give a team a sense of satisfaction for a job well done. The victim's family and friends, with the finality of the recovery, can now stop wondering/worrying and get on with their lives.

Vehicle Recovery: Recovering vehicles will be covered later in this book but for now it is sufficient to say that it is a significant part of most dive teams' work and a specialized skill that needs constant practice (Chapter 16).

ADVANCED DIVER TRAINING

Not all of the following specialties will be needed by every team. Specialty training will be based on need and location. Keep in mind that an actual operation is not the time to find a deficiency in your training and equipment, so a team should train for every possible eventuality.

Fast Water/River Rescue:
The sheer force of a swift river, not to mention trees, branches, rocks, rapids and undertows can make for a unique rescue or recovery operation. Fast water rescues require a familiarity with river conditions, strong swimming ability, complex rigging and careful planning.

Altitude Diving:
If there is a possibility of the team responding to a crater lake, dam or high mountain reservoir there should be training in altitude diving tables and the related diving risks. Teams that could be transported before or after an operation by plane should also look into the possible complications that may occur in a thinner atmosphere.

Helicopter Deployment:
Helicopters are one of the most efficient methods of transporting the initial response team, and in some areas the only method. Most law enforcement, fire and SAR personnel will have worked around helicopters at some point in their career. If the dive team is air-mobile, or expects to jump or rappel from helicopters, then monthly training should be scheduled, for the benefit of the pilots as well as the divers.

Survival:
In the remote areas of the Northwest, it is conceivable that a rescue team could be dropped into the water and then have weather conditions deteriorate to such an extent that recovery by boat or helicopter is impossible. These teams, like the Kodiak ASAP team, jump with survival kits and the training to support two men for three days should a pick-up be impossible. This level of training and preparedness is not for everyone, but it shows an awareness of and preparation for the unexpected.

Chamber Operation:
The injured diver's three best friends are trained Diver Rescue personnel, oxygen and the recompression chamber. It is only natural that all ᵔrofessional dive teams should have a familiarity and understanding of recompression chambers and procedures. Most professional commercial divers can run routine treatments on fellow divers who have exceeded the tables or suffered a DCS hit.

Divemastering:
All SRT divers should aspire to the level of Divemaster and be quite comfortable conducting the routine diving operations of his particular agency. Be aware that the sport Divemaster ratings have very little to do with conducting a professional recovery or rescue operation. Although the sport certification should be held by the SRT Diving Supervisor or Team Leader, it must be augmented by considerable in-house training and experience.

Sheriff's divers receive briefing on recompression chamber procedure from John Alexander, MD, of Northridge Hospital, California.

The hyperbaric facility on Catalina Island also offers emergency medical training and chamber operation classes for law enforcement.

Ice Rescue:

Ice rescue is a subject totally alien to California or Florida teams but a very real problem for the northern and sub-arctic states. Ice rescue has some very specialized equipment and procedural requirements that will be covered in Chapter 13. Cold water rescue also requires an understanding of hypothermia, and an in-depth study of "mammalian diving reflex" and the treatment of cold-water drowning victims.

Cave Rescue:

Caves and mines can flood as a result of heavy rain or changing river conditions, trapping the unwary within. Speleologists all over the world, and sport divers in places like Northern Florida, enjoy exploring and diving in these cave systems. Anywhere there is public access there is always the chance of accidents, so teams in these cave-infested areas should have a cave rescue capability — best coordinated through associations like the National Speleological Society — Cave Diving Section's (NSS-CDS) Rescue committee.

Wreck Penetration:

Whether it is rescuing a sport diver from an old wreck or having to penetrate a crashed plane, the techniques for safe penetration of the vessel must be learned well. Any time a diver has an obstructed, direct ascent to the surface, the dive will require special equipment and training.

Heavy Lift Procedures:

The heaviest lift required of any public service dive team would be light trucks or small planes, and whether they lie in 20 feet or 120 feet of water, the recovery carries with it special rigging techniques and unique hazards. Any lift greater than 4,000 pounds will probably go to a professional salvage contractor, under agency supervision.

A dive rescue team should have the equipment to do light and medium lifts and have a good working knowledge of lift-bag operation and rigging for staged lifts (Chapter 9).

Contaminated Water Diving:

Dive teams, like the New York Police SCUBA Unit and Imperial County Sheriff's URT, have a first-hand understanding of the problems involved in diving in polluted water and raw sewage. Any diver who has had the "pleasure" of doing a recovery in contaminated water knows that it requires special training, equipment and procedures.

Agencies in large metropolitan areas should take the time to have local waters tested, especially near large factories, chemical waste sites and sewage treatment plants. Parasitic infections, toxic chemicals and micro-organisms can be just as deadly as a Great White shark or a deranged gunman, and a whole lot harder to fight. See Chapter 6.

Author rappels into the Toroko Gorge in Taiwan in search of a missing American student.

N.Z. rescue diver rappels down cliff to access victim.

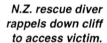

Author attends Santa Barbara City College advanced police diver program under the control of Mike Von Alvensleben (R) and Capt. Tony Rouhotas (L) of ICSURT.

Sheriff's divers practice strapping a victim onto a Miller board, with suspected spinal injuries.

All emergency dive procedures must be practiced on a regular basis.

4
SRT DIVING AND EQUIPMENT

The use of diving techniques and equipment by a special response team is essentially just a mode of transportation. The diving is only a means to get to the job: recovery, rescue, investigation or tactical — then the real work begins. As new divers are told in the commercial industry, "No one is going to pay you just to blow bubbles."

The careful selection of equipment and diving methods can greatly improve a team's chances of success. No one set of dive gear will meet all environmental and operational needs of a team, but all gear should be rugged, simple and streamlined. The following material will give some indication as to the application and limitations of various diving systems. A study of your own agency's tasks and geographic location will fill in the gaps.

NOTE: Many of the following topics are covered in greater depth later in this book.

RESCUE SWIMMER

The aviation branches of the Navy and Air Force have long recognized the need for surface rescue swimmers — as have public service agencies with a beach/surf or swift water responsibility.

The rescue swimmer is essentially a rescuer, equipped for local conditions, who can immediately enter the water and rescue a person in distress. It is important that the rescuer be a strong swimmer, with adequate training and equipment to dominate the situation.

Wet suits are usually essential to provide protection from cold and abrasion as well as provide flotation. Dry suits are used in colder areas but are very tiring to swim in and restrictive to the rescuer. Additional equipment utilized by rescue swimmers consists of:

- Mask, fins and snorkel
- Lightweight safety helmet

- Rescue harness
- Rescue "can" (as used by lifeguards)
- Throw lines and deployment bags
- Rescue ropes and carabiners
- Boogie boards, air rafts and small inflatable boats

Swift water river operations may require an advanced level of rigging, rope handling and the use of a tyrolean rope system.

SCUBA (CONVENTIONAL)

All SRT dive training and teams have to begin somewhere, and they usually have their origins in a handful of dedicated sport divers who have found a need for their skills. Some teams need never look beyond advanced SCUBA skills but even the selection of basic SCUBA gear can have a marked effect on the team's performance.

The biggest mistake many teams make is to allow personal prejudices, industry hype and fast talking salesmen to influence their selection of gear. It is not our place to recommend one brand over another, since there are many manufacturers of first-class equipment in the U.S. But consider the following before writing the check:

- Buy strong, top-quality equipment
- Keep the whole system streamlined and snag-free
- Study your agency needs and environment
- Visit other teams in your area to see what they use
- Test and evaluate everything before you buy it
- Be sure parts and after-sales service are available
- Avoid gadgets and "hot new ideas"
- Carry only the equipment you need — TASK LOADING
- Try to standardize the team's equipment in design and color
- Cultivate a working relationship with a local SCUBA shop that is staffed by real divers, not rookie salesmen, and is willing to give a discount to the team

It cannot be over-emphasized, the need to purchase equipment with local conditions and tasks in mind. A dry suit is essential in the frozen north but would create hyperthermia problems in Florida. On the same thought, diving in a polluted border river in Southern California, in the middle of summer, is still going to require the protection of a dry suit. It is now a trade-off between the discomfort of being too hot or the possibility of contracting a deadly parasitic infection.

Regulators that have worked well in the clear waters of the Bahamas may cease to function, or free-flow continuously, under ice or in heavy silt. The Navy tests have shown some regulators to have good breathing characteristics in shallow water but to have totally inadequate gas delivery for a hard-working diver at depth.

Buoyancy compensators (BCs) that look great in the family photo album may be shredded by the rigors of professional diving, especially around car wrecks and crashed aircraft. The BC is one piece of equipment that is a hindrance on some SRT dives, but absolutely essential on others. It is nice if the vest has a quick release feature, but more importantly, it must be durable, reliable and streamlined. Buckles, straps, gadgets and gauges, strung all over the vest will create drag, slow the operation and frustrate the divers.

Knives should be sharp, utilitarian tools, and not the heavy multi-purpose models marketed by several companies. Watches and gauges must be clear and rugged and stowed where they will not get broken.

Some equipment is manufactured from materials that may deteriorate under local adverse conditions, e.g., cold, petroleum product pollution or chemical waste.

The limitations of SCUBA are: relatively short air supply, lack of communications, exposure to contaminants and weight of equipment. The advantages are: freedom of movement, rapid deployment, availability of gear and well established standards and training methods.

A Sheriff's diver with OMS twin 108's.

A Sheriff's diver with twin 72's.

PARA-RESCUE SCUBA

Para-rescue usually refers to air mobility, jumping from planes or helicopters, and under very adverse conditions. The SCUBA requirements for this application are quite different from that of the boat or shore based diver.

Equipment must be stronger, more compact and better secured to the diver. Length of air supply is not as critical since victims and wreckage are often seen from the air before the jump. The dive capability is essential just in case the victim disappears below the surface before the rescuers can make contact. Victims may also be trapped inside planes or boats requiring the diver to drop below the surface to attempt an extraction.

The diver must wear a full, parachute type extraction harness, and carry additional slings to facilitate the hoisting of victim and rescuer back into the helicopter.

ASAP pararescue diver.

Early USAF PJ.

Halcyon Rapid Deployment PDF rescue system.

SCUBA COMMUNICATIONS

Ever since man first used SCUBA he has yearned for the ability to talk to his fellow divers under water. The use of hand signals served to fill the gap for essential communication but lacked the ability to convey detailed information or verbally share the diving experience. Time, research and technology have now brought the diver several forms of through-water communications ranging from the inexpensive sport units to the more sophisticated commercial and military systems.

The EXO-26 Full Face Mask from DSI was designed with the SCUBA diver in mind, although it can be used with an umbilical. The EXO-26 is a lightweight, rugged and dependable full-face mask that can be used in conjunction with most wireless, and all hard-wire, underwater communication systems. This allows clear and efficient diver-to-diver and/or diver-to-topside communications, all in a convenient package. If communications are not required on some operations, then the whole comms package can be quickly removed and stored without any special tools.

Interspiro's AGA mask, marketed through Viking America, can also be retro-fitted for in-water communications. The AGA is currently in use by several international police and government agencies, in conjunction with the AGA Divator Mk II SCUBA system. This system consists of the mask and a set of compact twin cylinders, that when filled to 4500 psi give the diver 80 cu.ft. of air in a very manageable package. NYPD SCUBA Unit utilizes the AGA mask in conjunction with conventional SCUBA cylinders for diving in the polluted waters of the New York harbor, East and Hudson Rivers.

Two companies that supply excellent wireless communication systems, to SRT teams worldwide, are Ocean Technology Systems and Life Technologies. Both companies offer a variety of wireless Single Sideband ultrasonic communicators, worn either on the side of the SCUBA tank or harness. The OTS systems provide the diver with either push-to-talk or voice-activated (VOX) capability and are U.S. Navy approved. The surface supervisor can be equipped with a compatible topside unit, complete with transducer, that will allow clear surface-to-diver communications without the inconvenience of a hard-wire link.

Another useful form of communication between the Diving Supervisor and the free-swimming SCUBA divers, is the OTS DRS 100 Diver Recall System. Unlike other recall systems that generate "tone only", the DRS 100 allows the divers to hear clear voice communications from top-side without any diver carried receiver. This is achieved by an omni-directional, underwater transducer that has a typical range of 500 meters, depending on biological and ambient noise levels. In addition to voice communications, the DRS 100 also features a non-oscillating siren or intermittent tone to recall divers. The whole package weighs 35 lbs, comes in a #1400 Pelicase, includes battery charger and hand-held microphone and is in wide use by the U.S. military.

OTS diver recall system, DRS-100.

OTS single side band acoustic, wireless communication system.

Diver holds push-to-talk button. Earphone is under the mask strap and against the bone behind the diver's ear.

Diving Supervisor lowers the transducer into the water for through-water communication with the diver.

Use of conventional topside radio (OTS Aquacom) in conjunction with tethered Scuba and AGA mask.

TETHERED SCUBA

A diver is never committed to the water on a commercial operation without some form of attachment to the surface. Most professional divers are using surface-supplied gear but even SCUBA dives require a safety line and diver-tender. This is an excellent policy that the SRT diver should try to adopt.

Sport divers use the buddy system as their safety factor, but in zero visibility water and around crash sites the buddy diver can be more of a hindrance than a help. A more effective system is the use of a safety line attached to the diver's harness (not the BC), a line tender and a safety diver (on the surface but fully dressed-in and ready to go). The tether can now be used for signalling through the use of pre-established line-pulls; distressed or unconscious diver recovery; to monitor the diver's depth, progress and location; and as a direct route for the safety diver to follow in the case of an entangled or non-responsive primary diver.

The safety factors far out-weigh the minor inconvenience of having to tow the line around. Ice dives, penetration dives, night recoveries and black water operations should all require a safety line on the diver, a standby diver, harnesses for both and a line tender for each.

There are diver tethers available that consist of a ⅜" static nylon kermantle rope with a four-wire communication line built into the core (OTS Mk 5 Buddyline). Voice communication is then possible if the diver is equipped with some form of light-weight mask that has a mic and earphone. The EXO-26, Kirby-Morgan Band-mask, DSI-18 and AGA masks can all be run off a conventional SCUBA system and give the added capability of voice communications — very useful when doing crash site evaluations, handling towing cables and rigging for heavy lifts. If voice communications should fail, the diver still has line-pull signals and the security of a strong attachment (5800 lbs breaking strain) to the surface.

Supervisor hits push-to-talk switch on OTS Aquacom.

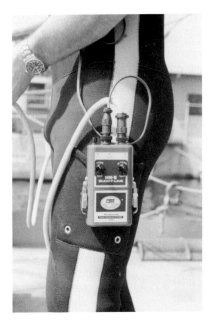

OTS hands-free, voice-activated (VOX) MK-5 Buddy-Line.

Police diver utilizes the Buddy-Line and AGA mask for hull search.

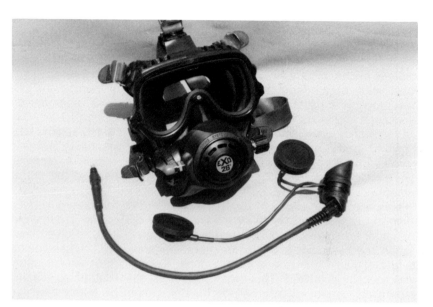

EXO-26 full face Scuba mask with optional comms package that is easily installed or removed as required.

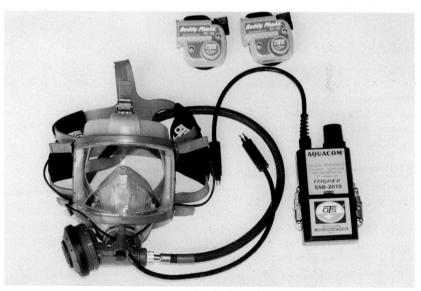

AGA mask with Aquacom SSB-2010 single sideband wireless transceiver and two receive only buddy phones.

CLOSED-CIRCUIT SCUBA

The closed-circuit SCUBA unit is commonly referred to as an oxygen rebreather, or simply a rebreather. Closed-circuit systems are used primarily by the military for covert assault swim and hydrographic survey work. Some police departments have had this type of training and one State agency is using the rebreather to capture the wily sea-otter for relocation.

A rebreather functions on 100% oxygen that is fed into a breathing bag, is utilized by the diver, then passed through a carbon dioxide filter and recycled to the diver. The oxygen metabolized by the diver is replaced from a small pressure cylinder, no bubbles are emitted, so the unit is termed a closed-circuit system.

There are closed-circuit mixed-gas systems used for extremely deep diving but beyond the needs or training of the SRT diver. The oxygen rebreather has many limitations and is definitely not a joy to dive. Since oxygen becomes toxic at depth, the rebreather should not be used below 25 feet of sea water, the preferred depth being 15 fsw, except under extreme circumstances. The system requires special training, careful preparation, cannot be cleared under water, cannot be buddy breathed and is a curse if leaking or flooded.

Chapter 19 of this text covers the rebreather in more detail. They are excellent for long duration, shallow water, covert operations but have very little application for rescue or recovery work.

SURFACE-SUPPLIED DIVING

Surface-supplied diving has become very popular with law enforcement because it allows extended bottom times, voice communications, diver safety and protection from bacteria in contaminated water. Surface-supplied diving denotes an air (or gas) source originating on the surface and being fed to the diver through a hose (or umbilical), under pressure. These systems come in several forms.

Hookah: Basically a conventional second stage regulator on the end of a long medium pressure hose, fed by a small compressor or air cylinder. Often used by scientific divers but not suitable for SRT.

Heavy Gear: Also known as Standard Gear, this is the classic old-time heavy brass-copper helmet, vulcanized canvas suit and lots of lead. Still in use by some commercial and clearance divers, the heavy gear is bulky, heavy, out-moded and unsafe without special training. The U.S. Navy has replaced the old Mk V gear with the newer Mk 12.

Light-weight Helmet: Now we are addressing equipment that is very useful to the SRT team. Light-weight helmets, like the **SuperLite-17** of

Diving Systems International, are ideal for diving in contaminated water and give the added benefits of good communications, a dry head and protection from sharp objects and falling debris.

The SuperLite can be mated to either a wet suit or dry suit through the use of various neck-dams supplied with the helmet. The light-weight commercial diving helmets have long been essential tools to the professional working diver, and are now demonstrating their value to the public service divers of the U.S.

Bandmasks: Originally known as the Kirby-Morgan Bandmask, the **DSI-18** has seen service all over the world in deep oilfield diving, civil marine operations, military roles, experimental dives and increasingly, by the law enforcement community. Lighter and more economical than the full helmet, the bandmask still offers good communications, head protection and excellent breathing characteristics. With an increased demand for an even lighter and more economical mask, DSI came up with the **EXO-26.** Designed primarily for SCUBA, but adaptable for surface-supplied work with a harness mounted manifold block — the EXO-26 is light, comfortable, affordable, a pleasure to dive and easy to maintain.

Author prepares to dive mixed-gas heavy gear (1977).

Complete portable surface-supplied diving system.

DRY SUIT DIVING

The dry suit has established itself as a valuable piece of equipment for any rescue/recovery team. Once considered essential only for ice diving, cold water rescue and long exposures, the dry suit is now the diver's primary protection against toxic waste, contaminated water, disease and parasitic infection.

If dry suits can be used to protect divers in nuclear power plants they are definitely suited to keeping out the microscopic killers of our polluted waterways.

The dry suit is not a piece of equipment that one just buys then goes out and dives. Dry suits require special training in donning, doffing, diving, buoyancy control, maintenance and storage. There are also some suits that are suitable for Haz-Mat operations while others are only suitable for sport diving or as splash suits.

Again, a realistic look at your diving environment and some expert advice will go a long way towards purchasing the correct dry suits for your particular agency. NYPD SCUBA Unit went with the **Viking dry suit** when it was found that their divers were ingesting tropical parasites from the polluted Hudson River. On the other side of the continent, Kodiak Alaska's ASAP team found the **KME dry suit** met all their needs for a cold water/ice para-rescue rig. SEALS and U.S. Special Forces use the Viking and DUI suits in conjunction with either SCUBA or the LAR-V rebreather for arctic or sub-arctic operations.

NYPD divers utilize the Viking dry suit for protection against cold, pollution and bacterial infection.

NITROX DIVING

Nitrox is not a new innovation to the diving industry. Primarily used by military and scientific divers, Nitrox is now being considered for use in the sport and public service diving fields. Nitrox is a gas mixture in which the percentage of oxygen has been raised and the nitrogen lowered. (Air being approximately 20% oxygen and 80% nitrogen, as opposed to nitrox which could be 40% oxygen and 60% nitrogen). The mixtures commonly used by deep cave and wreck divers in Florida are:

Nitrox 1 — 32% oxygen / 68% nitrogen
Nitrox 2 — 36% oxygen / 64% nitrogen

The reason for this increased oxygen level is to increase bottom times, usually at depth, without getting into decompression time. Even though No Decompression diving should be the general policy for most public safety teams, nitrox can greatly increase bottom times without getting into decompression. However, the use of nitrox does complicate the logistics and requires additional training and equipment. Nitrox also has depth limitations: 32% - 130 feet and 36% - 100 feet.

Two potential dangers with nitrox diving are the hazards involved in mixing the gases and dealing with pure oxygen, and the increased risk of oxygen toxicity at depth.

If your agency is anticipating the use of nitrox diving, then some careful study and very special training is called for. SCUBA tanks will require special filling, gas analyzation and distinctive marking.

5
SURFACE-SUPPLIED DIVING

The commercial diving industry has long understood the value of surface-supplied diving to the extent that SCUBA is almost non-existent on many jobs. The advantages of surface supply are increased bottom time because of unlimited gas supply, diver safety and constant communication between the diver and the surface. This constant communication allows the supervisor to monitor the diver's progress, condition and breathing while allowing the diver to coordinate complex tasks with the support crew. This could include requesting tools from diver tenders, directing crane operators, directing manifold operators on lift-bag recoveries and switch operations on burning or welding jobs.

Only in recent years, with the advent of smaller and lighter surface-supplied systems, has the law enforcement community also found the value and safety of this type of diving. Surface-supplied diving systems come in many types and configurations, depending on application and depth requirements. We will confine this chapter to those systems most used and most suitable for special response teams.

Surface-supplied diving (SSD) does require special equipment and special training. Initial training should be done in confined water under the watchful eye of an instructor experienced in surface-supplied diving operations.

The following is a breakdown of the equipment required for surface-supplied diving, assuming that the team already has all their conventional SCUBA gear:

- Helmet or mask suitable for SSD
- Diving harness
- Umbilical with fittings
- Communications
- Diving control manifold
- Air source — cylinders or LP compressor
- Back-up air supply

A team could conceivably function with only one set of surface-supplied gear and have the safety diver on SCUBA, but this does not allow for breakage or malfunction of the system. In areas of heavy contamination both primary diver and safety diver will need to be fully equipped for surface-supply. Two full sets would be good but three ideal for a small team that has a limited use for this type of diving. With three sets, two can be used for training and operations and one kept in reserve for emergencies.

HELMETS

The helmet usually consists of a fiber-glass or brass body with penetrators for gas supply, exhaust and communications, plus some form of neck-dam or seal that mates the helmet to the diver's neck ring or helmet collar. A strong viewing port, earphones and microphone, a non-return valve (check valve) where the gas line meets the helmet manifold block and a bail-out valve are also essential. DSI's **SuperLite-17B** is an excellent example of a helmet that is ideally suited to SRT operations.

The Superlite also has a demand regulator breathing system similar to a SCUBA second stage. This allows for more efficient gas consumption, improved communications and, in conjunction with an oral-nasal mouthpiece, reduced chance of carbon dioxide build-up.

Additional features that add to the popularity of the SuperLite are: a free-flow valve system that can double as a face-plate defogger; a comfortable, detachable head liner; a whisker bubble deflector; an adjustable nose blocking device; optional dry suit or wet suit neck-dam assemblies; clear and accessible communications; the "B" sideblock modification that will accept a dry-suit inflator hose; and good after-sales service and parts availability.

Warning: helmets with no oral-nasal mask are prone to carbon-dioxide build-up. To prevent this developing to a dangerous level (hypercapnea) the diver must adequately flush the helmet at frequent intervals.

Because of the large air space in diving helmets, there is a tendency for them to be positively buoyant. To prevent the helmet literally floating off the diver's head, helmets like the Navy Mk12 and Aquadyne AH3 utilize a system of jocking straps that run down between the diver's legs. The SuperLite-17B and Miller 400 do not require an uncomfortable jock strap since they have adequate weight built into the helmet itself. This makes the helmets a little heavier on dry land (SuperLite weighs 24 lbs) but virtually neutral in the water.

MASKS

The Kirby-Morgan type bandmask has seen more commercial, scientific and military diving operations than probably any other surface-supplied helmet or mask. Lighter, smaller and less expensive than the helmet, the bandmask has proven itself a comfortable and reliable piece of diving equipment. Although not as dry as a good helmet, the bandmask still offers excellent communication and breathing characteristics.

The latest in this line of masks is the **DSI-18** Bandmask (previously known as the **Heli-Ox 18** but equally suited to air diving). The DSI-18 consists of a fiberglass frame with Lexan face port, attached to a rubber hood and held onto the head by means of a five-fingered "spider." The DSI-18 has many of the design features of the SuperLite-17B: free-flow valve, bubble deflector, nose blocking device, non-return valve, bail-out valve, demand regulator with oral-nasal and excellent parts and service availability.

The **EXO-26,** although initially intended as a SCUBA mask, can also be used in conjunction with a surface-supplied system. A manifold block, similar to that found on the side of the SuperLite, is attached to the diver's harness and will accommodate an umbilical connection, LP inflator and bail-out. This system makes for a very light, comfortable and transportable dive package while still giving many of the benefits of the heavier duty systems.

U.S. Navy MK-12 surface-supplied diving helmet mated to the Viking HD dry suit.

DSI SuperLite 17B manifold and one-way check valve. Note plastic dust caps in place when umbilical and bail-out are not connected.

DIVING HARNESSES

When surface-supplied diving, there is a very real danger that strain on the hose/umbilical could result in the helmet or mask being pulled from the diver's head. To prevent this the diver must wear a special harness fitted with "D" rings and a quick release snap-shackle.

Simply attaching the hose to the diver's weight belt or bail-out bottle backpack (unless the bail-out bottle is attached to the harness) is not only unwise, it is extremely unsafe. Nothing must interfere with the drop path of the weight belt and the average SCUBA backpack is not strong enough to double as a harness. In a worst-case scenario the diver must be able to ditch all else and still be brought home on his umbilical and harness.

The **Miller** harness has long been the standard for the industry and is available from DSI or directly from Miller Diving of Harper, Texas. These harnesses come in several configurations, either with or without the bail-out bottle attached. The advantage of having the bail-out bottle attached to the harness (with stainless screw clamps) is that it eliminates the need for a separate SCUBA backpack. Harnesses are made from heavy nylon webbing with corrosion resistant rivets, buckles and "D" rings.

UMBILICAL

In days gone by, the diver's umbilical was a crude arrangement consisting of a heavy rubber air hose, a screw type control valve and a length of manila rope. We have come a long way since then. The modern diver's umbilical is actually a bundle of lines taped together, and made up of: a hard-wire communication line, a pneumo hose, an air line, and a safety line. Additional lines may be taped into the umbilical if needed. A hot water line, used in conjunction with the hot water heated suit, is used when diving for long durations in cold water. Some teams run a video/audio cable into the diver's umbilical so that a running commentary, complete with video, can be monitored/recorded from topside as the diver is working.

On commercial jobs the air/gas line is usually Gates ⅜" (inside diameter) non-floating air hose, with the appropriate fittings to attach the hose to the diver's helmet on one end, and the control manifold at the other. For police/rescue work a floating hose is preferable since it will stay above the debris on the bottom and have less tendency to get entangled. Synflex is one popular type of floating hose and DSI now has their own brand that is marketed with their systems. The two most common fittings used on the gas line are #6 JIC and 9/16" O_2.

The pneumo is a ¼" (ID) depth indicating hose, open at the diver's end and with a brass fitting (usually #4 JIC) topside, to attach it to the pneumofathometer (depth gauge). The communication line is usually an armor jacketed four-line hard-wire cable with post connectors at the surface end and a four-pin female waterproof (WP) Marsh Marine connector on the diver's end. The safety/lifeline can be omitted, but is usually a ⅜" poly or nylon line to add strength to the whole system and prevent hose or communications fittings being pulled out.

Umbilicals can be purchased fully assembled and ready to dive, in 100-ft to 300-ft lengths, or made up by the team from components. Whatever length the team needs, 100-ft for training or 250-ft for operations, the individual components of the umbilical should be continuous lengths with no unnecessary connections mid-line. The air and pneumo hoses will need to be pressurized before taping to accommodate hose shrinkage under pressure. (Shrinkage should be no more than two percent at 150 psig.)

Prior to assembly, inspect all umbilical components for damage or abnormalities. Install all fittings and connectors, pressurize the hoses, and then use two-inch-wide duct tape every 18-24 inches. The attachment of pressure fittings and communication connectors requires special training and oftentimes special tools. All umbilicals need to be thoroughly cleaned, blown out and pressure tested before diving.

After the umbilical is attached to the diver's helmet, it needs to be attached to the harness with a quick-release snap-shackle that will allow emergency release under tension. When selecting the attachment point on the umbilical for the snap shackle (usually on the left side of the diver), be sure to leave ample slack in air and commo lines going to the helmet. This will prevent these fittings pulling out when the tender takes-up on the diver's hose. At the same time, it is important not to leave too much slack in the lines between helmet and harness as this will only cause hang-ups and impede the diver's movement.

COMMUNICATIONS

The helmet or bandmask will usually have two earphones and one microphone, all of which must be submersible and impervious to the damp conditions in which they must operate. There will be a penetrator through the helmet's frame or shell with either post or WP connectors (4-pin male). This will connect into the compatible fittings on the umbilical and carry the signal to and from the surface.

The surface support team will need some form of radio to communicate with the diver. This could be a separate two-diver radio like the **OTS Mk 1-DCI Aquacom,** or built right into the diving control manifold as with the DCS-2. Both units offer separate Diver 1 and Diver 2 connections, the ability to talk to both divers simultaneously, and a diver cross-talk feature. When there is a high ambient noise level from boats, compressors or power tools, the diving supervisor can hook in a separate headset.

DIVING CONTROL MANIFOLD

The manifold is a control panel that allows the operator to monitor the diver's air supply, supply pressure, depth and air source. At one time these were custom made from available pipe, fittings, valves and gauges, but now DSI has the **Dive Control System-2** (a new and improved DCS-1) and Amron has the **Amcommand I and II.**

Both units are well suited to SRT diving. Features are:

- Light and portable
- Totally self contained
- Easy to operate
- Controls both depth and pressure
- Built-in communications
- Can be run from SCUBA tanks
- Air cylinders can be changed with diver down
- Rugged construction
- High visibility cases
- HP cylinder backup for LP compressor operations

The DSC-2 is small and light enough to allow operations to be run from a Zodiac and still carry adequate air tanks for the divers.

AIR SOURCE

The most convenient source of air for SRT divers is SCUBA tanks, since they are probably already in the supply system. These can be connected directly into the DCS-2, one on-line and one on backup. When the diver depletes one tank, the manifold is switched over to the other. The first tank can then be replaced with a fresh one that then becomes the backup air supply.

If the team does not have many tanks, then the empties can be filled from a portable HP compressor as they are used. An alternative is to have a mobile LP compressor as a primary air source and SCUBA cylinders as backup. This compressor could be truck, trailer or boat mounted, depending on the local requirements and anticipated needs. If the team has a dive boat it can be fitted with a bank of larger (240-cu.ft.) cylinders for use in conjunction with surface-supplied diving operations. The high bank pressure can be stepped down through the DCS-2 manifold regulator in the same manner as conventional SCUBA cylinders.

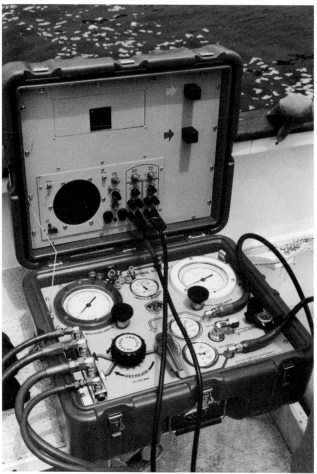

DSI diving control system DCS-2.

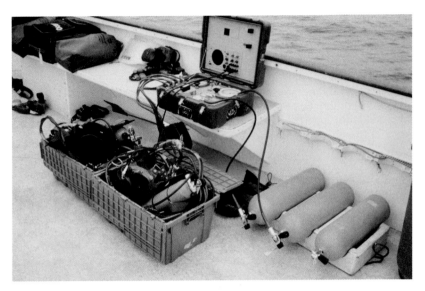

A well organized dive station with both umbilicals neatly stowed in plastic boxes, Scuba tanks in racks and DCS-2 ready for operation.

AMCOMMAND II features a wireless headset for the tender or supervisor to monitor all diver and surface communications.

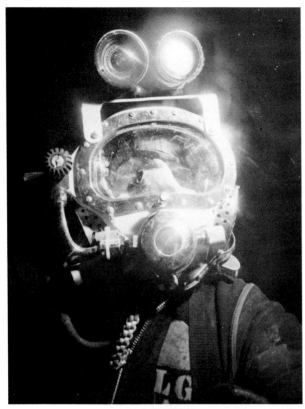

Author at 480 feet beneath the North Sea with helmet-mounted light and video that can be monitored from the surface.

Quick release snap shackle recommended for attaching the diver's umbilical to the D-ring on the Miller harness.

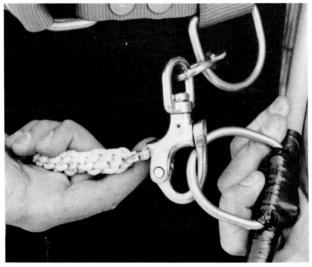

55

BACK-UP AIR SUPPLY

All surface-supplied divers should be equipped with an emergency bail-out bottle (also referred to as a "come-home" bottle by the Navy). Conventional SCUBA cylinders can be used for this purpose but are bulky and unnecessarily large for this function. The smaller pony bottles (15 to 30 cu.ft.) are more than adequate for this purpose, considering the limited depths of SRT diving.

The pony bottle can be banded directly to the harness and then connected to the bandmask or helmet by means of a conventional SCUBA first-stage regulator and intermediate hose, or with the addition of a mid-line quick disconnect (QD) fitting. It is not unusual to have the bail-out bottle inverted on the harness. This allows the diver to reach back and ensure that his emergency air supply is on at the bottle, or to turn it on if needed. Inverting the bail-out does increase the distance from the first stage to the helmet manifold so requires a longer whip to make the connection.

If the bail-out bottle is upright then the air should be on at the first stage and off at the helmet. If needed the diver simply opens the bail-out valve on the helmet manifold block and he will receive emergency air. If the bail-out bottle is inverted and the diver well trained, the air can be off at both first stage and helmet. This reduces the chance of the diver accidentally bumping the valve and unknowingly depleting his emergency air supply. In a "loss of primary air" situation the diver must reach down and turn the air on at the bottle, then open the bail-out valve at the helmet.

When diving SSD masks without a bail-out valve feature, it is necessary to have a second-stage regulator and a spare mask for emergencies. The second-stage should be positioned for easy access by the diver, and once he has air he can don the spare mask for the ascent to the surface.

DSI inverted twin bail-out bottles attached to a Miller harness.

SURFACE-SUPPLIED DIVING PROCEDURE

Once the decision has been made that the operation calls for surface-supplied diving, certain prerequisites must be met. Firstly, there must be sufficient personnel trained in SSD procedure to handle the scope of the operation. This may call for:

- A designated Divemaster/Supervisor
- A control system/gas rack operator
- A diver tender to handle the umbilical and assist the diver
- A stand-by safety diver
- A tender for the stand-by diver if he is also dressed for surface-supplied diving
- Support personnel to handle tools, ropes and recovery bags
- Additional divers for prolonged operations

The absolute minimum would be a Supervisor on radio/manifold, a diver, a tender and a stand-by diver on SCUBA. Now an equipment check needs to be done. Check:

- All essential equipment is on site including suits, helmets, neck dams, umbilicals, control system, harnesses and bail-outs
- Adequate air is available for the dive tasks anticipated and possible decompression (gauge all tanks)
- All hose, manifold, helmet and radio fittings are compatible
- Hose ends are sealed from contaminants with tape or caps
- Radio batteries are charged or fresh
- Bail-out bottle is full

At this point four things happen at once (1) The Supervisor directs the team and coordinates with first responders. (2) The control system operator sets up the radio, manifold and air cylinders and makes the topside umbilical connections. (3) The tender helps the diver dress-in, blows out the gas lines and connects the helmet to the umbilical. (4) The stand-by diver dons all his SCUBA gear except mask.

The diver should also verify the pressure in his bail-out bottle, test the breathing and communications in the helmet and defog the faceplate. The diver now sits quietly in full equipment, less the helmet, with the tender at hand, and awaits the Supervisor's pre-dive briefing. With suit, fins, harness and weight-belt the diver should avoid unnecessary movement and potential heat exhaustion. The stand-by diver will also be sitting quietly, ready to listen in on the briefing.

When the Supervisor is satisfied with all the pre-dive equipment checks (and there should be a written check-list) he will give the diver a briefing on what the situation is, what the objective of the dive is and how he would like it accomplished. The Supervisor will also review line-pull signals and emergency procedures for the diver, tender and stand-by diver.

The tender will now:

- Ensure the diver's air is turned on
- Attach the umbilical to the diver's harness
- Connect the bail-out whip to the bail-out bottle
- Check that the helmet bail-out valve is turned off
- Turn on the bail-out bottle if necessary
- Assist the diver in donning the helmet
- Do a final communications and breathing check
- Fasten the helmet to the neck yoke assembly and ensure a positive lock/seal. If using a bandmask, then simply zip down the hood and fasten the spider to the diver's comfort.
- Place the pneumo hose through the harness at the diver's chest level.

The diver now has restricted vision and is rather top-heavy. The tender must physically guide him to the entry point, hold his umbilical and assist him into the water. Once in the water the diver can do a final gear check as the tender gives him a leak check. The diver should stop just below the surface so that the tender can see if there are any leaks in the diver's umbilical, bail-out system, helmet or suit (if a dry suit is used).

If the diver is jumping into the water, be sure he has adequate hose out to reach the water and not be pulled up short.

LASD/ESD diver in Viking HD dry suit and holding SuperLite 17B. Note the special collar designed to accommodate this helmet.

Over-heating can ba a serious problem for divers in hot climates. The Author awaits his turn to dive on a homicide related weapons search (1998.)

The task of mating the SuperLite helmet to the dry suit is considerably easier with two diver tenders working together.

The tender can now pass the diver any necessary tools, camera, search line, body bag, lights or video. As the diver descends or swims away, the tender and D.S. will note the diver's time off surface and slack the umbilical. The tender must constantly try to feel the diver on the end of the umbilical — taking up slack when necessary and feeding out more as the diver needs it. Some common line-pull signals are:

From tender to diver
1 pull — "Are you all right?" or "stop" if descending
2 pulls — "Slacking hose" or "going down"
3 pulls — "Stand-by to come up"
4 pulls — "Come up now"

From diver to tender
1 pull — "I am all right" or "I am on the bottom"
2 pulls — "Give me slack" or "lower away"
3 pulls — "Take up my slack"
4 pulls — "Haul me up"

Search patterns (arc)
2 pulls — "Change direction"
3 pulls — "Found object of search!"

Emergency signals
2-2-2 pulls — "I am fouled and need assistance"
3-3-3 pulls — "I am fouled but can clear myself"
4-4-4 pulls — "Haul me up immediately"

The above line-pull signals are only a guide and may be changed or modified to suit the individual team/task requirements. The important point is that all team members should know the established signals and emergency procedures.

All line signals should be long, firm pulls and are only used when voice communications are lost. In general, the diver will simply tell the supervisor what he needs and the tender will comply immediately. It is useful if the radio is set up so that both the supervisor and tender can hear it.

As the diver works the supervisor will monitor and log the diver's progress, communications, breathing, depth, bottom time and air supply. If the supervisor hears the diver over-breathing the helmet he should tell the diver to slow down and regain his breathing rate. The supervisor should notify the diver when he is changing air bottles so that the diver can be alert to any gas contamination or pressure loss.

If the diver or his umbilical should become fouled, it is counter-productive to struggle since this will lead to fatigue and possibly panic.

The same rules apply as to an entangled SCUBA diver:

- Stop
- Think
- Regain breathing and composure
- Notify topside that you are trying to clear yourself
- Systematically try to find the cause and clear yourself
- Be very careful if using a knife to avoid cutting the umbilical or dry suit
- If all else fails, call for a stand-by diver to come and free you

The diving supervisor looks on as the rack operator monitors gas supply, depth and communications. The tender at left controls the diver's umbilical.

The surface-supplied diver must learn to recognize potential hazards and obstructions to the smooth passage or his umbilical. He must be especially careful when doing heavy lifts, salvage operations and working around jagged wreckage. With time and practice the efficient handling of the umbilical under water will become second nature.

Should the diver have a failure of the primary air/gas supply then he should calmly switch to bail-out by opening the valve on the right side of the hat (SuperLite-17B and DSI-18) and opening the bail-out bottle if it is turned off. Once on bail-out, the diver can notify the supervisor of the problem and make a normal swimming ascent or return to the down line and climb up. If the problem is easily corrected topside then the diver can go off bail-out and continue the dive (providing the diver is sure he still has adequate air in the bail-out bottle for another emergency). A safe procedure when the bail-out is used, even for a short time, is that the diver should surface and have the tender gauge the bottle. If the diver has a pressure gauge on the bail-out this may not be necessary.

If the mask has no bail-out feature then the diver will take his second-stage regulator in one hand and discard the surface-supplied mask with the other. Once the diver has air he can don his backup SCUBA mask and make his way to the surface. Once the primary mask is discarded, comms are lost and the dive must be aborted.

The Diving Supervisor must have a set of U.S. Navy Standard Air De-compression Tables on hand and a Dive Work Sheet. In surface-supplied diving, topside is responsible for monitoring the diver's depth and bottom time, and then establishing which schedule he will be decompressed on. SRT diving should be kept well within the U.S. Navy No-Decompression Limits but there are times when in-water decompression ("wet stops") may be required. Even if the dive profile is within the No-Decompression Limits, it is still good practice to get into the habit of doing 20' and 10' safety stops when ascending from deep or long duration dives.

As the diver ascends, the tender will take in the slack and coil or figure-eight the umbilical. When the diver surfaces, the tender can pull him to the exit point and assist him out of the water. Sit the diver down, remove the helmet and place it in his hands. (If the diver has been in polluted water he must be decontaminated before any seals are broken or the helmet removed.) Now the tender can shut off the bail-out bottle, disconnect the whip, release the umbilical from the harness, take the helmet from the diver and place it on the umbilical. Finally, assist the diver out of the harness, bail-out, weight belt and suit if necessary.

If the operation is over, the system can be rinsed off, shut down, broken down and hoses plugged or taped. If more diving is anticipated, then the next diver should be already suited up, getting into the harness and neck-dam and preparing to dive. The bail-out bottle should be gauged between each dive to make sure no air has been accidentally breathed or bled off. The helmet or mask oral-nasal can be rinsed out and wiped dry for the next diver, and the faceplate defogged. The previous diver should

The standby safety diver should be fully dressed in, fins on and ready to dive at a moment's notice.

LA Sheriff's divers prepare for a training dive at an inland lake. The table and chair can be a real asset when working prolonged search and recovery operations.

report any communication, breathing or leakage problems with the helmet, and a new one put on line if problems are serious. There is often some resistance to breathing, comms are seldom perfect and few helmets are perfectly dry (unless used in conjunction with a dry suit).

Operations requiring several divers will require an established dive rotation. The Diving Supervisor will have the final say on who does which dives based on experience, fitness and specialized skills. On normal rotations each man changes jobs after each dive. The diver exits the water to change and rest, the standby diver becomes the primary diver, a new man becomes the tender and the tender dresses in as standby. When the initial diver has changed, he can join the topside rotation until it is his turn to do a repetitive dive.

After cold, arduous, deep or long duration dives the diver must be monitored for any signs of decompression sickness. Where air embolisms become apparent almost immediately upon surfacing, a decompression problem could take some time to show itself. Divers should not be permitted to leave the dive site immediately, but required to stay around for an hour or two. Hot showers and hot tubs can also compound the problem by causing small bubbles to come out of solution and collect in joints or spinal areas. Any symptoms of the bends, whether it be a pain-only or CNS hit, require that the diver be put on **oxygen** and **immediately** transported to a **recompression** facility for treatment.

Only good instruction and regular training will get a team comfortable with surface-supplied operations. Once SSD has been mastered, and all team members are comfortable in both a surface support mode and diving mode, then SCUBA will be used less frequently. The safety and convenience of communications and an umbilical far outweigh the initial hassle of hauling a hose around.

No matter how murky the water the surface-supplied diver can always follow his umbilical back to his entry point.

Surface-supplied divers can get entangled in not only weeds but fishing line, rope, nets and other bottom debris. As with the Scuba diver he must first STOP, THINK and then try to free himself. If this fails the standby diver can come to his assistance.

Note: For additional information and a more complete study of surface-supplied diving, the author recommends the U.S. Navy Diving Manual and the NOAA Diving Manual. The helmet, bandmask and Dive Control System operator's manuals should also be studied by all team members before any diving operations begin.

Corroded 50 gallon drums should be treated with suspicion and only approached in HAZ-MAT diving gear.

Toxic waste flowing into Southern California from Mexico at the Calexico border crossing (New River).

6
HAZ-MAT DIVING

"Haz-Mat" is the abbreviation for Hazardous Materials and refers to any substance or chemical that may be hazardous to humans. This could include volatile fuels, heavy metals, toxic or corrosive chemicals or raw sewage. Fire departments have considerable expertise, training and experience in dealing with hazardous material spills. This training now needs to be utilized by dive teams that come in contact with, or are required to dive in, contaminated waters. These contaminants can have a wide variety of effects on the diver ranging from skin irritation or infection to corrosion of equipment.

The following is a list of dive sites that may endanger the health of a dive team:

- Rivers polluted by raw sewage and industrial waste
- Waters contaminated by toxic chemical dumping
- Beaches with sewage outfalls
- Harbors and docks in commercial ports
- Oil or chemical spills from tankers or freighters
- Crash sites of aircraft carrying pesticides or chemicals
- Canals where chemical trucks have crashed
- Irrigation ditches contaminated by agricultural pesticides
- Sewage treatment plants and oxidation ponds
- Stagnant ponds
- Waterways near municipal dump sites

The New River, flowing from Mexico into Southern California, was studied by health experts who found almost 30 viruses including typhoid, polio and salmonella, along with carcinogenic (cancer causing) chemicals like chloroform and benzene. In some areas the fecal coliform bacteria has been measured at 5,000 times the U.S. standard for safe human contact. It is not unusual to see human feces, bottles, bags, condoms, dead cats, dogs, cows and clumps of chemical foam float by. Even a human corpse on rare occasions. This is the same river that illegal aliens try to swim from Mexicali into Calexico to avoid the Border Patrol checkpoint.

At other sites on the border, like Tijuana, 5-10 million gallons a day of excess sewage is dumped into the Tijuana River, which requires the permanent closing of two miles of San Diego beach; at El Paso raw sewage floats untreated into the Rio Grande from Nuevo Laredo and Juarez — cities that have no sewage-treatment plants. Factories that could not do business in the U.S. because of EPA restrictions take their operations across the border and dump all the chemicals they want, without restriction.

New York has more than its share of pollutants in the Hudson River, East River and New York Harbor, and yet the NYPD SCUBA Unit still dives these waters daily for missing bodies, evidence recoveries and surface rescues. Tropical bacteria, brought into the U.S. by visitors and immigrants, is dumped directly into the Hudson from overflowing treatment plants. Once in the water the bacteria are accidentally ingested by the divers, and can result in a multitude of gastro-intestinal parasites. These parasitic infections can cause several disorders ranging from diarrhea to the loss of colon material, if not diagnosed early enough.

Diving in the vicinity of sewage outfalls carries the risk of disease caused by pathogenic microorganisms. Pathogens, such as bacteria and viruses are responsible for a multitude of respiratory and enteric disorders.

PREPARATION

Polluted Water: The first order of business is to bring in the health and environmental experts to do scientific sampling and analysis of the local waterways. Once the chemical, bacteria and other contaminants have been identified, and concentration levels established, the team can begin equipping themselves for the probability of having to dive these waters. Each chemical must be individually evaluated for concentration, exposure time and compatibility with the diver's equipment. For additional information in this area consult the Environmental Protection Agency's Manual of Practice for On-Site Coordinators.

The experts will also recommend which shots and inoculations the team should have in case of accidental contact with the contaminants. Suggested vaccinations/inoculations include:

- Typhoid fever
- Cholera
- Hepatitis
- Polio
- Tetanus
- Smallpox
- Diphtheria

The nature of the chemicals/bacteria will also have considerable influence on the decontamination procedures required for all divers, equipment and support personnel after a dive.

Haz-Mat Spills: In the event or anticipation of a chemical tanker crashing into a waterway, or some such similar disaster, the dive team should set procedures for establishing the risk factors involved in mounting a recovery operation. This will require some familiarity with the conventional haz-mat procedures utilized by fire departments to reduce the spread of chemical spills and facilitate the clean-up.

The Diving Supervisor must decide whether it is safe enough to dive, based on the nature of the chemicals and extent of the spillage involved. Haz-mat specialists should be consulted before the team even attempts to approach the site. The vapors from the spill could be just as dangerous as the chemicals themselves. If a supervisor needs to be able to identify spills, he can consult the **C.H.R.I.S. Manual** (Chemical Hazards Response and Information System) or the DOT Hazardous Material Handbook/Emergency Response Guidebook.

If the DOT chemical identification placards can be seen, or the supervisor knows the product code or number designation of the chemicals involved, he can telephone **CHEMTREC** at 1(800) 424-9300 for assistance. CHEMTREC is the abbreviation for Chemical Transportation Emergency Center. The **FBI** and **NCIC** computer system can also be accessed for this type of information.

Be especially cautious when dealing with pressurized containers or tanker trucks with exterior reinforcing ribs on the trailer rig. Flatbed trucks may be transporting the chemicals in 55-gallon drums, so it is important to know the exact number in the load and account for each and every one. Damaged or sinking ships will have a cargo manifest on the bridge that will detail the entire contents of the cargo holds and containers. This manifest will also indicate the exact location of hazardous materials within the ship.

Divers assist in EPA/Health Department water sampling.

EQUIPMENT

The equipment selected for contaminated water diving will have the greatest impact on the health and safety of the team members, equalled only by following strict procedures for diving and decontamination. The object of the exercise is to protect the diver from any physical contact with the contaminated waters — not a drop should touch his skin. The solution to this problem is a dry suit mated to a full helmet, with all seals water-tight, and the system run at positive pressure.

Although this equipment is not cheap, it will quickly pay for itself by the decrease in the number of man-days lost, due to sickness and infections contracted from diving in the polluted water. Some infections/diseases are incurable and may result in early medical retirements.

Dry Suits:

Vulcanized rubber suits have proved themselves most suitable for haz-mat diving and are the easiest to clean in the decontamination process. The vulcanized rubber dry suit has been found to retain less bacteria than the nylon or neoprene varieties, and is more resistant to caustic chemicals.

The **Viking Heavy Duty** Shoulder Zip Suit, delivered with a special collar to mate to the **SuperLite-17B,** is the first choice of many police, fire and government agencies that dive routinely in contaminated waters. These suits are made from the best materials, are strong, reliable and effective in their resistance to chemicals and bacteria. The **Viking Pro,** in conjunction with a full-face AGA mask, was the suit chosen by New York Police and Fire Departments for diving in the Hudson River. These suits are in use by the U.S. Navy, NOAA, EPA, Richmond, Baltimore, Houston, San Diego, Imperial County, Los Angeles County and probably every progressive agency with a polluted water problem and a public safety dive team. If they do not, they should.

The correct dry suit gloves (Viking #3154) and wrist seals will also be required to complete the package.

It is important to get special training in dry suit diving and additional training for haz-mat operations. A seemingly minor procedural error like not connecting the power inflator, from the "B" side block of the SuperLite to the suit inflator valve, can result in a small leak, a contaminated diver and an aborted dive.

The suit's cuff and neck seals, along with the zipper must be kept in good order and checked regularly for holes or leaks. A leak on a conventional dive is an inconvenience, but a leak in contaminated water can be a serious health hazard. Even the suit's inflation and exhaust valves will need to be stripped and cleaned of contaminants, after every dive.

Incorrect donning of the dry suit will destroy the seals faster than normal diving and wear. Similarly, incorrect cleaning, maintenance and storage will render a suit useless long before the end of its expected working life.

Viking HD dry suit and SuperLite 17 helmet.

NYPD Scuba Unit in Viking Pro suits and AGA masks.

Helmets:
The light-weight helmet is the optimum method of keeping contaminants away from the head, ears, nasal passages and mouth. Not all helmets are suitable for contaminated water diving. The DSI markets a **SuperLite-17B** that is part of a special contaminated diving package. Firstly, it is designed to mate directly to the collar of the Viking dry suit. Secondly, the side-block on the helmet has been drilled to accept the dry suit inflator hose. And finally, the SuperLite has a Double Exhaust System. This is a series/stacked exhaust system that ties the helmet main exhaust and regulator exhaust together. This helps prevent a back-flow of contaminants into the helmet.

The double exhaust system was designed by Diving Systems at the request of the National Oceanic and Atmospheric Administration. The **Miller 400** and **Aquadyne DMC-7** also offer double exhausts for diving in hazardous and polluted environments.

Masks:
The full-face mask, in conjunction with a dry suit and open-circuit SCUBA should only be used where surface-supplied helmets are operationally infeasible (helo jumps and rapid deployment). The full-face mask is less effective in protecting the skin, mouth and ears from waterborne chemicals and pathogens.

NYPD SCUBA Unit uses the **AGA mask,** U.S. scuba tanks and the Viking dry suit as their standard equipment for diving in the Hudson and related waterways. Even with this protection, several divers have been found to be hosts for unwelcome gastro-intestinal parasites. Oftentimes these infections can be traced, not to the fault of the equipment, but to the poor post-dive hygenic procedures employed by the individual divers.

If a mask must be used, for operational reasons, the **AGA** and **EXO-26** are probably the best full-face masks currently available. They have low volume oral-nasal fittings; are constructed from materials that are resistant to corrosion; can be fitted with communications; and have light-weight, low profile designs. The EXO is a more rugged mask and better suited to comms, while the AGA has a unique positive pressure air supply that is activated by the first breath.

The Positive Pressure air supply system ensures that if the mask's face seal is disturbed, the regulator will automatically free-flow and prevent contaminated water from entering the mask. The AGA is also equipped with separate inhalation and exhalation chambers to further protect the diver from ingesting contaminants.

SURFACE-SUPPLIED OR SCUBA

Surface-supplied diving in contaminated water will always be preferential to the use of SCUBA. Apart from the benefits already discussed in this chapter, surface-supplied equipment gives the diver the added security of communications, topside control, two separate air sources (umbilical and bail-out) and a lifeline.

It can be assumed that if the water is a danger to the diver's health, it is probably zero-visibility, pitch dark below the surface and possibly strewn with junk and debris. The topside communications will be a comfort to the diver, and the lifeline gives the stand-by safety diver a direct route to follow to an entangled or unconscious primary diver.

Another good argument against SCUBA operations in contaminated water is the out-of-air emergency. Even though this should never happen and is a sign of poor planning, in murky water it is impossible to see the submersible pressure gauge, and thus have any indication of remaining air pressure. Add to this the fact that the diver will be using more air as a direct result of the increased apprehension of diving in a hazardous environment.

The backup air supply for a full-face mask is usually a conventional SCUBA octopus second-stage and an extra face mask. For the diver to utilize this bail-out system he must remove the full-face mask, expose his face to the contaminants and then put a contaminated second-stage in his mouth. This procedure almost guarantees the ingestion of some bacterial filled water or toxic fluids. With this in mind, an additional second-stage is not recommended when diving in contaminated water. The diver must carefully monitor his air consumption and avoid removing the full-face mask at all costs — until decontamination has been completed and the Divemaster signals that it is safe.

The **AGA MkII Divator** system, used by the British Police and many European agencies, has a unique reserve air supply valve mounted on the right shoulder strap of the tank pack. This is a spring-loaded reserve valve that the diver can activate only when air supply drops below 20% of total volume (900 psi approx.). This is an excellent feature when diving in zero-vis water and prevents the need to doff the full-face mask in an out-of-air emergency.

DE-CON TEAM

An extremely important, and often forgotten, part of polluted water/haz-mat diving is the decontamination team (de-con). Decontamination requires both special training and specialized equipment not normally found within a law enforcement agency. This is one area that a local fire department could be of great assistance, since they will already have the training and equipment necessary. This will include:

• Haz-mat suits and boots
• Breathing apparatus (SCBA)
• Hoses, pumps and water
• Decontamination solutions
• Transportation containers
• Established procedures

The degree of protection required for the de-con team will be dependent on the threat level of the environment. There are basically three levels: Class A would be full suit and enclosed breathing system (SCBA) — used where contamination is bad, there are toxic fumes and corrosive chemicals. Class B is a hooded suit with exposed breathing system and Class C would be the suit, gloves, rubber boots but no breathing system.

The de-con team should also be trained in tending the diver's hose and assisting him in and out of the water. The de-con site should be well clear of the diving station and downwind of all unprotected personnel.

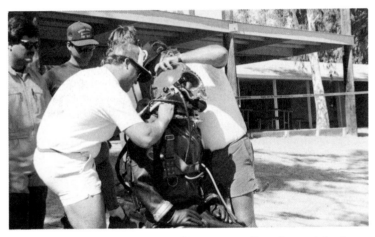

Diver must be carefully dressed to ensure all seals are intact.

Initial hose-down upon exiting contaminated water.

74

Hose down the umbilical that came in contact with the contaminated water.

Thoroughly scrub down diver.

Final rinse before seals are broken.

DIVING PROCEDURE

All diving operations in polluted water must carry with them a Risk/ Benefit Factor. That is to say, is it reasonable to risk a diver's health to achieve the objective? There must be a very strong reason to necessitate a dive that could have long-term negative side effects on the team.

If the operation is to proceed, then Contaminated Diving Procedures must be followed to the letter. Apart from all the normal procedures associated with surface-supplied diving, there are several more attached to haz-mat operations. Start by trying to select a dive site that is up-wind of the contaminated area so that smells/fumes will be carried away from the surface support unit.

1. The team should have an accurate evaluation of the concentration and nature of the pollutants.
2. Dive team should set up well clear of the water's edge, up-wind and up-current.
3. All support personnel, line tenders especially, should have protection ranging from gloves and boots to full haz-mat suits.
4. Carefully check the helmet-to-suit seals (the large helmet "O" ring is removed when mating the SuperLite to the HD Viking) and glove-to-suit seals, before allowing the diver near the water. Duct-tape zipper and cuffs as an added precaution. Be sure all hose connections are tight and power inflators are correctly attached.
5. Run the whole system at a positive pressure. Positive pressure in the dry suit and light free-flow in the helmet. In this way air passes out through leaks rather than contaminants finding their way in.
6. If there is any indication of a leak the diver will notify topside and the dive will be immediately aborted.
7. The diver must be extremely careful around crash sites and sharp objects that may puncture the suit.
8. The supervisor must be alert for any indications of stress and anxiety in the divers. (We are often more scared of what we cannot see than what we can.)
9. Divers with open cuts or sores should be kept away from contaminants that may further the risk of infection.
10. Keep dives and bottom time as short as possible to limit exposure and stress — 30 to 45 minutes. Diving in hot, chemically active sewage treatment plants may require some form of external cooling for the divers.
11. All divers must go through a thorough decontamination procedure before undressing or removing the helmet. Dive gear can be taken back to the fire department for a more thorough cleaning and drying.
12. Hose tenders and rope handlers must wear rubber gloves and avoid getting their hands near their mouths (smoking or eating is unsafe in a haz-mat environment).
13. Monitor divers after dives for any evidence of illness or adverse reac-

tion. If medical problems develop, the attending physician must be notified that the diver had been working in a polluted area. If possible, the hospital should be informed of the type of contaminants/pollutants present.

These procedures are only a broad guideline that must be modified for location, objective and types of contaminants.

DECONTAMINATION PROCEDURE

The decontamination procedure is broken into five areas:

- The dressed-in diver as he leaves the water
- The diving equipment
- The undressed diver
- Support equipment
- Support personnel

As the diver leaves the water he should be hosed down with uncontaminated water, at a reasonable pressure, and then scrubbed down with a strong detergent solution. Use both large and small brushes to get into all areas of the suit and helmet. Fire departments will be able to advise on other decon solutions needed to neutralize certain chemical and organic compounds.

At this point the weight-belt and bail-out can be removed, with the diver still on surface-supplied air, and a further decontamination is done with a strong chlorine bleach/water spray. In areas of high-risk contaminants the diver can be completely immersed in a large portable tank of bleach solution. Or the tank can be used for the final fresh water rinse in lower threat situations.

Before any seals are broken, the diver should be thoroughly rinsed down again with fresh water.

After the diver has undressed, the suit should be cleansed in a 50% by volume solution of chlorine bleach in hot water. After a final wash with soapy water and a fresh water rinse, the suit can be blotted dry and hung at room temperature to finish the drying process. Valves will need to be disassembled and cleaned, along with the weight belts, harness, bail-out, helmet, gloves, lights, tools, umbilical, etc.

Once dry the suit seals should be talcummed, the zipper waxed and the suit rolled and stored according to the Viking manual. The dry suit underwear must also be laundered according to manufacturer's instructions.

The diver should take a hot shower (providing he is not too close to the decompression limits) and thoroughly scrub his skin and scalp with an anti-bacterial cleanser. Special attention should be given to the ears to prevent otitis externa. After drying, an otic solution like Domeboro can be applied to the ear canal. Otic solutions can also be useful for general prophylaxis before working in a contaminated or humid environment.

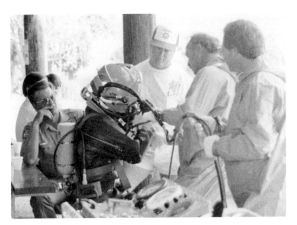

Mike Von Alvensleben supervises ICSURT's initial contaminated water training.

Diver is led to the water's edge.

Support personnel prepare to decontaminate the diver as he exits the water.

78

Tenders remove weight belt and bail-out bottle before decontamination.

Diver receives thorough hose down at water's edge.

Victims and objects recovered from contaminated water must also be hosed down.

Contaminated water diving requires considerable preparation, support equipment and support personnel (Alamo River).

Tenders in HAZ-MAT suits prepare to assist the diver from the Alamo River in Southern California.

80

Diver climbs from river and prepares for initial hose-down.

Diver is hosed down by tender in full Class A HAZ-MAT equipment.

Diver is carefully scrubbed with large and small brushes.

81

Diver receives second hose-down and moves to the DECON area.

Diver receives chlorine bleach spray.

Diver may be seated for complete decontamination. Drums are for transportation of contaminated diving gear to the Fire Station for additional decontamination.

Diver is wiped down.

Seals should not be broken or helmet removed until decontamination procedure is complete.

All support equipment that came in contact with the contaminated waters must also go through a decontamination and cleaning process. Support personnel should follow the same hygiene requirements as the diver: hot showers and bactericidal cleansers as soon as possible after the termination of diving operations.

ROUTINE HEALTH

The divers are the most valuable part of any diving operation. Their health and fitness should be of prime concern to their agency and team supervisors. Divers required to operate frequently in a polluted environment must also receive regular physical examinations. Of particular importance will be blood and stool samples to be sent in for analysis.

Stool and blood tests are a common, if unpleasant, part of being on a New York dive team. Early detection of some parasitic infections can mean the difference between a simple cure and major surgery. Giardia Lamblia, if not diagnosed early, can result in loss of the colon or even death. Milder parasitic infections like Blasto Cystis, that causes cramps and diarrhea, also need to be detected and treated in a timely manner.

Apart from medical examinations, the divers must maintain a high level of good health, exercise and nutrition. This will help the body to fight or resist various infections. Personal hygiene is also of utmost importance when handling hoses, ropes and diving equipment that has been in polluted water. Team members and support personnel should not place cigarettes, coffee cups or food near their mouths, until they are away from the decon site and have thoroughly washed their hands with bactericidal soap.

Line handlers and hose tenders must also wear gloves and practice good personal hygiene when working around contaminated water.

Breaking seals and removing the mask prematurely could result in diver contamination and future illness.

WARNING: STTU makes no recommendations for safe exposures in contaminated waters. Each site must be evaluated by the on-site supervisor and the diver himself. Hazards vary with the nature of the contaminant, time of exposure and concentration. Consultation with the Environmental Protection Agency, CHEMTREC or local health groups is strongly advised. Fire department personnel should be called in on all chemical spills, and to assist in the identification of hazardous materials.

For additional reading on this subject, obtain a copy of DIVING IN HIGH-RISK ENVIRONMENTS and THE DRY SUIT DIVING MANUAL by Steven M. Barsky, distributed by Dive Rescue International.

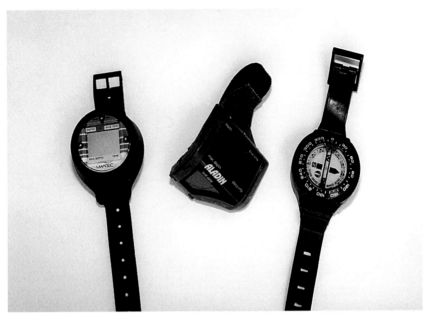

Essential instrumentation for diving operations: digital depth/timer, computer and compass.

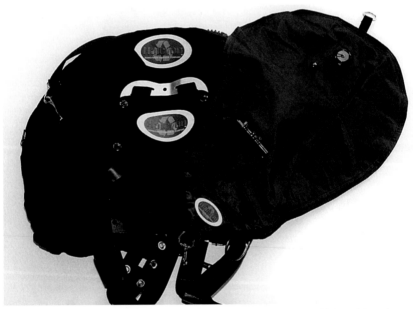

Halcyon wings and backplate complete with emergency lift bag/signal device for drift decompression.

7
SUPPORT EQUIPMENT

Apart from the equipment required to mount a diving operation, there is a wide variety of support gear that is essential for various types of rescues and recoveries. These requirements will depend on the local conditions, responsibilities of the SRT team, and could range from basic ropes and hand tools to heavy lift bags and recovery vehicles.

COMPRESSORS

Compressors fall into two categories: one for breathing air and the other for powering pneumatic tools and supplying air to airlifts and liftbags. Compressors designed for breathing air and diving then fall into two sub-categories: high pressure (HP) and low pressure (LP).

The HP compressor is the one with which most SCUBA divers are familiar and is found in any SCUBA shop or dive boat that does air fills. These HP compressors can range from small portable units like the **Bauer** Utilus to massive commercial units that weigh over a ton. Typically, these compressors are three-stage units that systematically increase the air pressure as it passes through three separate compression chambers.

A professional dive rescue team should have their own HP compressor of some form, whether it be a portable field unit, a trailer mounted system or a permanent filling station at their headquarters. Whatever compressor selected, it should meet the strict standards for compressed breathing air and be equipped with filters to remove excess moisture, oil vapor and gas contaminants like carbon dioxide and carbon monoxide.

Team members must be thoroughly trained in the operation, inspection and maintenance of the compressor(s). Many teams have large base units as well as small portable units for field use. All compressors should be periodically tested to ensure the purity of the air being delivered to the SCUBA cylinders or storage banks.

The low pressure (LP) breathing air compressor is used for surface-supplied diving operations and is usually truck, trailer or boat mounted. Since most SRT operations require rapid deployment and LP compressors are rather heavy and difficult to move, few teams utilize them. The alternative for surface-supplied diving is to fill SCUBA tanks from a HP compressor and then run these through a DCS or gas rack to give the diver the required LP air.

Teams that have a use for an LP compressor must run the compressed air into a volume tank before being routed through the manifold and umbilical to the diver. This volume tank prevents fluctuations in supply pressure and gives the diver an available air reservoir should the compressor run out of gas or cease to function. This system should be backed up with a bank of HP SCUBA tanks, controlled from the diving control panel, for added safety.

LASD portable HP compressor with air intake extended.

88

LASD Scuba truck.

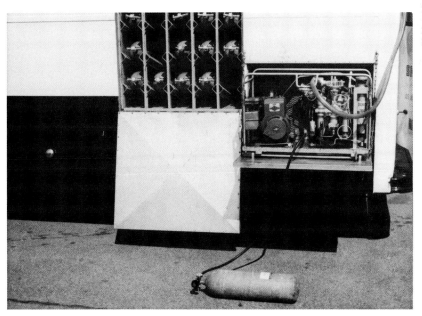

Scuba truck is equipped with HP compressor and 30 Scuba tanks in side racks.

SEARCH EQUIPMENT

Random shotgun type searches, without the use of search lines or a systematic plan, are ineffective exercises in futility. Only in the clearest of waters and under ideal conditions will the divers have any success. Most searches are in reduced visibility and require at least a minimal amount of planning and equipment.

At a minimum, the diver will need a marker buoy, an anchor line, a clump weight and search line. The first task on any police rescue or recovery operation is to establish a "last seen point" and mark it with a buoy as a reference point for the rest of the search. This will be covered in greater detail in Chapter 14 so for now we will simply list the items of use for searching:

- Several small bright marker buoys
- Two or three large buoys
- Several clump weights ranging from 10 to 30 pounds
- Several coils of ⅜" polypropylene rope from 70 to 300 feet long
- Rope bags for ease of handling in the water
- Various snap hooks and shackles
- Sketch paper and board
- Compasses for divers and Divemasters
- Flashlights, chem lights and strobes for night operations
- Local maps and nautical charts

RESCUE & RAPPELLING EQUIPMENT

Since many SRT teams are tasked with rescue operations and can be called on to operate in remote areas, there should be adequate rescue and rappelling equipment in the dive team's inventory. Local conditions will dictate the type and amount of equipment required but there are some pieces common to all teams:

- Personal rappelling ropes in 150' lengths
- Team rappel/rescue ropes in 300' lengths
- Rope deployment bags and backpacks
- Assorted locking and non-locking carabiners
- Assorted lengths of tubular webbing
- Individual harnesses/Swiss seats
- Gloves and helmets
- Assorted ascenders, pulleys and descenders
- Rescue litters and back boards
- Complete first aid/trauma kits
- Portable demand/positive pressure oxygen systems
- Portable radios on marine and rescue frequencies
- Survival rations, water and wilderness kits

RECOVERY GEAR

Most police diving is recovery work since it is only on rare occasions and in colder areas that rescue is a realistic expectation. The recoveries could range from guns and bodies to cars and boats. A professional team will have at least the following recovery gear in their dive truck:

- Assorted lengths of heavy nylon rope
- Body bags and liners
- Evidence containers for handguns and rifles
- Nylon straps and chains for vehicle recovery
- Small and large lift bags (50 lb to 3,000 lb)
- Lift bag inflation hose, connections and valves
- Ascenders, snap hooks and shackles for staged lifts

TOOLS

Fire departments have a wide variety of hand and power tools designed for rescue and extraction (Jaws of Life), just as SWAT teams have some very innovative methods for forced entry. Many of these tools and methods can be useful to the underwater recovery team but are often best reserved for use on dry land. The essentials for the dive team are basic hand tools for maintenance and a few extras for simple entries and extractions.

Light tools:

- Assorted screwdrivers
- Allen wrenches
- Adjustable and open ended wrenches
- Socket set
- Small and large hammers
- Pliers, side cutters and needle noses
- Specialty tools for dive gear
- Banding tool for hose fittings
- Knife
- Pipe wrenches and vise grips

Heavy tools:

- Crowbars and wrecking bars
- Sledgehammer and maul
- Large wrenches
- Heavy chisels and wedges
- Car jack and handle
- Marlin spike

Power tools:

- Jaws of Life/extraction tool
- Chain saw and cutting disc
- Cutting torch
- Thermic lance

LIGHTS

Apart from the personal dive lights that each team member carries, the response vehicle should have adequate lighting to operate in a night mode. Some boats and vehicles have lights permanently mounted to their exterior, where other agencies have portable emergency lighting that can be set up on stands and moved around.

Many diving operations will stop at nightfall and resume at first light because of the hazards or complications of searching in the dark. The primary reason is the increased probability of overlooking something in the search pattern. But if the operation continues into the night, the more light that can be thrown onto the dive site, the easier the dive team's job will be.

Additional lighting will require generators or power hookups on the response vehicles. The team will also need a good supply of hand-held lanterns and batteries for searching the river banks or related shoreline.

Strobe lights are useful for marking locations, objects or divers in the dark, since they can be seen at great distance. However they can also be very disorienting if too many are being used near one location.

Hurst power tools being used in an underwater extraction exercise.

8
EQUIPMENT MAINTENANCE

Several chapters in this book cover the maintenance requirements for specific pieces of equipment, e.g., dry suits, helmets, weapons, cameras, etc. So in this chapter maintenance is covered only in the broadest terms.

Because of the harsh conditions in which most teams operate: salt water, sand, dirt, ice, pollution and oil, equipment maintenance must be regular, routine and thorough. SRT equipment can be divided into two categories: life support equipment on which a team member may depend, and additional less critical support equipment.

The life support equipment that requires the most attention would include:

- All diving equipment, especially regulators and gauges
- Compressors and filters
- Rappelling ropes and rescue hardware
- Dry suits and umbilicals
- Decontamination suits and breathing apparatus
- Medical supplies and oxygen delivery systems
- All gas lines, connections and valves

After each training dive or call-out, all dive gear must be rinsed off in fresh water, washed in soapy water if necessary, and hung or laid out to dry. Repairs should be made, parts replaced or equipment trashed as necessary. When everything is 100% ready to dive, it can be repacked and prepared for the next operational alert.

The Operators Service Manual must be consulted when cleaning or servicing any of the above listed items. Each piece of equipment has unique cleaning and storage requirements, that if done incorrectly could render the item inoperable. Dry suits are a good example of a piece of equipment that can be more easily damaged by incorrect handling than regular use.

If any part of the diver's life support/breathing system becomes contaminated, it could cause serious problems on the next dive. Every fitting from the air supply, through the control system and umbilical to the helmet must be free from oil, chemicals, pollutants, and be capped or taped after every dive.

It is often hard to get a team motivated when it comes to cleanup, maintenance and repair work. Especially after a long day in the water when everyone is tired, cold and hungry. But the bottom line is that a team's professionalism can be judged by the status of their equipment **after** an operation. There is no predicting when the next call-out will occur so the equipment, like the divers, must be ready to go on short notice.

Maintenance duties should not fall on one or two team members. Everyone pitches in until the job is done and it is time to go home. Some repairs may have to be left until spare parts can be obtained, but it is better if a team has an essential parts inventory. If parts are used, log it in the repair log and make a note to replace them as soon as possible.

Some pieces of equipment require annual shop inspection and service by a trained technician, e.g., compressors, tanks, regulators, gauges, umbilicals, etc. These inspections and repairs should be logged in a team equipment log so that service dates are not missed.

All other non-life support equipment should also be carefully maintained so that it is ready when needed. Again, fresh water rinsing, drying and possibly a little oil on moving machine parts, will go a long way to preserving expensive equipment from salt water corrosion and rot.

Drying racks for suits and drying rooms for other equipment are almost essential for teams that dive regularly. Not all States are blessed with California sunshine, and nothing is more discomforting than having to don a cold, damp suit for a night dive. Diving equipment should not be repacked in bags and go-boxes until it is clean and dry.

Waterproof containers, covers and cases are essential for gear that is not routinely used. Especially cameras, videos, lights, batteries, weapons, etc. When a team responds to a call it is usually not known in advance what gear will be needed. It is time consuming and frustrating to have to clean and dry equipment that was never used, just for the lack of some way to keep it dry.

Rust and corrosion will develop very rapidly in a moist, salty environment. At the first indication of rust on any equipment: trailers, trucks, boats, tools, knives, support equipment, etc., it should be dried off, sanded down and given some form of protective coating. If allowed to continue, the corrosion will eventually weaken and destroy the host material.

9
RIGGING & LIFTS

So much of a diver's work involves ropes, knots and basic rigging, that the theory and practice of this subject should be stressed to all new team members. Divers with a strong construction, mountaineering or naval background will generally have most of the necessary rigging skills already, but other team members may be unable to tie even the most simple and essential knots. To have knots come undone, or ropes break during a recovery, will slow the job, require additional searching and possibly cause injury to a diver. To position ropes or hardware incorrectly can place unnecessary strain on the system and result in accident or injury.

There are several SRT tasks that require sound rigging. They are:

- Lifting light and heavy objects from the bottom
- Anchoring rappel ropes for descents down steep banks or cliffs
- Attaching submerged cars to recovery vehicles
- Doing staged lift-bag lifts of vehicles in deep water
- General mountaineering/rescue operations
- Setting boat moorings and securing deck equipment

ROPES

Ropes come in a variety of sizes, materials and construction for different tasks, and are made from either natural or synthetic fibers. Natural fiber ropes like cotton, hemp, manila and sisal are not suitable for use around diving operations since they soak up water, tend to sink, are slow to dry, and are subject to mildew and rot.

Synthetic ropes made from nylon, polyester (Dacron and Terylene), kevlar or polyolefin (polypropylene and polyethylene) are ideally suited to SRT work and have individual advantages and disadvantages. These ropes come in several sizes but the ones most common to the dive team

95

are ¼" to ⅝", and lengths from 100' to 300' (although longer lengths are available).

There are four basic types of rope construction, each with its own properties and specific applications.

LAID ropes are usually of the three-strand twist variety, and are not ideally suited to rescue work. Under load they tend to untwist which can cause spinning, stretching and kinking. The ⅜" polypro twist is a common utility rope found on dive sites and used as a search line or light hauling line.

SOLID BRAID ropes are a thick braid of fiber bundles with no core, that generally lose strength rapidly when subjected to abrasion. Most solid braid ropes are unacceptable as rappel/rescue lifelines.

DYNAMIC KERMANTLE ROPE consists of a high-strength inner core (kern) and an abrasion resistant, braided outer sheath (mantle). The "dynamic" refers to the rope's stretch or shock absorbent qualities when subjected to a drop load, etc. The manufacturers have sacrificed some of the rope's abrasion-resistant qualities to give the rope an added shock absorbent quality to prevent injury to a falling climber.

STATIC KERNMANTLE ropes also have an inner core and braided sheath but very little stretch under load. The safe working load of these ropes is about 1/15 of their breaking strength, and approximately 70% of the rope's strength is in the core. This allows the sheath to take a lot of abuse and abrasion without affecting the strength of the rope, but they do sacrifice some of the shock absorbent qualities of the dynamic rope when used for climbing. The ½" static rope is excellent for diving, caving and rescue operations (⅝" for heavier duty applications and ⅜" for light hauling and search lines).

The dive team's ropes should fall into two categories: those that are considered "lifelines" and used for rappel/rescue work, and those that are just work/utility lines. The lifelines must be given more attention and care than the work ropes so that they are not weakened prematurely by abuse or neglect.

- Store ropes in deployment bags in a cool, dry place
- Do not walk or drop objects on the ropes
- Keep ropes away from battery acids and contaminants
- Clean and dry ropes before storage
- Do not wash in chlorine or bleach compounds
- Use a chafing mat or rope guard on sharp corners

KNOTS

The strongest rope in the world is of no value if the knot which attaches it is not sound. There are only a few knots essential to good rope management but they must be well learned and practiced. The strength of a rope is reduced at the knot and different knots have different effects on rope strength, so it is important to utilize knots that are both secure and strength efficient.

The knots that an SRT diver must know are:

- Bowline
- Figure eight
- Square knot
- Clove hitch
- Sheet bend

Other useful knots are:

- Fisherman's knot
- Prusik knot/hitch
- Water knot
- Bowline on a bight
- Double sheet bend
- Rolling hitch
- Round turn and two half hitches

All these knots can be found in any good mountaineering, seamanship or rigging manual. The diver should also learn how to coil and stow ropes, handle boat lines, do basic splices and tie down deck equipment.

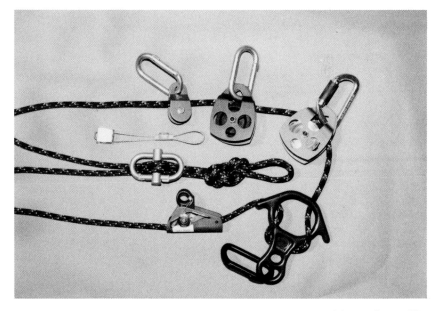

Essential rescue equipment includes assorted pulleys, carabiners, figure-8's, ropes and ascenders.

LIFT BAGS

The lift bag is a valuable tool for the recovery diver. They can range from small 50-pound units to large, sophisticated 3,000-pound pontoon bags, used for lifting boats and vehicles. The lift capacity of a bag will be dictated by the amount of water it displaces, and this will vary from salt to fresh water.

In the absence of professional lift bags one can use drums, buckets, trash bags or even plastic, gallon milk containers to create the needed buoyancy. It will be the diver's task to calculate the amount of lift needed, and the effect of the reduced pressure as the load rises in the water column. The lifting capability of the device should not be grossly greater than the weight of the object, since the air in the bag will expand on ascent and cause an out-of-control rush to the surface.

NOTE:

1 cubic foot in sea water = 64.0 pounds of lift
1 cubic foot in fresh water = 62.4 pounds of lift

1 U.S. gallon of sea water is 64 x .13368 = 8.56 pounds (approx.) so a 50-gallon drum gives 50 x 8.56 = 428 pounds of lift (less the weight of the drum and rigging)

1 U.S. gallon in fresh water is 62.4 x .13368 = 8.34 pounds so a 50-gallon drum gives 50 x 8.34 = 417 pounds (approx.)

Shallow lifts of less than 20 feet can be brought directly to the surface but deeper recoveries will need to be staged to avoid over-expansion of the gases and loss of control. Another risk of over-expansion is that the bag or container may burst and send the whole load back to the bottom. For this reason lift devices should be open at the bottom to allow venting, or have some form of relief valve.

Dive Rescue International students receive training in lift bag rigging.

98

When rigging a lift bag it is important that the diver not become entangled in the rigging, especially if on surface-supplied gear. As the bags fill and take shape the diver must again be cognizant of the risk of being dragged to the surface in a runaway inflation. Any boats in the area should stand clear so as not to be directly above the surfacing lift as well.

Rigging, lifting and light salvage are advanced diving skills that must be taught in the classroom, rehearsed on dry land, then practiced in confined water. Lift bags can be a valuable tool to the skilled diver, but a serious hazard to the untrained amateur.

Scuba tank with T connection used to inflate both bags simultaneously.

DSI students are also taught correct cable and chain rigging for vehicle extraction.

2,000-pound lift bags rigged front and rear; additional bag inside vehicle.

3000-pound pontoon bags rigged on either side of the vehicle.

Rescue rope, deployment bag and ascenders used for deep staged lifts.

Divers discuss lift bag rigging before attempting vehicle recovery.

Recovered vehicle in tow by San Diego Water Utilities barge.

RECOVERY HARDWARE

In addition to ropes, knots and lift bags a diver must be familiar with steel cables, chains, shackles, hooks, wire ropes, snatch blocks, winches, tuggers and capstans — the tools of heavy recovery and salvage. An overturned tanker truck in a deep river is not going to be pulled out with a few lift bags and a conventional wrecker.

Recoveries of this magnitude will bring in heavy recovery specialists with special equipment and large cranes, but it is still the diver's job to attach the slings and shackles and rig the direction of the pull/lift. For this type of task the SRT diver must be taught how to set chain-hooks, slings and to identify hard points for the lift.

For teams with little in-house knowledge in the area of heavy lifts, a visit to local commercial diving schools or salvage yards may be called for.

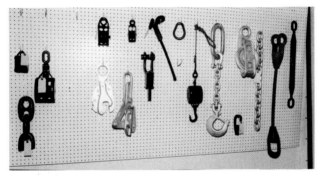

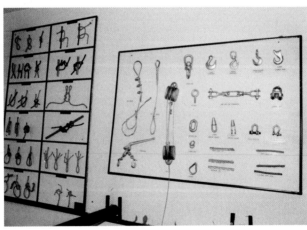

Assorted fittings and recovery hardware that all commercial divers are trained in at the College of Oceaneering.

TOWING

Once a car or boat has been floated with lift bags, it must be towed to a convenient point for extraction from the water. Avoid towing the vehicle over deeper water, on the off chance that the lift bags deflate and you end up with a more difficult task than before. As soon as the boat or car is on the surface begin moving it to shallower water, even if it means a longer route to the exit point.

It is also important to have a tow line that is longer than the greatest depth of the water. If the vehicle in tow sinks, it could drag down the tow vessel as well. A crew member should be ready to cut the tow line if this type of emergency develops, and the recovered object should have a long line and buoy still attached, so that it will not be necessary to search again before another recovery is attempted.

When working with tow truck operators it is essential that they come under the control of the Diving Supervisor. A dive team member should be stationed with the operator during all pulls to protect the interests of the divers. It is good policy to develop a working relationship with a few local wreckers, who have trucks of sufficient power to pull vehicles from the local waterways.

The more the team trains and works with one tow operator, the more comfortable and skilled both groups will become. A good operator will be able to suggest methods of rigging and recovery to the team, since this is a full-time occupation for him. More on this in Chapter 16.

Sheriff's divers prepare for a bottom search in the L.A. Harbor. Note large, high visibility buoy.

Sheriff's divers receiving briefing from top side incident commander

Amphibico housing with lights

10
PHOTOGRAPHY & VIDEO

Underwater photography and video have become invaluable tools in the preservation of crime scene evidence and accident data. However, underwater photography also requires expensive equipment and training in its use and maintenance. Situations that could require dive team photography or video recording are:

- Plane crashes and damage
- Submerged vehicles and their occupants
- Weapons and their relationship to bodies
- SCUBA victims and the state of their equipment
- Injuries to bodies
- Evidence that may be damaged during recovery
- License plates of suspected stolen vehicles
- Planning recovery operations
- Training slides and videos
- Recording injury to marine life
- Documenting commercial fishing violations
- Recording pollution and EPA violations
- Surveillance
- Planning tactical operations

PHOTOGRAPHIC EQUIPMENT

A photographic system is made up of four primary components: the camera, the lenses, the strobe and the film.

The most popular camera for U/W work is the **Nikonos,** since it is light, rugged and requires no special housings. Some divers prefer the **Nikonos V** for its automatic features and Through-the-Lens (TTL) metering while others prefer the Nikonos III for its rugged, manual simplicity.

Whichever is selected, the diver must still have a good understanding of the principles of U/W photography.

Lens selection falls into two categories: large-area, wide-angle coverage or macro/close-up photography.

The Nikonos is usually sold with a 35mm lens but the 15mm, 20mm and 28mm lenses are the most popular for wide-angle applications. Water magnifies the apparent size of objects to a point that a 35mm lens actually performs like a 50mm under water. Because of the limited visibility in most waters, it is essential that the underwater investigator get as close as possible to his subject. In addition, the optimum distance for flash photography under water is three to five feet, making the 15mm or 20mm lenses ideal.

For close-up photography of weapons, injuries and gauges, a close-up/macro attachment is required. This can be in the form of an additional lens added to the front of the existing lens or a tube placed between the lens and camera. In addition to the close-up attachment there will be a distance bar and frame to show exactly what the diver can expect to get in the final picture.

The SRT photographer will need to be able to operate at night, in deep water, inside vessels and planes, so a strobe is an essential addition to his camera. Since color is filtered out with depth, the light from the strobe will also give a more accurate depiction of the colors involved.

The strobe will require some form of arm/bracket to attach it to the camera. This arm should allow the diver to move or position the strobe for the best photographic effect. At times the diver will want to remove the strobe from the arm and hand-hold it to offset problems with silt and back-scatter (light bouncing off of small particles suspended in the water).

The film selected for SRT photography will depend on local conditions and operational requirements. The lower speed films like 100 ASA are most suitable and have a fine enough grain for the shots to be blown up for documentation and briefings. Faster films like 400 ASA may be needed in darker waters and 1000-3200 ASA may be needed for surveillance where a strobe would compromise the operation.

The faster films will also allow the use of higher "f" stops (f11-f22) and thus greater depth of field. Depth of field refers to the amount of the scene that will be in focus, in front of and behind the selected focal distance (e.g., 10 feet). This is important when photographing large objects like planes or showing the relationship between two or three spaced objects (e.g., a body and a weapon or an engine broken from a wing). Whatever the film speed, always use 36 shot rolls fo reduce the number of times the diver must surface to reload. Most scenes will require less than one roll of film, but the divers should be encouraged to shoot the whole roll to guarantee good results.

The selection of slide or print film will depend on the ultimate use of the photos. Slides are good for briefings and lectures but prints are easier to pass around or reproduce in documents. With "one-hour" developing readily available, prints can be developed and studied on-site before any decisions are made with regard to disturbance of the evidence.

It is a good policy to document, sketch, map and photograph all crime and accident scenes for future reference and testimony. It may be months or years before the diver is required to appear in court and the memory cannot be relied upon for minute details.

Nikonos V with additional 20mm lens and 103 strobe.

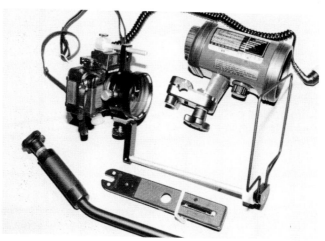

Nikonos V with Macro attachment, 35mm lens and optional strobe.

State of the art Amphibico VH1000 marine video housing for 3CCD digital 6 mm video.

CAMERA MAINTENANCE

Many a good roll of film has been lost to a flooded camera because of poor loading and unloading practices. Underwater cameras are not cheap and flooding one can be an expensive and inconvenient proposition. The Nikonos cameras have a set of "O" ring seals on the main body, lenses, strobe connectors, winders and rewinders.

The main body and lens "O" rings need to be kept cleaned and siliconed at all times. Before each operation the seals should be carefully removed, cleaned and lubricated with a light coating of silicon grease. The grooves and seats that come in contact with the "O" rings also need to be cleaned of any visible sand, dirt or water.

If a strobe is to be used, then the "O" rings and seats on the connector/sync cables will also need to be tended to. The battery cover on the strobe also has "O" ring seals.

When entering and exiting the water the camera should be handed to the diver carefully. Do not jump in with the camera in your hand and be sure to attach it to your person when swimming or working under water. As soon as the camera exits the water it should be rinsed in fresh water (preferably immersed completely), and then dried. Do not leave cameras, film or accessories sitting in the hot sun or exposed to salt spray.

Dry the camera and your hands carefully, before removing or changing film. Be aware of the potential for water to drip from your head, hair or equipment into the open camera body while changing film.

Store and transport cameras and accessories in rigid, padded cases of the Pelican variety. Clean and dry all equipment, and remove the batteries before it goes into the case. The spare parts kit should include a full set of "O" rings, a tube of silicon grease, essential tools and extra batteries.

PHOTOGRAPHIC TRAINING

Photography is a specialized skill and underwater photography even more so. Personnel will require photographic training if they are to get acceptable results in recording U/W evidence and crime scenes. Once the recovery has been completed, there are no second chances to record or photograph the site.

U/W photographic training must begin with a thorough understanding of conventional photographic techniques. This can be obtained through police forensic departments, professional photographers within the agency, college extension programs or police science seminars.

For underwater crime scene photography there are several contract instructors that run U/W investigator/photographer programs. Florida has a two-week State approved course and the major sport SCUBA associations all have related specialty certifications. Supervisors should try to select team members who show an interest or aptitude for photography and help develop their skills.

Finally, there is no substitute for just getting wet and shooting a lot of film under various conditions. Books like "The Nikonos Handbook" by Jim and Cathy Church, are also invaluable sources of tips and techniques for the SRT diver who cannot get the formal training.

LA Sheriff's diver with Nikonos III, 15 mm wide angle lens and dual strobes.

CRIME SCENE & ACCIDENT PHOTOGRAPHY

The investigative photography of a dive site begins before the diver enters the water. Photos should document points of entry, "last seen points," the surrounding crime scene and physical evidence leading up to the accident. This is best done with a conventional SLR camera. Once the senior investigator is satisfied that the shoreline evidence is well documented the divers can prepare for the underwater phase.

After the camera is loaded, "O" rings are cleaned and siliconed and the strobe is checked for function, the diver must enter the water in such a manner as to avoid disturbing the evidence or available visibility. This may mean entering and approaching from down current so as not to stir up the bottom and cloud the water. The diver should also avoid unnecessary use of his fins and try to keep them clear of the bottom. If sediment does get stirred up, the diver should stop and remain motionless until it settles and he can get the best possible shots.

The film is the cheapest part of the whole operation and there are no second chances, so shoot as much as necessary to cover the entire scene. It is also a good policy to "bracket" important shots by shooting them at one "f" stop higher, and then one lower, than the recommended setting. The angle of the strobe head can also be changed to give different lighting and reduce the chance of "bounce back" or hot spots ruining the shot. Remember to change the focal distance (feet to object) as you move in and out framing your shots.

Aircraft crash sites should be photographed from the eight points of the compass, then four shots of the fusilage and finally from directly overhead. The balance of the 36-shot roll can be utilized to document damage to propellers, landing gear, wings, and the relationship of any bodies thrown from the wreck.

Once the overall scene shots have been completed, the diver can either change lenses or cameras and go in for the close-up shots of smaller pieces of critical evidence. These could include:

- Injuries to bodies
- Weapons
- ID numbers on vehicles, ships or aircraft
- Gauges, altimeters, compasses, clocks, etc.
- Depth and pressure gauges, timers, weight belts, BCs and regulator on SCUBA victims
- Light switches, ignitions, gear shifts and emergency brakes on vehicles

When the cameras are dried and unloaded, the film must be tagged with the date, time and diver's name, since it is now part of the chain of evidence. Small film canisters are easily misplaced so they must be passed to someone reliable, and processed as soon as possible.

It is important to photograph Scuba victims before recovery to assist the Medical Examiner / Investigators in establishing a cause of death.

Many Scuba victims die with their weight belts still in place.

Attempt to photograph diver's console to indicate air pressure remaining, depth and time.

VIDEO PHOTOGRAPHY

Technology has given the diving community a wide range of compact video systems that are ideally suited to law enforcement diving. The team can now video all training and operations for future review and evidence can be preserved indefinitely.

The new line of video cameras and underwater housings are very user-friendly and are easier to learn than conventional photographic systems. This does not mean that one does not have to study the Owner/User manuals that come with the cam-corders and housings, or take at least some elementary training in their use. A flooded video system can be more expensive and just as inconvenient as a flooded Nikonos. "O" rings must still be cleaned and siliconed, housings tested for water-tight integrity and batteries kept charged.

Video systems come in two forms: the commercial grade topside mounted monitor/recorder with a cable running to the diver's hand-held camera/light system, and the smaller compact units that utilize a cam-corder in an amphibious housing.

The commercial video systems allow the diver to give topside a running commentary on his findings as they watch on a monitor. This allows the Diving Supervisor to direct the diver under water and make on-the-spot decisions. At the same time all the visuals and dialog are being recorded. The less desirable features of these units are the cost, weight and size that makes them unsuitable for many teams tasked with rapid deployment.

The smaller, self-contained systems allow the diver to swim freely, recording as he goes. However, the Supervisor must wait until the diver surfaces to replay the scene and make decisions. These units can also be equipped with lights and filters to get the optimum results, either under water or on dry land.

Mike Gast of Metro Dade Underwater Recovery Team demonstrates his agency's underwater video system.

112

Underwater video techniques are similar to those used for still photography, in that the diver must learn not to stir up the bottom and to film from down current. An additional skill the diver must develop is the ability to pan slowly and smoothly without any apparent jerky movements.

Do not remove video cameras from wet housings; keep the lenses protected and covered; do not store any equipment without thorough drying; keep batteries charged; and transport systems in shockproof, waterproof cases.

NYPD diver with hand-held, topside-controlled and monitored video camera.

NYPD diving supervisor monitors diver's progress and records data while watching the video monitor on the boat's bridge.

A good example of back-scatter as strobe light bounces off particles suspended in the water.

Sharp, clear pictures are possible when the photographer waits for silt to settle.

PART II

DEPLOYMENT

Sheriff's divers working off of 28' Skipjack

11
BY LAND & SEA

Most U.S. dive teams will respond to an incident by either vans, trucks, boats or helicopters. A few will have call to use commercial or military fixed-wing aircraft, if the distances involved are considerable. Whatever the means of transportation, there will need to be a certain amount of equipment preparation and organization common to all operations.

The dive unit must maintain a high level of both individual and team skills. Personal fitness is of prime importance since there is no way to anticipate the distances that one may need to swim, the sea state, the water temperatures or the magnitude of the disaster/rescue. When in doubt, train for a worst case scenario.

Equipment must be packed in such a way that personal dive gear and team equipment is easily identified and transported. Each diver should have a full set of SCUBA gear in a strong dive bag, with his name on the outside. He should have all the necessary spare parts, small tools and batteries for his personal kit.

Team equipment, surface-supplied gear, search and recovery items should be packed in clearly labelled Go-Boxes. Cameras, videos, lights, compasses and gauges should all be packed in padded rigid cases with "O" ring seals. Spares must be packed for all specialized equipment.

Search and rescue (SAR) equipment will need to be packed in comfortable mountaineering packs, butt packs or lighter day-packs. Oxygen delivery systems, medical kits, radios, lights and emergency rations will also need to be included in the backpacks. Rescue/rappel ropes should be set up in rope deployment bags for ease of handling and reduced chance of tangling.

Check-lists should be included with each individual pack and Go-Box and team check-lists should be made up to cover all the equipment required for different types of call-outs. Not all equipment need to be taken on all operations, but it is essential that important items not be left at HQ when the team is in the field and possibly hours away.

RESPONSE PROCEDURES

Team leaders and administrators will need to establish a set of written procedures for team call-outs. This should cover such points as:

- Types of emergencies and tasks assigned to the dive unit
- Who can authorize a call-out?
- Contact numbers and addresses of team members
- Shift rotations and on-duty personnel available
- Availability of beepers/pagers/radios
- Which response vehicles are in the field
- Which divers have their gear with them, on/off duty
- Response time to headquarters or incident location
- Vehicles/boats/helos available
- Loading of Go-Boxes and specialized equipment
- Cooperation with other agencies
- Chain of command on site
- Minimum number of dive team members necessary on site
- Availability of recovery vehicles/cranes
- Proximity of recompression facilities/chambers
- Response time of paramedics/ambulances
- Skills of local emergency rooms/hospitals and knowledge of dive-related injuries
- Team's rights to refuse a hazardous dive/recovery
- Availability of divers from neighboring agencies
- Availability of commercial divers for deep operations

Once the team gets to the dive site there must be a second set of procedures relating to the actual diving operations. These will be covered in PART III of this book.

VEHICLES

Upon touring the U.S. we have found a wide variety of vehicles in use by law enforcement U/W recovery units. They range from patrol cars and small vans to converted trucks and 28' mobile command posts. Obviously the vehicles that are custom made for rescue/recovery diving operations are the best, but also the most expensive.

Some agencies have gone to several smaller vans or utility trucks, while others have opted for the one large response vehicle that is capable of carrying all essential personnel and equipment. The smaller vehicles definitely give the greater flexibility and ability to respond to multiple locations.

Four-wheel-drive can be of considerable value when operating around beaches, ponds, river banks and mountainous lakes. The 4WD rescue trucks should not be used for recovery operations — that is the job for the wreckers and tow trucks. The 4WD is simply to get the team and equipment as close as possible to the dive site while reducing the

Three Rivers, Michigan Dive Rescue truck utilized by the combined teams of Three Rivers Fire Department, Lockport-Fabius-Park Fire Department and St. Joseph County Sheriff's Department.

Broward County Sheriff's Dive Rescue truck.

chance of getting stuck. Some rescue trucks are set up with winches and booms for personnel and litter recovery but they should not be committed to trying to pull out vehicles. 4WD is also useful on slippery launch ramps and soft ground when launching the team's trailered boats.

The accompanying photos will show several modifications that can be made to trucks to make them suitable for SRT operations.

When a team arrives on site in their dive truck, it is important that the support personnel work out of the storage compartments and that the divers dress out of their dive bags. There is nothing more unprofessional to see than gear strewn all over the dive site with no sense of order. Excess dive gear, clothes, towels, uncoiled ropes and hoses, tools, etc., are the most common items that are not correctly stowed.

Law enforcement personnel will also need to establish a procedure for securing their firearms while involved in diving operations. Hanging gun-belts on rear-view mirrors, throwing loaded handguns into dive bags or leaving them on the seat in an unlocked patrol car is unacceptable and extremely unsafe. If they cannot be secured under lock and key, one officer should be assigned to watch over the divers' weapons.

With the crowds that gather at crime scenes and dive sites, it is only a matter of time before expensive equipment (dive gear, gauges, knives, radios, etc.) will begin to go missing. By only taking out that which is needed or being used, and stowing the rest, the scene security will be maintained and the team will appear neat and professional.

A large plastic ground sheet is very useful for keeping gear out of the dirt and providing a clean, dry spot for the divers to dress-in. Yellow police line tape should be strung around the dive site to keep crowds back, even if it is not a possible crime scene. It is amazing the power that a thin strip of yellow plastic has on a crowd, especially when it says "Police line — do not cross."

One of four vans owned by the Metro Dade Police Underwater Recovery Unit.

NYPD Scuba team's dive van with separate wet and dry areas, showers, changing rooms and lunch area in the rear.

LA Sheriff's ESD Rescue trucks are used in support of the Scuba van shown in Chapter 7.

As with all equipment that is subjected to salt water and harsh conditions, the response vehicles must be carefully maintained and serviced. After each operation, all bags, boxes and equipment should be unloaded from the truck to allow the salt water to be hosed and wiped off, and then allowed to dry. Pools of water in utility boxes, in the trunk or on the deck will result in unnecessary rusting and corrosion. Winch cables will need to be run out, cleaned and lubed. Damage should be repaired, spares replaced and equipment reloaded when dry. All of this should be a priority to the whole team as soon as they return to base, and not be left to just a few.

LASD new Rescue trucks have a rear-mounted 1,000-pound winch and boom backed up by a capstan for personnel and victim recovery.

Clean, organized and inventoried storage compartments are essential for rapid deployment and efficient operations.

BOATS

As with vehicles, there is a wide variety of boats in use by police dive teams. These range from two to ten-man inflatables all the way up to 38' to 52' plus motor launches. Some divers could even find themselves being deployed from the USCG's large, heavily armed, ocean-going ships.

Many agencies prefer not to incur the costs (and they are considerable) of maintaining a large boat and instead, work out agreements with Harbor Patrol, Coast Guard or local commercial operators. This also eliminates the need to hire and train a skipper and deck crew. However, there are many advantages to having a designated dive/rescue boat that the SRT team can consider their own.

- Modifications can be made to make the boat more suitable for dive operations
- Compressor and tank racks can be installed
- Dive/rescue equipment can be kept on board for immediate deployment
- VHF radios, radars, side-scans, LORAN, U/W video, navigational charts, etc., can all be added to improve emergency response capabilities
- Swim steps can be added, hand rails in the dive area can be modified, storage for wet suits and dive bags can be organized, decontamination and shower tanks installed
- Safety and fire-fighting equipment can be kept current
- Spotlights, light bars, sirens and agency identification can be added
- Additional weapons and tactical equipment can be secured aboard for call-outs that escalate unexpectedly

All of these things cost money, but for a large agency with a significant maritime responsibility, the convenience (and pride) of having their own boat is tremendous.

NYPD Scuba launch.

LASD SEB/ESD 28-foot Skipjack used for dive rescue operations.

Boats up to 28 feet can be trailered for relocation to inland lakes and rivers.

Boston Whalers are ideally suited for dive rescue operations.

INFLATABLE BOATS

The smaller inflatable boats, of the Zoviac/Avon variety, have long been valued by military and police dive teams for several reasons:

- Availability
- Ease of handling, storage and transportation
- Relative light weight
- Buoyancy and stability
- Ease of entry and exit
- Relative low cost
- Minimum maintenance and long life

Inflatable boats fall into three basic categories: less than 14 feet that can be easily assembled and deployed by two people; boats 13-16 feet that are normally permanently set up on trailers; and the larger commercial boats that go from 17-30 plus feet.

Commercial/military grade boats in the 14-16 foot class seem to be the most suitable for special response teams and dive rescue operations. Smaller boats do not have the deck space or capacity for additional personnel and their essential diving gear.

Inflatable boats are available with either rigid or non-rigid keels. The rigid boats of the RIBs (Rigid Inflatable Boats) design come with a full fiberglass hull and inflatable sides. The rigid hull allows for greater speed and a smoother ride, and when combined with the inflatable sides are more stable than conventional boats. But there is a drawback with the RIBs system — one sacrifices the compact storage, light weight and versatility of the non-rigid units. A RIBs boat must be trailer mounted and cannot be deflated, rolled up and transported in the back of a truck. The deep V of the fiberglass hull also restricts the boat's movement in shallower waters, but provides excellent performance in open waterways.

The UM line of Sillinger boats have a unique feature that makes them well suited to SRT diving operations — a removable, collapsible keel. When assembled, the boats have all the performance of a rigid hull but with a shallow draft and the ability to disassemble the boat for ease of storage and transportation.

The UM Sillingers are extremely rugged boats, constructed from very high-resistance 1880 decitex Hypalon Neoprene that is impervious to gasoline. When working around marinas, ports or boating accidents, the gasoline in the water can turn the PVC materials of other boats very stiff and brittle. This will not occur with the Hypalon/polyamide materials found in the Sillingers and other high quality boats.

There are many instances when it is very useful to be able to unload, unpack and assemble a small inflatable boat at a remote dive site, lake or river. Keep in mind that a boat "recommended" by the manufacturer for eight people may only hold four or five divers with all their equipment, and fewer if surface-supplied diving is anticipated. When in doubt about procuring an inflatable boat, it is better to err on the side of a little too big than too small and cramped.

LA Sheriff's helicopter deploys an inflatable Sillinger in a rapid deployment exercise.

Sheriff's Deputies assemble a smaller inflatable boat in a dive rescue exercise.

Inflatables in the 16+-foot range are usually permanently trailered.

Avon R-310FRB.

Achilles SH-156 is a good example of the minimum size boat for surface-supplied diving operations.

SEALS prepare to deploy from Zodiac, F-470.

TRAINING & SEAMANSHIP

For an agency that has their own boats, large or small, it is essential that all members of the dive team receive training in handling and maintenance. Apart from the designated skipper(s), all team members should receive instruction, training and experience in:

- Basic seamanship and navigation
- Docking and line handling skills
- Location of fuel valves and electrical systems
- Fueling procedure
- Engine start and stop procedures
- Familiarity with radio, depth finder, LORAN, side-scan, etc.
- Anchoring and anchor recovery
- Cleaning and maintenance
- Operation of bilge pumps and fire system
- Local and State boating regulations

There is no telling when an emergency may arise that will require the immediate and skilled reactions of a member of the dive team. In addition, law enforcement personnel operating in a marine environment must be conversant with the local and State Boating Regulations, so that they can correctly handle any accidents, disputes or violations that may arise with, or aboard, other vessels in the area.

MAINTENANCE

Because of a boat's prolonged exposure to water, especially salt water, corrosion is a major problem. Much of a boat's engine and electrical system is designed to function in a salt water/sea-air environment, but preventive maintenance, wash-downs and periodic inspections will greatly increase the life and dependability of a boat. After use, anything that can be rinsed in fresh water should be; anything that can be covered or sealed should be; and even if the boat is not used it must be inspected regularly for corrosion and deterioration. Boats that are not taken out on a regular basis, still need to have the engines run on a weekly basis to keep the lubricants circulating and to prevent internal and external moving parts from seizing up.

The divers will probably be tasked with periodic hull cleans if the boat is kept in the water. This is to remove marine growth, weed and barnacles that can damage the finish, create drag and increase fuel consumption. Water cooling intakes should also be cleaned of potential blockages that could result in engine overheating, and zinc blocks can be checked for deterioration and replaced if necessary. The propeller(s) and steering gear should be inspected for damage and freed of any weed, line, rope or net that may have been picked up on previous outings.

Boats that can be trailered (usually less than 28') should be hosed down, scrubbed down and kept in a clean, well maintained state that will lend credit to the professionalism of the dive team and their agency.

SEAL rescue swimmer reenacts the rescue of a Navy pilot during the Gulf War.

12
BY AIR

HELICOPTERS

The helicopter has been the work-horse of search and rescue (SAR) ever since it proved its value in troop deployment and medical evacuation (medi-vac) in Korea, Malaya, Borneo and Vietnam. The helicopter's ability to land or hoist personnel from confined areas, and then transport them directly to support units or hospitals, has resulted in the saving of many lives that would otherwise have been lost. Dive rescue teams can also take advantage of this rapid deployment capability.

There are several U.S. agencies with dive teams that utilize the helicopter for transportation and deployment of their teams and the recovery of victims. While some make the helicopter a pivotal part of their standard operating procedures (SOPs) others use them infrequently and only when alternate methods are unsuitable, unavailable or time is of the essence.

Helicopters are extremely expensive to purchase and maintain, so there are several alternatives to ownership. If your agency has an aero bureau for patrol and SWAT functions, then the dive team can develop a working relationship that will give them air time for maritime call-outs. For an agency with no air capability, a mutual aid agreement can be worked out with a neighboring law enforcement agency, Coast Guard or National Guard unit that does have suitable helicopters and trained pilots. The final option is to establish contact with a commercial helicopter operator who is willing to donate or hire out his services in emergencies.

Whichever of the above categories a dive team falls into, it is not enough to just have a pilot and craft available. Time must be allocated to train the team in helo deployment and recovery methods, while the pilots will need to gain experience in servicing the team's needs. Having divers jump from a low-flying craft, often in adverse conditions, is not a skill that helicopter pilots pick up in basic flight school. Each new technique, whether it be helo-casting, rappelling, fast roping, skid riding or hoist recovery, needs to be practiced by both pilot and team members, under ideal conditions, before it is attempted on an operation.

Kodiak, Alaska's ASAP team, has a good working and training relationship with the local U.S. Coast Guard station, for all their dive rescue related helo ops. But since the Coast Guard helicopter pilots rotate out every six to eight months, training with the dive team must be a bimonthly event. This is the minimum to keep pilots and divers at a safe and functional skill level.

TYPES & MODIFICATIONS

Not all helicopters are suited to SAR and SRT operations. Some are specifically designed for this role while others can be modified to deploy divers. Not all helicopters have the flotation equipment for prolonged operation over water, and others can only drop but not recover the dive team.

U.S. Air Force Pararescue teams (PJs) make good use of the HH-3, HH-53 (extra H is for mid-air refueling capability) and MH-53 (advanced navigational system) for their rescue needs. All are equipped with floating litters, ample room for a full team with equipment, and recovery hoists. These are supported by the smaller UH-1 Huey and the newer UH-60 Blackhawk from Sikorsky.

The U.S. Coast Guard deploys the large HH-52A (Sikorsky S-62) and the HH-3F Pelican (Sikorsky S-61-R) for extended range search and rescue work, while the newer Aerospatiale SA 366 Dolphin is utilized for shorter range operations. These helicopters are stationed all the way from the chill of Alaska to the heat of Florida and equipped with extremely sophisticated navigational, night vision and recovery equipment.

New York Police SCUBA Unit pre-positions two divers each day at their Air-Sea Rescue Unit. They will generally be the first divers on site, dropping from their pontoon equipped UH-1 Huey, anywhere in the vast reaches of the New York harbor or coastal waterways.

Los Angeles Sheriff's SEB/ESD divers can be skid deployed from one of Aero Bureau's several 500s, but utilize their Sikorsky S-58T (T for turbine converted) for larger operations that may require more than two divers and/or hoist recovery capability.

Other helicopters in wide use by SAR dive teams are the Bell 206B-3 JetRanger and 206L-3 LongRanger; the AS350 AStar and the AS355 TwinStar; and the McDonnell Douglas MD500E.

There are many factory options and after-sales additions that can make a helicopter a more valuable rescue tool:

- Sliding or removable doors
- Hard points for rappelling or fast roping

- Recovery hoists with special slings or seats
- FLIR — Forward-Looking Infra-Red
- NVDs — Night Vision Devices
- Nightsun remote controlled external lighting system
- WSPS — Wire Strike Protection System (wire cutter)
- Floating rescue litters and attachment points
- Crew Chief's belt and retaining harness
- Additional external hard points and slings for skid deployment
- Pontoons or emergency flotation systems for use over water
- Advanced navigational systems; GPS, Inertial, Dopler, etc.
- Radio systems compatible with law enforcement/rescue and maritime frequencies

NYPD Air/Sea Rescue helicopter equipped with pontoons.

USAF Pararescue UH-60.

SAFETY & LIMITATIONS

Helicopters, by nature and reputation, are extremely sensitive to over-loading, weight distribution, weather conditions and temperature/altitude changes. It is only through complex engineering, skilled piloting and the grace of God that they succeed in flying at all. Helicopters are not rugged pieces of machinery, will not sustain much abuse and operate only within a narrow set of limitations.

The person ultimately responsible for the loading, unloading, flight operations and safety in a helicopter is the pilot. Since only the pilot understands the flight characteristics, loading limits and performance limitations of his aircraft it is essential that there be constant communication between him and the dive team in both training and operations.

All flights should begin with a briefing that involves all participants in the rescue. No matter what the dive team requests or needs, it is the pilot who will have the final say as to whether their requests are reasonable, possible or safe. With time and training a good, professional relationship will develop between the pilot and the rescue team.

The pilot may delegate many of the loading and unloading duties to a Crew Chief or Flight Engineer. This will include the boarding and deploying of the divers and their equipment. In this case the Crew Chief's word is final since he is in constant contact with the pilot by means of a head-set and throat or boom microphone. Where helicopters are too small to accommodate a Crew Chief or even a co-pilot, then the crew chief responsibilities may be given to a member of the rescue team. This should be a member with considerable experience in helicopter operations and intimate familiarity with the dynamics involved in helo jumping and recovery procedures.

Florida Police divers prepare to board the helicopter under the watchful eye of the pilot and instructor.

LASD ESD divers skid ride an MD500 in surface rescue gear.

Note rope handles anchored to helicopter's exterior hard points. It is important that divers drop simultaneously.

HELICOPTER OPERATIONS

The helicopter is not the answer to all prayers for a dive team. There are many instances when a helicopter is of no value: inclement weather, poor visibility, night operations or response to areas that are closer to the team by land or sea. Unless the dive team is routinely stationed at the heliport and the helicopter has engines running, there can be significant delays in getting a team airborne.

The team must be assembled and transported to the helipad; the flight crew must be notified, assembled and briefed; engines must be run up, weather checked and navigational calculations made; equipment and divers must be loaded; some equipment and personnel may have to be discarded because of weight limitations; and only then does the team become mobile. Now, providing the helicopter does not have engine trouble, the rescue site must be found from the air; an evaluation of conditions made; and the team dropped in.

On the bright side, there are more than enough instances to justify the use of helicopters. Back-country rivers and lakes inaccessible by boat or truck; large counties with many waterways; offshore islands and dive sites popular with local fishermen and sport divers; areas with adverse sea conditions that would make boat deployment hazardous.

Whenever a rescue team is deployed from a helicopter, especially one with no recovery hoist, there is always the possibility that the helicopter may have to leave the team because of low fuel, mechanical problems or deteriorating weather conditions. For these reasons, helicopter operations should be supported by a boat deployment at sea or on lakes, and a truck deployment in wilderness areas.

The NY Police SCUBA divers who are dropped by Air Sea Rescue are routinely the first on site for a rescue, and even though the Harbor Patrol SCUBA launch is en route, it may be 20-40 minutes away. With 146 square miles of navigable waters and 576 miles of waterfront, response time by boat or truck alone could be too slow to effect a rescue.

Each member of Alaska's ASAP team jumps with a survival kit that can support two men for three days, on the off chance that the Coast Guard helicopter may have to leave them to fend for themselves if a recovery becomes impossible. This requires special training in cold weather, wilderness survival for all the members of this hardy, volunteer team.

Alaskan ASAP Team dressed in and ready to go for helicopter deployment training.

ASAP divers drop from US Coast Guard Sikorsky.

Police divers helo-cast for surface swim operations.

NYPD divers jump from Air/Sea Rescue helicopter from a little greater height than necessary.

Sheriff's divers drop into an inland lake from Aero Bureau 500.

HELO-CASTING

Helo-casting, also known as helitac or helo-jumping, refers to the technique of jumping from a hovering or slow moving helicopter to effect a rescue. The optimum height and speed for a dive team to jump is "low and slow," 10 feet and 10 knots (20/20 max.).

Although some military spec. warfare units, like the SEAL teams, work their way up to 40/40s (40 feet at 40 knots), the average dive rescue team has no use for these high-speed, bullet dodging maneuvers. The risk of injury or equipment loss is too great for anything faster than the absolute minimums.

The divers should board the helicopter in full SCUBA with all loose gear secured and fins and mask in hand (or over the wrist). About 3-5 minutes out from the distress location the divers will make last minute equipment checks and adjustments, buddy checks, and then wait for an update on the site when the team leader or pilot can get a visual.

The helicopter pilot should approach the drop site from down-wind (or up-current if the divers may have difficulty swimming against it) so as not to buffet the survivors with the rotor wash. Then, holding head into the wind, he will drop to 10 or 20 feet and slow to 10 knots for the jump. As the pilot is doing this, the crew chief will open the doors (if they are not already open or removed) and signal the divers to stand by in the door. On command, the divers will grip their masks with one hand and vests or belts with the other, face into the wind, step from the door or skids, get their feet together and prepare for the impact.

Some teams prefer to jump with their masks off to avoid losing them on impact. PJs tape their fins on with duct tape (100 mph tape), while others tie a string from fin to leg to avoid getting them knocked off. All teams tilt their heads forward to avoid getting hit by the tank valve in the back of the head. On impact, divers should surface, give the OK sign and buddy-up for the tasks ahead. The amount of equipment, type of suit and size of tanks will be dictated by local conditions, nature of the rescue and response time of surface units.

When jumping into contaminated water, near oil spills or in heavy pollution, the dive team should be equipped with dry suits and full-face masks. Jumping from too great a height, although "macho" and impressive for the news cameras, will blow the seals on the dry suit and mask and result in the diver being exposed to contaminated water, bacterial infection and toxic or corrosive chemicals. Under these conditions it is no simple task to pull the diver from the water and put him through a decontamination process. He may have to wait several minutes or even hours in a contaminated state until support arrives.

FAST ROPING & RAPPELLING

Neither fast roping nor rappelling are of great use to an SRT dive team unless they also have a tactical responsibility. Rappelling is of use when doing SAR operations in mountainous, uneven terrain or heavily wooded areas where a helicopter cannot land. Fast roping is an effective method for getting a tactical unit on to the deck of a ship or oil rig in as short a time as possible. Both of this will be discussed more in the tactical section of this book (Part IV).

If the dive team is to get involved in helo-rappel there are a few points worth considering. Firstly, all team members should be trained in rappelling and rigging on dry land before attempting helicopter descents. The high ambient noise level, increased costs and increased stress make for a very unsatisfactory training environment.

A local fire tower, cliff or bridge can be utilized for valuable low stress training. The divers must be taught not only how to make a smooth, safe descent but also rope management, knots, rigging, hardware, anchor points, hand signals and emergency procedures. Equipped with their own harnesses, figure 8s, carabiners and gloves, the team should practice until their skills are flawless. Emphasis should be put on a clean drop-off, a smooth descent, no violent or unnecessary braking and a controlled landing/splash-down.

After a lecture on safety, hand signals and helicopter dynamics by the pilot or crew chief, the team is ready for their first helo-rappels. The signals should be for "Stand by," "Hook up," "Get in the door," "Get on the skid," "Wind down" and "Go!" The order and signals will vary from team to team so it is essential that signals be established, standardized and learned by **all** team members.

The descent should be smooth with no "jumping" from the skids that will rock the ship unnecessarily and make it harder for the pilot to stay on location. The same is true for violent braking or premature drops before the team member(s) on the other side of the ship is ready to go.

It is usually more practical for divers to skid ride smaller helicopters than to deploy from inside.

FBI HRT practicing fast roping techniques prior to the Los Angeles Olympic Games.

ESD diver rappels from Sikorsky S-58T to assist in the apprehension of a suspect overboard.

WET RECOVERY

Wet recover or hoist operations are used where the helicopter is equipped to recover divers, victims or survivors from the water. There are several ways this can be accomplished:

1. **Conventional hoist:** This can only be done if the helicopter is equipped with a power driven winch, sufficient cable and some form of recovery sling, litter or seat. In a litter recovery the diver secures the victim in the litter and then sends or rides it up to the door of the helicopter. The diver enters first and then assists the crew with the litter. Some seats and slings are rigged so that both the rescuer and the victim can ride up together. With these the diver enters backwards, then drags the victim in.

2. **Platform recovery:** Some helicopters, like the Coast Guard H-3, can land on the surface of the water and lower a platform out the side door. With this the diver swims the victim to the platform, assists them in and enters last.

3. **Pontoon landing:** Helicopters like NYPD's Huey are equipped with large inflated pontoons with steps, so the divers can swim the victims to the side and then assist them into the craft.

4. **Cargo/personnel nets:** This is a system where a helicopter that has neither hoist nor water landing capability can effect a recovery. It consists of a special semi-rigid net slung on a rope or cable below the helicopter, into which the diver swims with the victim. The pilot then lifts the load from the water and deposits it on dry land or a ship's deck.

PJ rescue swimmer hoisted back into UH-1.

142

When divers are working in conjunction with rescue helicopters it is very useful if they carry Mk-13 Day/Night flares. When the diver is ready for a pick-up, of whichever variety, he can ignite the flare and hold it above the water. The smoke or flame will signal the pilot that the diver is ready, but more importantly, it will also give the pilot the wind direction and velocity.

The helicopter should not hover over the rescue site after the diver drop or during the early stages of the operation. This will only stress the survivors, eliminate the possibility of voice communications and subject the divers to a 100 mph downdraft from the rotors. The pilot should hover down-wind so that he can observe the rescue site and be prepared to move in on the divers' signal.

If the helicopter lands on the water in a strong current, the pilot can tilt the main rotor disc forward to hold his position or even make headway against it.

Helicopter pilots are trained in the use of the Spare Air (HEED) as a helicopter emergency escape device.

Rescue seat/penetrator on a USAF Pararescue helicopter.

SIMULATED HELICOPTER TRAINING

Since helicopters are so expensive to have on site for training operations, a lot of value can be extracted from a mockup. This consists of a wooden frame, constructed to the same specifications as the helicopter's door, and mounted on the side of a dock or pier.

Find a site that gives the trainees a good 10-15 foot drop into the water. In this way they can polish their technique and sort out equipment problems without wasting precious time and fuel on actual training days. All training should be done in full kit and under as realistic conditions as can be created.

To practice the hoist recoveries, a local crane operator can be borrowed or hired to drop his hook in front of the mockup door so that divers and victims can be hoisted up and retrieved. If possible, set the crane hook up with the same lift gear or slings found on the local SAR helicopters.

Many fire departments, SWAT teams and military installations have pole mounted helicopter hulls, complete with skids and hard points, for the sole purpose of practicing helo-rappel and fast rope techniques. Again, a few phone calls and a polite request may go a long way to getting your dive team some economical training.

Actual helicopter training days must be anticipated, planned and prepared for so that no time or money is wasted while the rotors are turning.

ASAP divers utilize wooden frame to simulate helicopter door exits.

Jumping in full Scuba requires rugged equipment and special training.

A crane is used to simulate hoist recovery.

FIXED-WING AIRCRAFT

Fixed-wing aircraft do not have the versatility of the helicopter but still have a significant role in SAR and SRT operations. This is especially true where the team must cover a large area or respond on a national or international level. The planes that a special response dive team would use fall into four primary categories: small aircraft for local rapid deployment outside of the range of helicopters; larger aircraft like the C-130 for prolonged search and/or parachute deployment; float planes to access mountain lakes and rivers or off-shore areas; and commercial aircraft for national or international exercises or callouts.

SMALL AIRCRAFT

The small aircraft that an SRT team would normally use would be of the light single or twin engine varieties. The actual plane used would greatly depend on the number of team members and the amount of support gear to be transported. Fuel capacity, instrumentation, range and cost may also be factors in the selection equation.

145

The average dive team member of 180-200 pounds will be carrying all his SCUBA gear, tanks and a 20-35 pound weight belt, which will give an "all up" weight of more like 300-plus pounds. Not to mention the space that this gear occupies. So a small plane rated for six people may carry only three or four divers and this is not counting rescue ropes, hardware, medical supplies, an inflatable boat and extra tanks or compressor.

If the callout is to an area of high altitude, like a mountain lake at six to ten thousand feet, the plane's engine will need to be turbocharged to operate efficiently in such rarefied air.

Whatever the aircraft selected, all equipment will need to be packed with space availability in mind. Most small planes will not have the cargo space for the normal SRT go-boxes, so dive gear should be packed in duffle-type dive bags. Place wetsuits and towels in the bags so that they protect the harder or more delicate equipment. Only cameras, lights, instruments, etc., should be packed in small, hard cases of the Pelican variety. Ample spares and small tools should be packed for any eventuality and each diver should supervise the loading of his own equipment. Two hundred miles from the nearest dive store is not the time to lose an "O" ring, break a fin strap or forget a vital piece of equipment.

HEAVY TRANSPORT

Air Force Pararescue and U.S. Coast Guard make good use of the C-130 for long-range deployment and extended searching offshore and in the wilderness areas of the continental United States. In some areas, like Kodiak, Alaska, the Coast Guard have a strong working relationship with local dive rescue teams, and in other states the Air Force will supply aircraft to transport rescue teams to anywhere they may be needed. This can be arranged by calling the **United States Air Force Rescue Coordinating Center/Scott Air Force Base Search and Rescue Center, 1-(800) 851-3051.** (It is suggested that this call be made by a local law enforcement official, and only in emergencies.)

One significant advantage of these heavy lift aircraft is that the entire dive rescue truck, boat, trailer and all support equipment can be driven right into the cargo hold of one of these monsters. On arrival, the whole system can be driven right off and is ready for work as if the team were within their own county. The military regularly deploys in this manner and civilian rescue teams have also been airlifted in this manner when necessary.

Pararescue (the PJs) will generally try to respond by long-range helicopter but have no hesitation in parachuting from a C-130 when the mission calls for it, and the rescue site is many miles offshore. Downed aircraft, ships in distress, mid-ocean collisions or rapid response to small islands could call for the special skills of the PJs. Pararescue personnel are all highly skilled paramedics with extensive training in helicopter deployment, parachuting, rappelling and diving (to mention just a few of their skills).

When jumping into a dive rescue or surface rescue operation from a fixed wing aircraft, the diver must be prepared for a long wait until additional assistance or recovery vessels arrive. It may be several hours before a ship can be summoned to the site; weather could close in and delay a recovery; even with mid-air refueling the HH-3 or HH-53 could be well behind the C-130.

One of the Pararescue procedures for this type of operation is to make one pass in the C-130 to identify the distressed vessel or rescue location. On the second pass the divers' inflatable raft, emergency supplies and a marker smoke is dropped. On the next pass, and only when the raft has inflated, the smoke is giving wind direction and the whole package is up-current/up-wind of the rescue site, will the divers be dropped. In this manner the divers will at least have the added security of the raft and supplies should further assistance be slow coming. The C-130 will try to stay on location and guide in the additional support elements. In wartime and in hostile territory this can be a very hazardous assignment for the PJs and air crew.

Pararescue divers are trained in STABO extraction.

Diver/Parachute deployment is a highly specialized skill requiring specialized equipment, extensive training and regular practice. The PJs, as with Special Forces and SEALs, have been doing this for many years and have refined the techniques and equipment to an art. In all reality, it is a skill beyond the job requirements or expectations of the average dive rescue teams. Nonetheless, if one has a yen to pursue this avenue of endeavor, there are many sport parachute clubs that combine jumping and SCUBA diving in their list of activities. But to see how it really applies to rescue work one must pay a visit to the PJs and 1550th Combat Crew Training Wing at Kirtland Air Force Base in New Mexico.

PJ Para-Scuba diver.

PJ under canopy.

Current PJ Para-Scuba rig.

148

FLOAT PLANES

Float planes can vary in size from the small bush planes of the Northwest to the large Coast Guard aircraft like the HU-16 Albatross. Their unique advantage is that they have the speed of a fixed wing but can still land on water and in remote areas. The disadvantages are that they are not common and cannot handle rough water. Even a two-foot chop can prevent the landing of a float plane. The float plane, like any fixed wing, also requires adequate landing and takeoff room for safe operation.

Once on the water, the plane can be driven around like a boat and serve as an adequate dive platform. They can even be anchored, under ideal conditions. The larger planes can carry a whole team and then some, but the smaller planes have the same space and payload limitations of the light aircraft mentioned earlier.

Dive gear and rescue equipment must be packed with these limitations in mind and the pilot will have final say in what goes, what stays and how it needs to be packed and distributed.

COMMERCIAL AIRCRAFT

Whether it be flying to Colorado for a Dive Rescue class, travelling to another State for a seminar, going on a dive vacation or an actual call for assistance, a dive team should know how to pack and travel with their equipment.

First and foremost, commercial airline baggage handlers are notoriously hard on luggage. On smaller aircraft and helicopters the divers can supervise and assist in the loading of their own equipment. With large commercial airports this is often not possible or practical, especially if connections are being made at various airports en route.

Make maximum use of go-boxes, aluminum and plastic cases and adequate padding around dive bags that must be checked. Try to carry on all sensitive gear like cameras, gauges, regulators, radios, etc. If possible, make contact with airport security or airline ground supervisors and advise them that the bags/boxes contain rescue equipment that requires special care and handling.

The next order of business is a complete CHECKLIST of all essential equipment including spares and tools. Each go-box should have a separate list inside the lid of all equipment that should be in that box. Check it and double-check it before heading to the airport and then check off each box and bag as it is taken away by the baggage handlers. On arrival at the final destination check off each box as it comes off the conveyor belt to make sure of its safe arrival. Report lost luggage immediately to the airlines to expedite the recovery of a box that may contain equipment vital to the dive.

It is also good policy to call ahead to the town or final destination to ascertain what diving resources are available: SCUBA shops; filling stations; dive rescue teams; heavy lift equipment; suitable boats; availability of service, repair or spare parts; etc.

FLYING AND DIVING

Divers must be careful about flying or even travelling in mountainous terrain, after diving. The sport diving guidelines are very simple: wait 12 hours before flying after a no-decompression dive and at least 24 hours after a dive requiring decompression or if the dives have been close to the limits of the no-deco tables. This is for flying in a commercial airliner with an internal cabin pressure of 8,000 feet (0.74 atmosphere), or an unpressurized aircraft not above 8,000 feet.

The reason for this is quite obvious. When we reach the surface after a dive, even a no-decompression dive, we still have a certain amount of dissolved gas in our system. By increasing our altitude we decrease the ambient pressure and can eventually reach a point where the gas comes out of solution, creates bubbles and results in decompression sickness (DCS), the bends.

The **NOAA Manual** takes this a step further and says that a diver must wait at sea level, breathing air, until he becomes a Group "D" diver according to the U.S. Navy Repetitive Diving Table, before flying in an aircraft with a cabin pressure of less than 8,000 feet. This Surface Interval Time before flying can be reduced by the breathing of oxygen instead of air.

**Optional Oxygen-Breathing
Times Before Flying After Diving:**

Repetitive Group	Time on Oxygen — Hr:Min
M thru Z	1:30
H thru L	1:00
E thru G	0:30
A thru D	0:00

In the case of an emergency evacuation of a diver the aircraft must be kept at the lowest safe altitude (below 800 feet) or in a pressurized aircraft with a cabin pressure not to exceed 800 feet. Imperial County Sheriff's Underwater Recovery Team have a unique problem in this area. Their nearest recompression facility is San Diego but there is a 4,000-foot mountain range between Imperial County and San Diego. The solution was to establish a contract with a Critical Air unit to transport injured divers in a pressurized jet if the need arises. A smart piece of forethought and emergency planning.

PART III

SAR OPERATIONS

L.A. County lifeguards coordinate a victim evacuation with U.S. Coast Guard Helo.

AQUATIC RESCUE

Search and Rescue (SAR) operations can take many forms and require a variety of skills. The SAR effort could be undertaken by local law enforcement personnel, volunteer civilians, professional mountain rescue teams, the Coast Guard, Air Force Pararescue or a specialized NSS cave rescue team. Conditions could vary from sub-zero, high altitude alpine areas to blazing hot deserts or dense forest. Whatever the team and wherever the rescue, time is always critical when operating in a search mode.

Until the victim(s) have been found, there is no way to ascertain their condition. Exposure, hypothermia, hyperthermia, dehydration, starvation, exhaustion, traumatic injury, shock and even panic are all potential killers when left untreated or uncontrolled.

Techniques for wilderness search and rescue have already filled several manuals, many of which should be studied by the rescue dive team, so for now we will concentrate on aquatic rescues.

CRITICAL RESPONSE TIME

There is a considerable distinction between **Rescue Mode** and **Recovery Mode** in SRT diving operations. The decision between Rescue or Recovery is usually dictated by the possibility of survival of the victim(s). If there is even the faintest possibility of saving a life, the team will go into a fast Rescue Mode, but if there is no chance of a "save," the team will fall into a slower, more methodical Recovery Mode.

The possibility of a save/rescue will be directly tied to time, and this can vary from operation to operation. Obviously a submerged victim or potential drowning is more time-critical than a diver missing in a cave system where there may be air pockets, or a capsized ship where survivors may be able to cling to life for several hours or even days.

Temperature also plays a big part in survivability. In general, a person missing in sub-zero temperatures is given less chance of survival than one in a more moderate, less hostile environment. Victims of a disaster at sea will survive longer in tropical areas than they will in arctic or sub-arctic waters (providing the sharks don't get them).

It would appear then that colder water temperatures reduce one's chances of survival, and there are many times when this is true. But there is one unique situation where cold water can play a big part in the possibility of a successful rescue. This is what has become known as COLD-WATER NEAR-DROWNING and is attributed to a human response similar to Mammalian Diving Reflex.

COLD-WATER NEAR-DROWNING

The Mammalian Diving Reflex in air breathing mammals such as whales, dolphins and porpoises is a physiological response in which the breathing stops, vital signs slow and blood is shunted away from the extremities/non-essential tissues to better supply the vital organs. This allows the mammals to make prolonged, deep breath-hold dives.

In humans we have observed a similar response to cold water immersion, especially in infants and young children. The general belief is that hypothermia is a big contributing factor in the survival of cold-water near-drowning victims. Under these conditions the body's need for oxygen is greatly reduced and the circulation of blood to non-vital organs, tissues and muscles is slowed. In this manner the blood is diverted to essential organs like the heart, brain and lungs.

Where sea mammals will remain conscious and active under these conditions, a human will lose consciousness and give a convincing appearance of death. The near-drowning victim will not be breathing, skin will be pale or bluish, pupils will be fixed and dilated, muscles will become rigid and pulse will be absent or so faint it will be barely detectable.

Rescues and successful revivals have been performed on victims that have been immersed for over one hour (although 20-40 minutes is the more common occurrence). Even though the greatest success has been experienced with young children, older victims should not be denied every attempt at resuscitation after extended submersions (there have been saves of victims in their sixties).

Public awareness of cold-water near-drowning can be greatly attributed to the research of Dr. Martin Nemiroff in the early '70s. As a faculty member of the University of Michigan Medical Center, Dr. Nemiroff compiled records of victims who had survived long submersions, and when he submitted a paper on this subject in 1975, he caused considerable controversy in the medical community.

Dr. Nemiroff found a more receptive home for his ideas and research when he enlisted with the U.S. Coast Guard and, by 1985 had been involved in over 300 successful resuscitations while stationed at Kodiak Island, Alaska. Other agencies and rescue teams in the United States are also having considerable success in saving lives in cases that twenty years ago the victims would have been declared dead-on-site or DOA at the emergency room.

Research is still being done into the subject of cold water drownings so dive team members should stay open to new developments and techniques. Although the ideal candidate for resuscitation is the young victim in clean, cold water, who has been submerged for less than 60 minutes — more awareness and effort in this area is resulting in saves of older victims in warmer waters and we are now seeing resuscitations of young children submerged for over one hour.

EMERGENCY MEDICAL TREATMENT OF THE COLD-WATER NEAR-DROWNING VICTIM

There are many environmental and physiological factors involved in cold water drownings and the treatment of such victims is even more complex. Apart from the specialized equipment and techniques that an emergency room must have, the physician must contend with a multitude of factors that call for an individual approach to each case.

A full study of this subject is beyond the scope of this book, and research is still on-going, so we will limit ourselves to a brief look at some of the techniques in effect today:

- Recover victim as soon as possible
- Initiate CPR immediately
- Be ready to clear the airway before and during CPR
- Insert artificial airways if trained to do so
- Transport victim to nearest emergency medical facility
- Continue aggressive CPR during transportation
- Maintain highest percentage of pure oxygen during CPR
- Start IVs if it does not delay transportation
- Rewarming of victim must be done from the inside out
- Do not use external techniques of rubbing, etc. (Cold, stagnant blood may flood the heart and lungs; this blood can be highly acidic and prove toxic to the vital organs.)
- Administer pre-warmed oxygen to raise lung and heart temperatures
- A flexible probe can be fed down the esophagus to monitor heart temperature
- The heart should be reheated to at least 90 degrees Fahrenheit before use of restarting attempts such as defibrillation

HOSPITAL CARE

- Administer heated and humidified oxygen
- Monitor arterial blood gases and EKG
- Normalize acid-base levels of the blood
- When ready apply electroshock defibrillation to stimulate full heartbeat

All this will be supported by:

- Chest X-rays
- Monitoring of cardiac output
- Lab studies of: blood gases & electrolytes
    blood urea nitrogen & creatinine
    serum hemoglobin and blood clotting profile

It is not uncommon for victims who have been successfully resuscitated to succumb later to complications. Careful monitoring and lab tests are designed to prevent such an occurrence.

All of this is a little beyond the need of the average dive rescue team, but it is sufficient to know that speed is of the essence and the first 60 minutes (the Golden Hour) is critical. Also, the rule of thumb of most emergency medical staffs is, "Do not declare a COLD patient dead." Continue efforts for resuscitation until the victim's body temperature has returned to normal. Only then, if the victim shows no signs of responding to resuscitation should medical assistance be abandoned.

It is good policy to establish a strong working/training relationship with local EMTs, paramedics and emergency medical facilities to ensure that everyone is up to speed on the latest advances and research in this field. The deep satisfaction of actually saving a life, rather than just recovering a body, is an experience that any dive team will carry for a long time.

FIRST RESPONDER

The skills of the First Responder to an incident that may require the services of the dive rescue team, are vital to the final outcome of the rescue. When time is critical, the First Responder can perform several tasks that will greatly aid the dive team:

- Do not delay in calling for the dive team in an aquatic environment
- Do not allow any witnesses or bystanders to leave the scene
- Study the physical evidence and compare it to witness descriptions of the incident
- Set up a cordon to preserve evidence
- Establish the most reliable witnesses and keep them at hand
- Try to establish a Last Seen Point (LSP) from the witness description
- Establish the time that the victim was last seen and how long submerged
- Return witnesses to their original view points when the accident occurred

- Study winds and currents for any changes in speed or direction
- Keep everyone calm, comfort the victim's friends and family until the Incident Commander and SRT Dive team arrive.

When the dive team and Incident Commander (IC) arrive on site the First Responder (FR) will pass control to them. He will then give the IC and dive team leader a detailed description of events to date.

As the dive team begins setting up and suiting up for Rescue Mode the IC will continue to interview witnesses, work with the FR, evaluate the scene and establish a LSP for the victim/vehicle/plane/boat.

It may be necessary for the dive team to run seminars and classes for local law enforcement personnel so that they can be trained as First Responders. The FR needs to be given a solid basis in exactly what the dive team needs to effect a successful rescue or recovery.

SCENE EVALUATION

From a dive rescue standpoint, the scene must be evaluated not just for the rescue considerations and LSP, but also for the physical characteristics that could add danger to the task. The Diving Supervisor must decide if the risk of committing his team to the water is justified by the chance of a rescue.

This has become known in the industry as the **RISK/BENEFIT FACTOR.** There is definitely no point in throwing good life away trying to recover someone who is already dead or has a low probability of survival. The diver must be assured of a good chance of a rescue with the minimum personal risk.

Strong currents, jagged metal, icy water, deep water, night operations in unknown areas, local irrigation flood gates, dangerous wildlife ('gators), difficult entry points, poor visibility and weather, approaching storms, lightning, heavy boat traffic, polluted water, toxic waste, chemical contamination or a combination of the above must be considered by the Supervisor, and every individual diver, before anyone is committed to the rescue/recovery.

If the following information has not already been collected the IC will need to establish: nature of the accident, number of vessels/vehicles involved, number of victims involved, names and ages of victims, etc.

The next steps are:

- Decide if this is to be a Recovery or a Rescue based on time
- Attach a Risk/Benefit Factor
- Establish a Last Seen Point and mark it
- Select and brief the divers
- Prepare emergency personnel to handle the victim(s)
- Review dive procedures and signals
- Initiate dive

WITNESS INTERVIEW

Trying to find a submerged object in a large expanse of water, when no witnesses were present to see it go down, can be a very frustrating, if not futile exercise. Ask any would-be treasure hunter of lost Spanish galleons. Therefore consider every witness a valuable resource, with the potential of being helpful to the rescue/recovery effort.

Most police divers will have ample experience in dealing with the public, taking statements and interviewing witnesses. Other civilian volunteer rescue teams may want to draw on law enforcement's experience in this area.

Guide to witness interview:

- Establish most reliable witnesses (not drunk or drugged)
- Separate witnesses and assign interviewers
- Approach and initial contact is important
- Maintain control and an objective attitude
- There may be high emotion, chaos and confusion at the outset
- There may be a need to comfort and calm
- Balance compassion with firm authority
- If dealing with family members of the victim then explain the mechanics of the Rescue but make no promises
- Child witnesses may respond better to female interviewers
- Some witness/survivors may be stressed, disoriented and unreliable
- Be aware that the witness may also be the perpetrator of a homicide
- Return witness to the location at which he was standing when the accident occurred, to get a better perspective
- Use reference points like boats, surface swimmers and buoys to establish a Last Seen Point
- Do not ask or expect witnesses to give accurate measurements in yards or feet across water
- Try to use a reference object similar in size to the last seen object so that the witness can get a size/distance relationship
- Have the witness direct the dive boat or swimmer to the LSP
- Immediately start sketching the scene and noting witness observations
- Be sure to see the witnesses' ID and establish an address and telephone number so that a witness can be called back if necessary

This somewhat covers the surface aspects of a rescue operation. Now it is time to take a look at the more relevant dive-related aspects and exactly what the dive team's task is in Rescue Mode.

DIVE RESCUE PROCEDURES

Not all emergencies that a dive rescue team is called to, will require diving. Some may be surface river rescues, survivors clinging to an upturned boat, partially submerged cars that can be negotiated in nothing

Witness interview is an important part of establishing the Last Seen Point.

more than a wet suit or ice rescue suit (Gumby). Others will require all the diving skills and resources of the team. The Golden Hour of the cold-water near-drowning is a critical factor in the northern States where water and temperature are found in the right combinations. Warmer areas like Florida will seldom, if ever, have to deal with this phenomenon. Many responses in Rescue Mode will disappointingly turn into recoveries once the team gets on site and does their initial evaluation.

Whatever the nature of the call, and wherever in the United States, an SRT team should be able to respond in a timely manner on the chance that it may be a rescue with a very real opportunity to save life. Rapid response requires trained personnel, pre-checked and loaded equipment, reliable methods of transportation, rehearsed callout procedures and efficient communications. These procedures will change with geography, topography and responsibility.

Once the team arrives on site, the nature of the rescue will dictate the techniques and equipment to be used.

SURFACE & SWIFT WATER RESCUE

Surface rescues are somewhat less complex than dive rescues but can be equally hazardous. The surface rescue will seldom take place on calm, sheltered waters since there had to be some sea state or river condition to cause the emergency in the first place.

159

Agencies should be trained and equipped for whatever aquatic conditions exist in their area. West Coast teams will need to be able to negotiate heavy surf and possibly strong currents; teams in the Rockies or near fast flowing rivers/irrigation canals will need to train in swift water river rescue techniques with the possible use of Tyrolean rope systems. Pararescue is equipped to drop into mid-ocean to assist distressed boats or downed aircraft; the Navy trains surface swimmers to rescue pilots who have either ditched or punched-out over water.

But back to reality. The most common surface operations for a dive rescue team will be the swift water variety. This will usually consist of rigging a Tyrolean rope system across the river; equipping the rescuer with wet suit, helmet, knife, gloves, harness, boogie board and fins; preparing a standby diver, similarly equipped; rigging safety ropes downstream; and then trying to reach the victim. Once the rescue diver has made contact with and secured the victim, both can be hauled in on ropes and pulleys.

Swift water rescue is a team effort where each man must know his job. A fast flowing river has tremendous energy that can sweep the inexperienced rescuer away, pin him against rocks, hold him under in turbulence or skewer him on sharp branches or wreckage.

Colder rivers will require the use of dry suits and thermal underwear. Small boats can also be rigged to a Tyrolean rope system and maneuvered close to a victim clinging to a rock or branch.

LASD Reserve SEB divers practice with the Miller backboard for dealing with victims who may have sustained spinal injury.

Where the victim or vehicle has disappeared below the surface, the same techniques and rigging will have to be used but with a diver instead of a surface swimmer. Before going in to a dive rescue mode, the diving supervisor must make a reevaluation of the Risk/Benefit Factors. Logs and debris being carried down-river can snag, injure or kill a diver trying to operate in a strong current and probably limited visibility. If the operation is turning into a recovery, it may be advisable to wait for the river level to drop and for conditions to become more favorable. Search personnel should be positioned down-river in case the body surfaces and is carried below the bounds of the immediate search area.

Surface-supplied equipment with good communications can greatly increase the safety factor in river diving, even if one does sacrifice a little mobility and freedom. The helmet or bandmask will also give the diver a certain amount of head protection from loose rocks and debris.

Not all surface rescues will be in swift water. Water skiers, jet skiers and swimmers can get run over by power boats and require assistance. Some unsuccessful suicidal bridge jumpers may achieve nothing more than knocking themselves out, or getting winded on impact. Victims that accidentally fall from bridges, cliffs, piers and ships may also require surface rescue.

In all of these cases there is a good chance that the victim has sustained a back or neck injury. The SRT team should be equipped with back-boards (Miller Board), and trained in securing victims to these in the water. Once a victim is strapped into a back-board, complete with C col-

Rescue swimmers will usually deploy with just mask, fins, snorkel, knife, harness and exposure suit.

lar and head support, there is reduced chance of further injury to the spine during removal from the water.

Responding to capsized boats in open water and rescuing the survivors frequently becomes the responsibility of a dive rescue team, especially if the divers are air-mobile. New York Police SCUBA team have two divers, twenty-four hours a day, stationed with their Air Sea Rescue helicopters. Kodiak's ASAP team also responds to shipping accidents, and commercial fishing boats in distress, by use of the Coast Guard helicopters. Although many of these problems could be handled by surface swimmers, it is good policy to jump in full SCUBA, so that if the victim should sink during the swim in, the diver can dive after him immediately. There is also the possibility that additional survivors may be trapped in or under the inverted hull, and the diver will have to dive to effect a rescue.

STTU dive team searches a river in central Taiwan for a missing American student.

DIVE RESCUE

The first hour of any dive involving submerged victims should be treated as a potential rescue. Upon arrival on site the designated divers should suit-up, as the support team rigs lines and prepares the additional equipment. All this should be done in a quiet, efficient and professional manner since the victim's family, and the news media, may be on hand.

Once the Incident Commander and Dive Supervisor have completed their preliminaries, they will brief the divers and initiate the rescue. The diver should also be doing his own site evaluation and deciding if the dive task is beyond his capability, training or experience. The diver always has the right to refuse a dive.

Some rescues may allow the diver to drop right onto the vehicle while others may require considerable searching just to find the victim. If using surface-supplied gear or surface communications, be aware that the press and victim's family may be within earshot of the radio. Keep voice communications on a professional level and to a minimum.

Once the victim is located by the diver, the diving supervisor should be notified. Pre-established procedures will dictate the diver's actions. Usually the diver will:

- Signal the tender with three pulls on the tether, or if communications are being used, discreetly notify the supervisor
- Secure a firm grip on the victim and swim directly to the boat or beach; or secure a rope to the victim and allow the surface team to effect the recovery

The tender will:

- Tie a knot in the search line or note how much umbilical was out
- Notify the team leader of the find
- Either pull the diver in or allow him to climb his own line
- Alert the other team members or paramedics to prepare for resuscitation procedures

It is essential that the diver maintain a firm grip on the victim, either under the arms and around the chest or by the belt, back or the pants or jacket. The diver's primary objective is to get the victim topside and onto a hard surface for CPR, as soon as possible.

Procedures to follow when the rescue has turned into a recovery are covered in Chapter 16.

Dive team members should not talk to the press and should refer all inquiries to the IC or press relations officer. Throughout the rescue the team is being judged and evaluated on their speed and professionalism by all concerned. Only practice and experience will hone the skills necessary to stand up under the harsh lights of public exposure.

STTU divers searching intakes of dam in central Taiwan for student swept down river.

ICE RESCUE

Frozen lakes, ponds and rivers are subtle invitations to an accident. Recreational use of these areas by skaters, fisherman, snow mobilers, back-packers, hunters and skiers result in many incidents each year. The police and fire departments of the frozen North have established a remarkable track record in successful saves and recoveries.

Ice rescue and ice diving both require specialized training that can only be found in areas with the climate to suit. Not only the victims and divers, but even the surface support personnel, are subjected to the possibility of hypothermia, frostbite and injury. The ice is a slippery platform from which to conduct a rescue operation.

Before venturing onto the ice the team must establish that it will in fact support their combined weight. From there, safety lines, harnesses and ladders can be used to ensure safety.

A triangular hole will need to be cut, chopped or hacked in the ice; divers with adequate thermal protection, lights, harnesses and safety ropes will drop through to find the victim. Ice rescue is one instance where the chances of resuscitating the victim are very much in the team's favor, as long as the victim is recovered within the first 60 minutes (research indicates that this may go to 120 minutes with new techniques and greater understanding of cold water drowning).

Divers may only be able to tolerate short durations under the ice, so additional pairs should be suited up early and ready to dive. Support personnel must have suitable clothing, food and warm drinks — especially if there is any wind-chill factor. Only divers and tenders secured with ropes and harnesses should be permitted to approach the hole or entry point.

ASAP instructors training students in ice rescue.

165

Surface-supplied diver prepares for ice dive.

Supervisor monitors air consumption and communications as support personnel tend umbilicals.

Scuba divers prepare to drop below the ice.

Support personnel control safety rope to diver as standby diver in EXO-26 prepares to render assistance.

167

Rescue diver and victim are recovered from below the ice.

Victim is given oxygen and prepared for transportation.

Movement on ice can be a slippery and dangerous experience.

DIVE PLANNING & BRIEFING

Like any SWAT operation, the most successful dive rescues will be ones that are carefully planned and professionally executed. Between the planning and the execution comes a most important part of any operation, the briefing.

Again, training and experience will give the team leader the repertoire of skills and knowledge to develop a functional rescue plan. Just as non-SWAT personnel do not brief tactical teams, non-divers cannot run a successful dive operation (even though many may try!).

The divers, as with the support team, must be in full possession of all the facts and dynamics affecting the rescue. A clear understanding of their individual assignments, and how they relate to the big picture is essential if the team is to appear smooth and professional and the rescue is to be deemed a success. The divers should be a part of the planning process since only they truly understand their own limitations and strengths. It may be necessary, in some circumstances, for a diver to make a quick dive on the site to establish water and bottom conditions, or wreck location/attitude, before a final plan can be formulated.

The briefing should include:

Situation
A brief overview of the entire operation:

- What led up to this rescue/recovery
- Sea state or water conditions
- Number and description of victims
- Last Seen Point
- Availability of additional emergency personnel

Mission
A short statement of purpose, e.g.:

- Recover the victim from the vehicle, or
- Locate the vehicle and attach recovery cable, or
- Rescue boat survivors, etc.

Execution
A detailed dive plan of exactly how the mission is to be accomplished, leaving no doubt in anyone's mind as to the mechanics of the rescue attempt:

- Divers' role, dive time and maximum depth
- Tenders' role
- Divemaster's responsibilities
- Coordination of EMTs, recovery vehicles, etc.
- Procedures for body or vehicle recovery
- Contingency plans

Administration & Logistics
An overview of the entire support effort and equipment requirements:

- Dive equipment required
- Tools, ropes and rigging
- Location of safety check-points and entry-points
- Air fills or air source for surface supplied
- Transportation and evacuation
- Emergency medical assistance for dive-related injuries
- Nearest decompression chamber and mode of medi-vac
- Availability of cranes and heavy lift gear
- Preservation of evidence
- Disposition of recovered bodies, vehicles, etc.
- Filing of reports

Command & signals

- Who is the Incident Commander and Diving Supervisor
- Assigned dive team leaders
- Diving rotation on prolonged operations
- Who is the PR officer and how to respond to the press
- Line-pull signals, hand signals or voice codes
- Day/night flares and procedures
- Availability of radios and frequencies to be used
- Local marine and emergency frequencies
- Abort and emergency abort signals

Most dive rescue operations will be extremely simple in nature, and as long as basic procedure and common sense rule, the operations will be successful. Major disasters like passenger airliners, trains or buses going into the water may grossly overtax the capabilities of any one team. If a team anticipates working with neighboring agencies in a mutual aid mode, the policies, procedures and command structures need to be hammered out ahead of time. In the midst of chaos, at a major aquatic disaster, is not the time to be discussing politics or feeding petty jealousies.

Large SAR operations function extremely well with several agencies involved: Forest Service, County and Federal law enforcement, fire departments, EMTs and ambulance operators, Air Sea Rescue, civilian mountain rescue, local volunteers and dog tracker teams. A professional dive rescue team must be able to mesh with all these agencies as well as other dive rescue teams. Long underwater searches burn up divers very quickly, so other agencies should be called early to give them time to assemble and respond.

Upon arrival, all new dive teams, fresh divers and support personnel will need a thorough briefing to bring them up to speed on the situation and efforts to date. If the site is congested, fresh teams can be kept in a staging area until needed. Fatigued workers and burned-up divers can also move to this holding area for rest, debriefing and food.

DEBRIEFING

Every major (and most smaller) rescue/recovery should end in a debriefing of the entire operation. There is much to be learned from each experience so that improvements can be made to future operations. The whole operation should be broken down step by step to find fault, make constructive criticism and possibly rewrite policy and procedure.

The areas to look at are:

- Response time of the team and individuals
- On-site setup and professionalism
- Witness interview and information movement

- The dive plan and briefing
- The actual rescue/recovery
- Support personnel assistance
- Team weaknesses
- Equipment breakages
- Equipment deficiencies
- Post-recovery procedure
- Press/Public relations
- Possible policy and procedure changes

There is one other area that can be covered in the post-dive debrief, the effect on the team of the rescue or the disappointment of the body recovery. This is known in some circles as Critical Incident Stress Debrief (CISD). Emotions, feelings and job related stresses can run quite high when dealing with death, serious injury, grieving families and especially injury to or loss of teammates. The CISD should be initiated by all teams to ensure past mistakes are not repeated; team members have an opportunity to vent their feelings or frustrations; the team develops a healthy growth and flow of information; deficiencies in individual performance can be targeted and remedied.

These debriefs may or may not require the attendance of a professional counselor, but all meetings should be conducted in private, with only team members present. All individuals must feel free to speak their mind and heart. The need for a counselor will probably be dependent on the stress of the previous rescue/recovery and the level of injury or loss of life involved. Recovering decomposing bodies from a jagged wreck, in cold, swift, limited visibility water can be quite stressful for some divers. Especially if children or teenagers are involved.

PJ instructor and Sheriff's Rescue specialist inventory pararescue medical kit. Note HALO/Freefall parachute rigs in rear.

172

NYPD diver assists surface victim in icy waters.

Helicopter dunker training

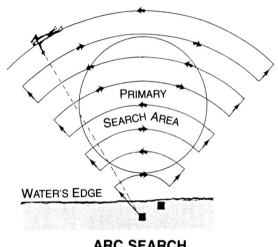

PRIMARY

SEARCH AREA

WATER'S EDGE

ARC SEARCH

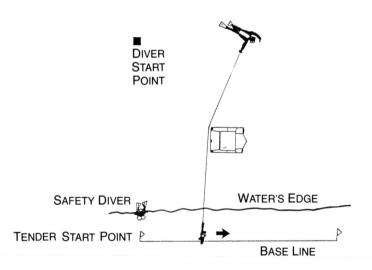

■
DIVER
START
POINT

SAFETY DIVER

WATER'S EDGE

TENDER START POINT

BASE LINE

SNAG SEARCH

174

14
UNDERWATER SEARCH METHODS

One of the primary tasks in any rescue or recovery operation is to find the object to be recovered. There are several well established and proven search methods to choose from, depending on the location, depth, water conditions and size of the object. Techniques and patterns that may work well for finding a gun thrown from a wharf may not be suitable for finding a body in a fast flowing irrigation canal. Although most teams depend on one or two methods that are best suited to their needs, teams should have a good working knowledge of all the available options. Just as a Hostage Rescue Team develops a wide range of skills and tactical options, the dive team must be equally prepared to cope with any foreseeable, and some unforeseeable, situations.

A successful search, like an investigation, requires patience, thoroughness, determination, a systematic procedure and an attention to detail. It is essential that the initial search be thorough and systematic so as to avoid repeatedly covering the same area unnecessarily and to be able to document the search accurately.

Before a search can be initiated the dive team must establish a **LAST SEEN POINT (LSP)** and then mark the outer boundaries of the search area. The **LSP** will come from witness interview, suspect interrogation or the physical evidence of the crash site. Tire tracks, abandoned clothes, broken guard rails, oil slicks and floating debris are all obvious indicators.

When planning a search for a weapon or piece of evidence that a suspect may have thrown into a body of water, it is advantageous to have the suspect brought to the scene and indicate where and how the object was thrown. Basing the search on the second or third hand accounts of the investigators can be very unreliable. If possible, have the suspect throw a dummy gun, or an object of similar size and weight, from the same point and in the same manner as the original incident. Providing the suspect is cooperating, this is probably the most accurate way to establish a start point for the search.

The outer boundaries of the search area will be dictated by the type of incident, the strength and direction of current, tidal movement, wind direction, water depth and the accuracy of the **LSP**. Conflicting stories or vagueness in the witnesses' statements may all contribute to a larger possible search area. This area should be marked and controlled for the preservation of evidence.

The shore line should also be searched in case the suspect's toss was not strong enough to get the weapon into the water, as intended (or strong enough to land it on the opposite bank). There is also a chance that the missing body is trapped in the rocks or weeds near the anticipated dive site.

After initial surveys and interviews, the team leader will select the search method most suited to the location and the object to be found. Study all of the following patterns, acquire the necessary equipment and have the team practice all of them under local conditions.

SHOTGUN PATTERN

The shotgun or random pattern should only be utilized in near ideal conditions: good visibility, known area and high probability of success. The shotgun pattern consists of a series of random dives and irregular patterns that will hopefully bring the diver onto the object. This may work for finding large objects in clear water but is considered the least professional and the hardest to document.

ARC PATTERN

Also known as the fan pattern, the arc has proven itself on numerous occasions with agencies all over the U.S. The arc pattern is generally used as a shoreline search (beach, lake or slow river) and consists of a diver swimming increasingly larger arcs as he is tended/controlled from the shoreline. As the diver reaches one side of the arc, the tender gives a two-pull line signal, lets out the appropriate amount of line and the diver continues in the opposite direction. The amount of line the tender lets out will depend on the size of the object and the visibility. Obviously a car can be found with larger arcs than a weapon or body.

A modification of the ARC pattern is the SNAG search. With this the diver begins with considerable line and a large arc with the hope of snagging the plane or boat on the first pass (see diagram).

PARALLEL PATTERN

The parallel pattern is another popular and effective shoreline search that can be used in both rivers and the ocean. The parallel search can be swum with a compass but is usually tended from the shore with a line. The diver swims parallel to the shore as the tender walks at the same speed holding the search line. When the boundary of the search is reached, the tender gives two line pulls, lets out a few feet of line and reverses direction with the diver. This can continue as long as the diver has air and energy.

Broken trees are a good indication of the violent passage of a motor vehicle.

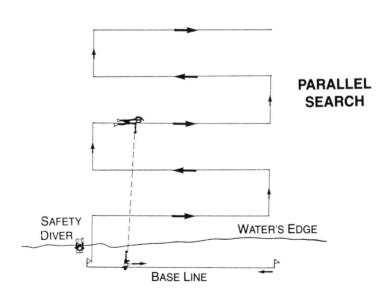

PARALLEL
SEARCH

SAFETY
DIVER

WATER'S EDGE

BASE LINE

The parallel pattern can also be modified as a snag search if the object is large enough. Both the arc and the parallel are ideally suited to surface-supplied diving techniques where the diver's hose is used in place of a line.

CIRCULAR PATTERN

The circular pattern has been credited with many successful finds in all areas of the diving industry. The circular pattern consists of the diver swimming a series of increasing circles, either tended from the surface, tended from the bottom by another diver or controlled by himself. Again the size of the circles and the amount of line let out each orbit will be dictated by visibility and the size of the object: two to three feet each time for a gun, three to six for a body, and six to ten for a car.

The clump weight for the marker buoy on the LSP is generally the center of the circle search. A ⅜" floating line makes the ideal sweep line and can be tied off to the object when it is found.

The circular pattern is best suited to mid-water searches where currents and tides are not too strong. The search can be swum by one diver with a standby safety diver on the surface or by two divers in a buddy pair (two divers do tend to get in each other's way and stir up the bottom unnecessarily).

LINEAR PATTERN

There are several variations of the linear search but the one that we have found most practical is the one frequently used by the NYPD SCUBA Unit. This pattern requires a length of rope (50-100 feet) with a clump or grapple on each end and a marker buoy coming up from one end. This pattern can be used in mid-water or as a shoreline search.

The clumbs are set on bottom and the line pulled taut between them. The divers now search either side of the line until they come to the end. That end is moved in the direction of the search three to six feet and then swum in the opposite direction. At the end of each length the ends are moved creating a systematic crab-like movement across the bottom.

The linear pattern is not tended from the shore and is best suited to a fairly even bottom contour. When the divers have done their time or are low on air, they can simply surface to be replaced by a fresh team. the marker buoy being the reference for their progress and the start point of the replacement teams.

GRID PATTERN

Working the grid pattern is a slow and tedious task but often the only effective way to find very small pieces of evidence. The entire search area can be mapped out on the bottom with ropes or long poles, then parallel lines are laid within the enclosed area. PVC frames are then used to thoroughly search a small 2-3 foot square area. When one grid is done the frame is flipped into the next grid and it is then searched.

The grid pattern would be used to find a small weapon or piece of jewelry in a muddy/silty bottom in a very specific area.

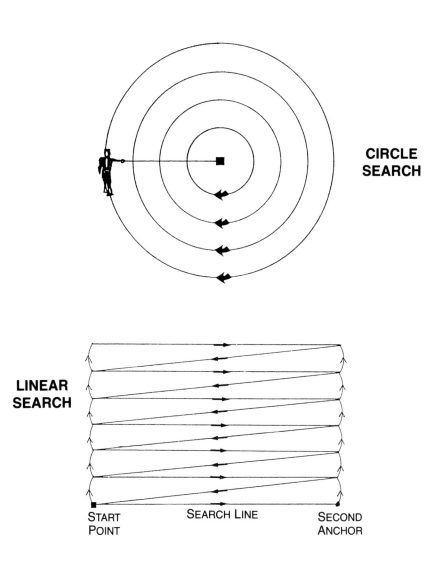

CIRCLE SEARCH

LINEAR SEARCH

START POINT   SEARCH LINE   SECOND ANCHOR

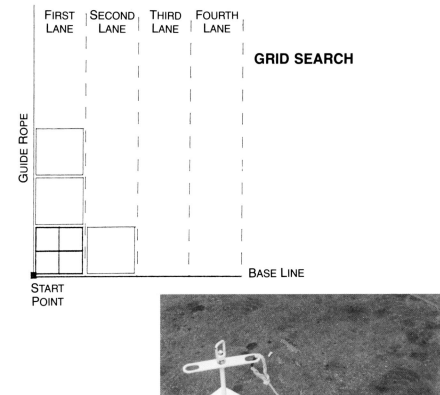

```
FIRST    SECOND   THIRD   FOURTH
LANE      LANE    LANE     LANE
```

GRID SEARCH

GUIDE ROPE

BASE LINE

START
POINT

Useful device for circle search patterns.

COMPASS SEARCHES

Compass navigation is a skill in itself and compass searches require practice and experience. The most effective compass search is done by a two-man team, one diver swimming course and the other playing eyes (commonly known as "course and eyes").

The three most common compass patterns are heading, box and parallel. The HEADING is a simple matter of being deployed at one point and swimming a direct heading on the hope of over-swimming the object. Often used in deep, clear water where the team swims at 80 feet while scanning the bottom at 100-150 feet. This can also be used in a strong ocean current where the team is dropped up-current from the probable crash site.

The BOX pattern is similar to the line-circle search but with the diver swimming a set course for a given time or distance and then turning 90 degrees and repeating the procedure. The box could be an increasing or decreasing pattern with the length of the sides being estimated by time or kick cycles. For example, swim three minutes, turn 90 degrees, repeat on all four sides and then reduce the swim times to two minutes 30 seconds and repeat, etc., etc. With kick cycles one can swim 100 kicks, turning 90 degrees each time, then reduce the sides to 90 kicks, 80, 70, etc.

The PARALLEL pattern is like the parallel-line search except that the diver swims a heading for a set time, then moves left or right four to ten feet (depending on visibility) and then swims the reciprocal bearing for an equal amount of time. This procedure is repeated until air pressure is low or the diver is fatigued.

All these compass patterns are best done with a navigation board or what the military calls an "attack board." Again, one diver on the compass and the other scanning — course and eyes. These free-swimming patterns are difficult to document, are susceptible to navigational inaccuracies and current drift, and leave a wide margin for error. They are best suited to deep, clear water where other more systematic methods are impractical.

RIVER SEARCH

Many of the previously mentioned techniques will prove effective in slow moving waters but swift water will require modifications and additional rigging. First, the shoreline search will need to be initiated well

Compass boards utilized by LASD divers.

181

Scooters are well suited to reef searches.

Tracking dogs have proven very effective in finding submerged victims or the location that they may have entered the water.

down-current and a study of the river conditions will need to be made. The Risk/Benefit Factor will be the major consideration. Some rivers cannot be searched until the conditions subside.

Bodies can get hung up in submerged stumps, roots, branches, lines, rock crevices and weeds. The team may choose to dive some of the more obvious features of the river before doing the bottom search. Cars and guns may be less affected by the current and will require a systematic search pattern.

The ARC pattern has proven very effective when tended from a boat in midstream or from an anchor rope across the river. A modified PARALLEL pattern can be worked across the river bed when done in conjunction with a correctly rigged Tyrolian rope system. Both patterns should begin down-current and worked up-river so that the diver is not disturbing his own visibility and is continually moving into undisturbed bottom material. The diver will need to add additional weight to his belt just to remain stable on the bottom.

Swift water searches are extremely hazardous to the dive team and ample safety precautions must be taken. Safety ropes, harnesses, rescue swimmers, safety divers, chase boats and good anchor points will all need to be in place before divers are committed to the water. Surface-supplied gear is also very useful in this application.

HULL & STRUCTURE SEARCHES

The dive team may be called on to check boat hulls for explosive devices, drug pods or damage. This will all be covered in more detail in Chapter 22 of this book. For now it is sufficient to say that the team leader must ensure that the ship's engines are shut down or at least out of gear. All water intakes and electronic equipment must be shut off and the ship's captain notified of the diving operation. As an added safeguard a dive team member should be stationed at the controls to make sure no one engages the engines unknowingly.

Two divers can now systematically swim the hull, paying special attention to grates, intakes, recesses and screw area, or a whole team can cover the hull in one sweep, connected with buddy-lines or a search rope.

Structures like bridges, docks, power stations, dams and restaurants over the water may need to be swept in conjunction with a presidential visit, a VIP/DVP security operation or in response to a bomb threat. A careful study of the structural drawings will need to be made, engineers consulted, machinery shut down and a dive plan developed. Each diver will be assigned specific piles or supports to sweep and then report back as they are cleared. Suspicious objects should not be touched, a safe perimeter cleared and the EOD (bomb squad) notified.

Through-water/wireless communications systems should not be utilized on EOD searches, since the radio emanations could initiate the explosive device. Hardwire systems are acceptable unless the EOD specialists indicate otherwise.

Florida police divers practice hull search techniques utilizing several divers on one rope.

SPECIALIZED SEARCH EQUIPMENT

Technology has brought us several items that can be very useful for search operations, especially when a large area or deep water must be covered. Side-scan sonar, ROVs, metal detectors, Nitrox and tow bars have all been used with varying degrees of success by the teams that have access to them.

The side-scan sonar can cost up to $40,000 but will allow a dive boat to detect large objects like planes or cars on the bottom. This is very effective when a large area must be covered in zero visibility water. Most units require a trained operator to get the most out of the system and interpret the data.

The ROV (remote operated vehicle) is a small, surface controlled, self-propelled video camera, often with a manipulator arm that can be maneuvered under water and used to scan for lost objects. L.A. Sheriffs have used Santa Barbara City College's ROV to do body searches in the deeper waters (190'-plus) off Catalina Island. This piece of equipment is too expensive to buy but possible to borrow, and a lot safer than diving at extreme depths without a decompression chamber on hand.

Smaller hand-held metal detectors can be very useful when searching for weapons in the mud or silt often found in ponds, lakes, rivers and harbors. The divers will need to be trained in the metal detectors' setup, maintenance and function, along with the interpretation of the various signals and tones that they may produce to indicate a find.

The tow bar is a more economical addition to a team's search equipment that can prove very time-effective when trying to cover large areas with reasonable water clarity. Two divers ride the bar, as it is towed behind the dive boat at a slow speed (1-3 knots), searching the bottom. The boat will require a skilled operator who understands the dynamics involved for the divers and is able to follow an accurate bearing. When the divers see the object of the search they can drop off the bar and mark the location with a small buoy or notify the deck team by means of hard-wire or wireless diver communications.

Some teams in Florida have trained their personnel in the use of Nitrox so as to increase their bottom times in deeper water (50-130 feet) without getting into the decompression requirements of the U.S. Navy tables. Nitrox 1 can double the divers' bottom times at 50-130 feet by raising the oxygen percentage in the gas mix from 20% to 32%.

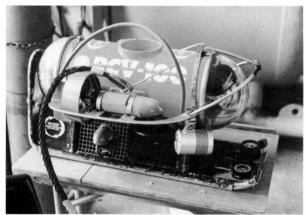

SBCC RCV-100.

Phantom 500 remote operated video camera.

185

DISCOVERY

Before the diver enters the water he must be briefed on the procedure to follow if he finds the object. There are several options open to the Dive Supervisor or senior investigator:

- Notify topside but do not touch the object
- Recover it immediately
- Mark it for the next team and return to the surface
- Sketch it and/or photograph it
- Bag it in the water

The procedure may depend on the nature of the object (gun, body, evidence, car), the location (river, sewer, deep water, mud), its evidentiary value (murder weapon, drug bust, suspicious accident) or whether the operation is a rescue or a recovery. Obviously rescue victims must be surfaced and given medical attention immediately.

Whatever the situation, the dive team must be clear on the procedure expected of them before diving. If the diver has communications this can greatly simplify the problem and allow the investigators to make decisions based on the diver's immediate observations.

SBCC ROV/RCV monitor being utilized during Advanced Police Rescue Class.

Author testing Fisher metal detector in Wilmington Harbor.

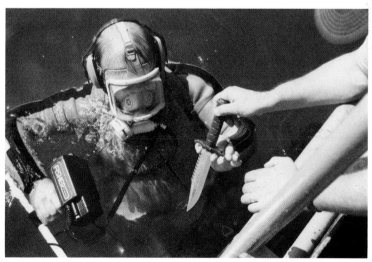

Weapons are easily found in mud and silt with the patient and systematic use of a metal detector.

Reefs and rock crevices must be systematically searched for trapped bodies.

Rescue divers should be trained in inwater decompression, if only for safety stops, on the off chance that search and recovery operations will take place in deep waters.

15
PENETRATION DIVES

A penetration dive is any dive where the divers must enter into a situation where they do not have a clear, unobstructed path to the surface. This situation will be found in wrecks, crashed aircraft, caves, pipelines, sewers or even under large barges or super-tankers. In an emergency, the diver cannot make a normal swimming ascent or buoyant emergency ascent because of the overhead structure.

All penetration dives require special training, equipment and preparation. The depth from the surface, the type of structure, the horizontal depth of penetration and the nature of the rescue or recovery will all have an effect on the equipment, techniques and personnel to be deployed. Some are considerably more complex than others.

PIPES & SEWERS

If an area has any form of large sewer system, storm water drainage system, irrigation system or even industrial water cooling pipes, it is only a matter of time before the dive team will be required to enter these pipes/tunnels in search of lost children or unfortunate flood victims.

There are several points that the team leader must consider in his Risk/Benefit evaluation and pre-dive survey:

- Probability of victim's entry into the pipe
- Diameter and construction of the pipe
- Level of contamination — chemical or bacterial
- Flow rate in or out of the pipe
- Length/depth of system
- Flood gate control in irrigation areas
- Potential for rain or increased flow
- Physical hazards such as rusty metal, broken concrete, etc.
- Dangerous inhabitants, alligators, snakes, eels, etc.
- Visibility
- Possibility of a primary diver rescue
- Need/availability of specialty extraction equipment

Surface-supplied diving is, without a doubt, the safest way to approach a pipe job and will be absolutely essential in the case of heavy contamination. The next best option would be SCUBA with surface communications, a strong safety rope and a second independent air source.

SCUBA divers should not enter without a harness, a safety line, preferably a braided rappelling/rescue type rope, and an extra air source. This does not mean an octopus or Air II but a totally separate SCUBA tank complete with regulator. A lot can be learned from cave divers about penetration dives and additional air supplies. Keep in mind that there is no easy way out, no direct ascent to the surface, probably no visibility and usually not enough room to turn around — in head-first and out feet-first!

The separate tank may have to be pushed ahead or dragged behind if there is insufficient room to wear it. The safety diver should be equipped with an emergency air supply complete with a 5-6 foot hose between the first and second stages; this to permit the second stage to be passed up past the entrapped diver's body to his mouth — there may not be room for the whole tank.

Buoyancy compensators will be of little use and possibly considerable hindrance, but extra lights and strong gloves are essential. The rescue diver on SCUBA should use the cave divers' **"one-third rule"** — one-third of your air going in, one-third to come out and the final third for emergencies and hangups.

One case in New York, where a small child had to be recovered from a sewer, came about as a result of some evil individual removing a manhole cover and then covering the hole with a carpet. The child stepped on the "trap" and fell through. The body was found nine feet down and twenty-five feet back in a pipe full of raw sewage with zero visibility. In such cases, full contaminated diving procedures and equipment must be employed. The decontamination team must be in place before the diver gets wet.

WRECKS

Since submerged shipwrecks are a popular dive site for sport divers it is reasonable to assume that in time, some poor wretch with a shortage of training and experience, will meet his demise deep in one of these attractions. Now the local SRT dive team must locate and remove the body.

The rescue team should all be experienced wreck divers, especially if the local waters are known for their wrecks. This is typical of areas like South Florida and Key Largo. It will also benefit the team if the divers can locate, dive, map and record all the local wrecks, just as a SWAT team does studies of local banks and potential barricade locations.

Unlike pipelines, wrecks can be complex mazes of passage-ways, cabins, holds, engine rooms, debris and jagged metal. To compound the problem the wreck may be inverted, angled or on its side, which can further disorient the unwary diver. Some wrecks have had bulkheads cut open, hatches removed, holds welded shut and debris removed to make them safe for sport divers. Others have aged naturally and remain as the day they sank.

There are several situations that can result in danger to a diver that enters a wreck without lights, safety lines, independent air sources, a knowledge of wreck diving and an experienced partner:

- Out of air and no direct ascent possible
- Malfunctioning breathing equipment
- Narrow passages that hinder buddy-breathing efforts
- Lost or disoriented
- Failed lights and no safety/guide line out
- Hatches closing and jamming behind the diver
- Possible movement of the wreck
- Dangerous territorial marine life
- Strong surges or currents
- Injury on sharp, rusty metal
- Entanglement in lines or nets
- Failure to monitor depth within the wreck
- Heavy silt and sediment can reduce visibility to zero
- Lack of experience or training
- Panic or stress from dark, confined spaces

Police divers prepare to penetrate a wreck during the State Police Diver Program run through Broward Community College.

191

With all this in mind the rescue team must prepare and train accordingly. Site surveys are essential and safety procedures must be followed to the letter. Safety divers should be stationed at the point of entry and maintain communication with the penetration team through line pull signals or through-water communications. Essential equipment would be:

- Lines and reels to mark the divers' progress
- Extra lights, minimum three per diver
- Independent air supplies, not just an octopus or Spare Air
- Adequate protection from sharp edges
- A slate and pencil to mark progress or draw plans
- Tools to open hatches; wedges and rope to keep them open

Divers should keep fin strokes to a minimum to avoid stirring up the silt that gathers in sheltered areas of the wrecks. The "one-third rule" also applies to wreck penetrations.

Many wrecks lie in deep water that will also require rigging for deep diving as well. Extra tanks at the exit point, hang-off tanks for in-water safety or decompression stops, down-lines and tag lines from the wreck to the down-line may all be necessary for a safe attempted rescue.

CRASHED AIRCRAFT

A plane crash may well turn into a penetration dive if the team must enter the fuselage to remove bodies or vital equipment. The larger the plane the deeper the penetration. Light aircraft like two- and four-seater Cessnas may require only that the diver reach in, release the safety belts and remove the passengers. Larger commercial planes may require the diver to climb completely into the cabin area to complete his tasks.

Before the team even considers entering the submerged aircraft, a site survey and evaluation must be completed. Although the chance of survivors clinging to life in air pockets within the airframe is remote, it must be considered. If the team can get on site quickly, locate the wreck and force entry in the first critical hour or so, a rescue may well be possible. In reality, the forces involved in a crash into water, where the aircraft sinks completely, greatly reduce the chance of survivors within the fuselage.

A more probable rescue may result when the airframe breaks up on impact and flings passengers away from the wreckage. They may stand a better chance of survival on the surface if they can stay afloat until help arrives. In the case of a controlled crash landing some passengers and crew may have had the opportunity to exit the aircraft before it sinks.

In shark infested areas, the magnitude of the crash, bodily injuries, deaths and decomposition may result in heavy shark feeding activity, prior to the divers' arrival. These eating machines may now pose a threat to the rescue efforts and the dive team. Working divers in shark country have made use of 50-gallon drums with the tops cut out as dive stages.

The divers can be raised and lowered standing in the drums, as some form of protection. If a shark becomes aggressive the diver can duck into the drum or use a pole to fend it off.

If the aircraft has been submerged beyond the limits for a rescue, certain investigative procedures will need to be completed for the FAA/National Transportation Safety Board (NTSB). These are covered in Chapter 16.

There is some additional information the Diving Supervisor will need:

- Type, size and capacity of aircraft
- Number of passengers and crew
- Location of doors and emergency exits
- Operation of aircraft doors from outside
- Water depth
- Type of cargo on board, toxic fuels or chemicals, etc.

A quick dive on the airframe will tell the supervisor:

- Attitude of plane
- Amount of wreckage
- Whether the fuselage is intact
- Probability of survivors
- Best access points
- Number of divers required
- The need for cutting tools, lights or safety lines

The key difference between penetrating a crashed aircraft and entering a pipe or shipwreck is the amount of razor-sharp, torn metal, loose cable and wreckage and the spaghetti of exposed wiring and cabin lining. There is some chance of becoming disoriented in an inverted aircraft, or being confused by the fact that everything has floated to the top of the cabin. But by far, the two greatest dangers to the rescue diver are being cut by the torn skin of the plane or being entangled in the cable and wiring in the cabin. A BC could well be punctured or torn before even effecting an entry, and divers should carry wire cutters at all times.

On large commercial jets the number of bodies and extent of tissue damage may also be stressful for the divers. If the jet has been down for some time, especially in warmer tropical waters, the stench and decomposition may be overpowering.

So again, make maximum use of safety divers on the surface and at the point of entry into the aircraft; doors are preferable to ragged holes resulting from the crash; try to photograph as much as possible before disturbing the wreckage; utilize independent air supplies or surface-supplied gear; beware of sharp metal and loose cables/wires; carry wire cutters; stabilize the wreck before entry; maintain contact with the safety diver at the point of entry.

CAVE DIVING & CAVE RESCUE

Cave rescue, as with cave diving, is a very specialized form of diving that should not be attempted by untrained personnel. Modern day cave diving can involve significant penetrations and may include notable depth. Furthermore, the complexity of the cave systems, the uniqueness of this environment and the narrowness of certain passageways can greatly complicate operations and put team members at significant risk. Given the danger of these operations one point is clear - the untrained rescue diver has no business venturing into this specialty.

Cave divers have always been considered the "extreme" of the recreational diving community but their work in research, deep diving techniques and long duration subterranean travel laid the foundation of what we now know as technical diving and is definitely worthy of respect. Long before technical diving came into vogue, cave divers were routinely doing decompression dives and mixed gas diving had become the standard for deep cave exploration.

The Global Underwater Explorers organization, working in concert with the Florida based WKPP have expanded cave exploration well beyond what anyone thought possible. In 1998 representatives Jarrod Jablonski, George Irvine and Brent Scarabin set a world record in Wakulla Springs in northern Florida by penetrating 18,054 feet from the spring entrance. To accomplish this record setting dive the team utilized Halcyon rebreathers, mixed gas (10% oxygen, 70% Helium, 20% nitrogen), five different deco mixes, specially built propulsion vehicles and over 30 safety tanks. The significant experience, training, and logistical planning that lead up to this effort had to support the team for more than six hours at 300 feet, along with an additional 15 hours of in water decompression.

Record setting cave dives are by no means the norm in cave diving. Nevertheless, "recreational" cave diving is consistently expanding in scope and popularity, resulting in the common occurrence of more ambitious diving profiles. Public Safety divers with an interest in cave rescue operations should first become **certified cave divers**. Becoming a truly proficient cave diver is a time intensive activity. However, cave rescue personnel can greatly increase their personal skills and prepare for limited cave operations by pursing formal cave diver training. Typically cave training is divided into roughly three phases, each lasting about a week. Despite this training, rescue personnel should remain aware that in some cases local experienced cave divers may be the most qualified for recovery operations.

This chapter is not, in any way designed to prepare individuals for cave operations. Instead, it is designed to highlight the complexities of this specialized environment and prevent a rescue team from venturing into an area well beyond their capability.

Diving in any body of water carries the possibility of drowning but there are several additional dangers that are unique to cave diving:

- No direct route to the surface
- Complete absence of light
- Excessive distance from the entrance to a cave
- Maze-like formations with numerous side tunnels
- Narrow restrictions can slow or trap a diver
- Fine silt can eliminate all visibility with only one incorrect move
- Equipment dependence resulting from an inability to surface in times of trouble
- The stress and task loading created by the above dangers

Cave diving fatalities are commonly the result of human error. The most common causes of cave diving fatalities are listed below and include:

1. Lack of formal **training** in cave diving
2. Failure to run a **continuous guideline** to open water
3. Failure to reserve at least **two-thirds** of starting air supply for the exit swim
4. Exceeding the **maximum depth limits** for their level of training
5. Failure to use at least **three lights** – one primary and two backup

As with any penetration (overhead environment) rescue dive there must be a period of fact-finding, interview and investigation. Cave operations require the discovery of additional information, including the following.

Missing Diver Information:
- Number of missing divers and description of equipment used
- Was the diver cave certified and equipped
- How long has the diver been down or missing
- How much gas/air was the diver carrying
- Where was the diver was last seen; conscious or unconscious
- What was the proposed dive plan and depth of penetration

Sport divers may often venture into caves without realizing the dangers of exploring an "overhead environment."

Not all caves have signs that make the dangers this clear.

Cave Information:
- Current map of cave system
- Location of entrance and position of permanent guideline
- Depth and length of main tunnel
- Possibility of finding air spaces or dry caves
- Flow characteristics of this cave (spring, siphon etc)
- Expected weather changes; possibility of rainfall
- Natural hazards such as restrictions, low visibility, or silty conditions

Some rescues may not be for cave divers but for dry cavers that have been trapped by rising water or incapacitated by injury, hypothermia or exhaustion.

The following is a list of equipment considered the minimum for one cave rescue diver:
- ❐ A set of Double Tanks with Isolation Manifold
- ❐ Harness, Back-plate and Wings (45 – 55 pound lift)
- ❐ 2 Regulators with clean "DIR" cave configuration
- ❐ 7 foot Second Stage Hose on Primary Regulator
- ❐ Digital Bottom Timer / Depth Gauge
- ❐ Compass / Redundant Instrumentation
- ❐ Primary Light with canister mounted on Right Hip
- ❐ Two Back-up Lights attached to Harness Shoulder Straps
- ❐ One Primary Reel (300'- 400') – This is run from open water to the mainline in the cave
- ❐ One Safety Reel (100'-150'), One Jump/Gap Reel (50'-75')
- ❐ Directional Line Markers
- ❐ Small, Sharp Knife on Harness
- ❐ Dry Suit or Wet Suit (depending on water temperature)
- ❐ Fins, two masks, weight belt (where necessary)
- ❐ Diving tables
- ❐ Repair kit and spares
- ❐ Clips on lights, reels, stages etc should be stainless steel bolt snaps for maximum reliability.
- ❐ Long penetration recoveries may require specially trained cave divers and underwater vehicles

If using Decompression Gases:
- ❐ Deco Tanks of Nitrox and/or Oxygen with MOD (maximum operating depth) clearly indicated
- ❐ Additional decompression regulators with SPGs (submersible pressure gauge)
- ❐ Cylinder attachment that can be cut because of clip failure or diver entanglement

Trips to the recovery site may be overland or through dry caves, necessitating adequate support personnel. Operations may also require an assortment of camping gear, sleeping bags and food to sustain a prolonged search.

Operational requirements for both wet and dry cave rescues may include:
- ❐ Communications systems
- ❐ Body bags
- ❐ Medical supplies, oxygen, back boards, litter
- ❐ Hypothermia bags, warming tents, warm air breather
- ❐ Strobes, lights, additional reels and lines
- ❐ Rescue ropes and hardware for raising and lowering systems
- ❐ Air Compressor for remote areas
- ❐ Special gasses (nitrox or trimix) where applicable

Incorporating the techniques for safe cave diving, the team can proceed with the search, rescue or recovery. Special attention must be given to the following:
- Plan the dive carefully and select a turn around point using the "one third rule" One third to go in – One third to come out – One third for emergencies
- Maintain a continuous guideline out of the cave system
- Operations must include all relevant cave equipment & lights
- Maintain neutral buoyancy at all times
- Utilize proficient, anti-silting swimming techniques
- Don't go deeper than the Equivalent Narcosis Depth (END) that the back gas will safely permit
- Mark all travel and deco bottles CLEARLY with the Maximum Operating Depth (MOD)

Frequently there are clues that can help direct a search team to the missing diver(s). Rescue divers should look for disturbed silt, bubbles on the ceiling, abandoned equipment, chipped or scraped walls, gathering of catfish and possibly guidelines or markers placed by the victim(s). Panicked divers frequently try to surface in the cave and are often found in overhead cracks but may also be found wedged in side areas or simply on the floor. Rescue teams should initiate a search based upon the lost teams dive plan (if known) or last seen point (where applicable). Barring any information about the lost teams location rescue personnel should go directly to the deepest point/ maximum estimated distance of the penetration and then search on their way out. This procedure will make the best use of their gas supply and decompression procedures while allowing later search efforts to be conducted at progressively reduced penetrations.

As with any homicide, crime scene containment and rules of evidence apply to cave fatalities. Prior to moving cave victim(s), crime scene information should be recorded (see chapter 16).

The actual transportation of victim(s) through the cave can be a difficult and tiring task, placing the recovery divers under greater risk. If the victim has been in the water for a prolonged period several complications arise. Rigor mortis can greatly increase the difficulty of managing a diver in restrictive areas. Furthermore, when decomposition has begun the body can become positively buoyant, requiring additional weight to keep the body off the ceiling and simplify the extraction. In cases of extreme body degradation, bags or webbing wraps can be used to transport, stabilize, or weight the victim. Since few passages will allow the rescue divers to swim on either side of the victim most operations result in one diver pushing and one pulling. This can result in further damage to the body, especially the face and exposed areas when being dragged or pushed through restrictions.

Injured divers or cavers can be transported through the water in a sump litter which consists of a heavy nylon bag, is open at the head end and is complete with zipper, cinch straps, attach-ment points and handles. The survivor can be strapped into the sump litter and equipped with a full-face SCUBA mask (like the AGA) and head protection. The SCUBA tank can be strapped to the bag between the victim's legs and the whole package guided through the sumps and chambers to the exit. The victim should be given the opportunity to become comfortable with the bag and SCUBA unit before being fully submerged.

Cave rescues and recoveries are generally cold and arduous operations at best. The dark, inhospitable and often claustrophobic environment adds to an already difficult task. For rescue teams with caves in their jurisdiction divers should get specialized training; make necessary equipment modifications; select rescue personnel with an aptitude for working in confined spaces; learn the local cave systems; and practice regularly. Search teams should never engage in cave operations that are beyond their abilities nor hesitate to abort a rescue that evolves beyond team capacity.

For more information on cave diving and specialized equipment, check out:
Global Underwater Explorers / GUE www.gue.com or 800/762-3483(dive)
Extreme Exposure gear at www.extreme-exposure.com or 800/378-7820
Halcyon dive gear at www.halcyon.net
Dive Gear at www.divegear.com

Double manifolded tanks with wings, harness, back plate, and lights configured for "Doing it Right."

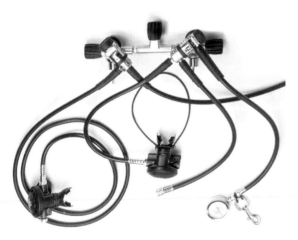

Primary reg on right post with 7 foot hose. Back-up reg on left with SPG and dry suit inflator.

200

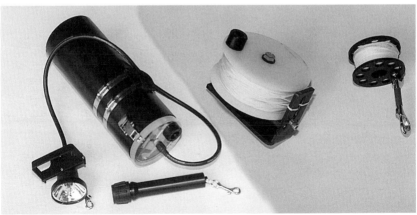

Lights and reels critical to safe cave diving. Explorer cannister light, Scout back-up light, Extreme Exposure primary reel and emergency spool.

Halcyon mixed gas rebreather used to set world deep cave penetration record.

16
INVESTIGATION & RECOVERY

The type of search, the object and how it found its way into the water will dictate the investigative requirements and the method of recovery. Where a drowning victim will be recovered to the surface immediately, the victim of a suspected homicide will have to be handled in the same manner as any topside crime scene. A car in a river will usually be pulled immediately but a downed aircraft will require on-site study by the NTSB and considerable dive time invested in collection of evidence and underwater photography.

The actual mechanics of the recovery can vary greatly with the size, weight and nature of the object, and the body of water it is to be pulled from. A submerged tractor trailer rig poses more problems to a dive team than a Japanese compact, just as an airliner in deep water is more complex than a light plane in a local lake.

Whether it be bodies, vehicles, aircraft, evidence or boats, each has its own investigative and recovery procedures. Where some recoveries may be time-critical, such as rescues and evidence that may sustain water damage, others can be run in a slow, methodical manner so that no clue will be left unturned.

BODY RECOVERY

Body recovery is not a pleasant or rewarding task but unfortunately it is one of the primary assignments of a law enforcement dive team. If the dive team is to survive budget cuts and media scrutiny they must be able to handle this task with professionalism and efficiency.

Body recoveries can fall into several categories:

- Missing persons near a body of water
- Boating, skiing, swimming or fishing accidents
- White water rafters or kayakers
- SCUBA divers
- Victims of shipping or aircraft accidents

- Victims of motor vehicle accidents
- Victims of foul play, homicide and suicide

Some of the on-site considerations will be:
- Is it time-critical?
- Has a crime been committed, or suspicion of a crime?
- Are criminal investigators on hand?
- Do other agencies need to be notified, e.g., NTSB?
- Is the Medical Examiner or Coroner on-site?
- Are suitable evidence containers/body bags on hand?
- Will photographic equipment be required?
- Is recovery equipment available?
- Is the chain of custody for evidence established?
- Have sketches, measurements and bearings been completed?
- What is the location/proximity of the victim's family?
- Are the press and news media at a discreet distance?

When in doubt, photograph, sketch and document the entire scene as if it were a crime scene. Before a body is moved be sure to search the surrounding area for victim's possessions, evidence or related debris. If the body must be moved immediately, the location should be marked with a weight and buoy.

In many cases it is advisable to bag the body in the water to protect the evidence and spare the family on the beach unnecessary grief. Bagging a body under water is no easy task and will often be left until on a hard surface, especially if no foul play is suspected.

Where there is a suspicion of foul play, full investigative and crime scene skills go into play. Bag the hands separately to preserve tissue samples under the nails, or in case the victim is grasping an article of critical evidence. The divers must make sure that nothing falls from the victim's clothing or pockets during the recovery, and that under the body be searched for evidence. Even after prolonged periods under water the body can still yield vital clues, as to the cause of death, to a medical examiner or skilled investigator. It is important that the divers do nothing to hinder the investigation.

Bodies that have been submerged for some time may be suffering from various levels of decompositon. Bodies in warm, shallow water will decompose and putrify faster than those in colder, deeper waters. Just as victims who were sick (AIDS, cancer, syphilis) or had a high bacterial content will deteriorate faster than healthy bodies. After rigor mortis (muscle rigidity) has set in, usually very quickly, the body is fairly easy to handle. With time and decomposition another problem will manifest itself and that is skin slippage. The exterior of the body becomes slimy and soapy and begins to rot away. A diver can accidentally pull the skin right off the victim's extremities if not correctly handled. This is one good reason for in-water bagging, but even if the dermis is pulled from the hands it can still be fingerprinted for identification purposes.

Other contributing factors to body deterioration are:

- Marine life feeding on exposed areas
- Critter and insect attack
- Wave action or currents moving the body around
- Abrasion on rocks, debris or coral
- Injuries sustained prior to death or submersion

Water, in many cases, can serve as a preservative, but the body will rot at a fantastic rate once it hits the air, especially if left in the sun.

The surface crew must be prepared to photograph and fingerprint the body as soon as possible, if necessary, then get it bagged and transported to the morgue without delay.

Divers surfacing with a decomposing body are advised to keep their masks on and regulators in place. The stench of putrefaction and natural purging can be quite overpowering. Also keep a line attached to the body or body-bag during the recovery process on the off chance that the divers may lose their grip. This will eliminate the need for a second search and the embarrassment of delay. Back-boards can also be used to minimize damage to the body.

The family of the victim(s) should be gently encouraged to leave the recovery site before the body is surfaced, and to view it at the morgue or Coroner's office. In the same context, news photographers should be prevented from getting any graphic or tasteless pictures of the victim.

The only satisfaction a diver can draw from a body recovery is the success of the search and the finality for the victim's family. The recovery will end the doubt, the waiting, the uncertainty for friends and relatives and allow the healing process to begin.

NYPD Scuba unit sergeant logs all information during the underwater search for a murder weapon.

Diving supervisor confers with investigators before divers search for a weapon utilized in a drug-related murder.

ICSURT retrieve body from a Southern California river.

Note the rope attached to the body to assist in the recovery operation.

Although it is recommended to bag the bodies in the water it is usually easier on dry land.

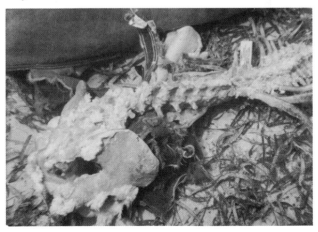

When a victim is reduced to nothing more than bones, identification can be very difficult.

DIVING ACCIDENTS

Teams operating in areas with an active sport diving population will be called upon to search for and recover victims of diving accidents. On rare occasions there may be suspicion of foul play, but in most cases these deaths are a result of diver error, poor training, stupidity and inexperience.

The dive team should make every effort to record and photograph all the details of the accident in case of future litigation. In our present "sue happy" times, and with the pressure from hungry attorneys, the victim's family will invariably try to go after the manufacturers of the diving equipment in a court of law. Dive team members may be subpoenaed to appear as expert witnesses for either party.

It may take years to get to court, so notes, sketches and photographs could prove invaluable where the memory may have faded. Note the following:

- Depth and time of recovery
- Position of the victim's weight belt
- Mask and regulator in place?
- Air in the BC and pressure remaining in the tank?
- Emergency inflation device pulled (CO_2)?

Victims of Scuba accidents should be photographed before recovery.

Photograph:

- Depth and pressure gauges
- Weight belt and buckle
- Mask and regulator
- Body position
- Condition of the BC

If possible recover the victim to the surface with his gear intact, for further examination. This can be done with a recovery line or lift bag. If the weight belt must be removed, note this and recover it also. Do not use air from the victim's tank to inflate the victim's BC — this will only serve to disturb the evidence.

On deck the diver can be photographed again before the dive gear is removed. Note each piece of equipment as it is removed and pay special attention to the SCUBA set and power inflator. If the tank is turned off, note how many turns of the tank valve this took. Note the remaining air pressure before the tank is moved. Do not remove the regulator or back-pack on site and send the whole system to the examiner's office. Note the amount of lead on the weight belt and the overall condition of the gear.

Gates underwater video housing with Sony VX1000 camera for high-end video applications.

PERSON/DIVER CHECKLIST AND PHOTOGRAPHY
TAKE PHOTOGRAPHS AND MEASUREMENTS

Important Note: Photograph all gauges and equipment as first seen underwater, before removing body(ies).

Investigating Officer _____ Department _____

Phone _____ Date _____ Time Start _____ Finish _____ Case Number _____

LOCATION OF ACCIDENT: Intercoastal _____ Nearest channel marker _____
Distance (feet or miles) _____ Open Ocean _____ Nearest channel opening name _____
Distance from opening (feet or miles) _____ Distance from shore line (feet or miles) _____
Direction from shore line: North _____ East _____ West _____ South _____ What degrees _____
_____ Nearest boat ramp (feet or miles) _____ Name _____
Additional Comments:

WATER CONDITIONS: Calm _____ Rough _____ Choppy _____
Wave direction _____ Wave heights _____ Current direction _____ Current speed _____

WATER VISIBILITY: Clear _____ Silty _____ Low Visibility _____ Night _____
Distance of visibility: 0'-3' _____ 4'-6' _____ 7'-10' _____ Max. visibility _____ ft.

WEATHER CONDITIONS: Small craft _____ Storm _____ Gale _____ Hurricane _____
Sky: Clear _____ Partly Cloudy _____ Cloudy _____ Raining _____ Night _____
Visibility _____ Wind direction _____ Wind speed (if possible) _____

POSITION OF VICTIM(S):
Face up _____ Face down _____ Right side _____ Left side _____ Sitting position _____
Additional Comments:

VICTIM(S) CLOTHING:
Bathing suit _____ Wet suit _____ Shortie _____ Full _____ Jacket _____
Farmer John only _____ Shirt: Long sleeve _____ Short sleeve _____
Pants: Long _____ Short _____ Jacket _____ Additional Comments:

VICTIM(S) DEPTH FOUND (MEASUREMENTS):
Head _____ Feet _____ Right side _____ Left side _____
Additional Comments:

VICTIM(S) WAS ENT/ANGLED: Yes _____ No _____ If yes, what was the victim(s) _____

BODY REMOVAL: Is extrication going to be easily accomplished? Yes _____ No _____ If no, explain why?

BODY DISMEMBERMENT: Describe location on body and to what degree the body is dismembered:

WATER CONDITIONS: Calm _____ Rough _____ Choppy _____ Wave Direction _____
Wave Heights _____ Current Direction _____ Current Speed (if possible to determine) _____

WATER VISIBLE: Clear _____ Silty _____ Low visible _____ Night _____
Distance of visible: 0'-3' _____ 4'-6' _____ 7'-10' _____ Maximum visible _____ feet

SUBMERGED OBJECT: Yes _____ No _____ If yes, answer the following.
Height _____ Material _____ Did boat hit submerged object? Yes _____ No _____ If yes, describe
what was seen under water:

TIDE INFORMATION: High _____ Low _____ Med. _____ Tide time _____
Tide different in feet at location of boat/vessel, if possible. _____ Time _____ Depth _____

WEATHER CONDITIONS: Small craft _____ Storm _____ Gale _____ Hurricane _____
Sky: Clear _____ Partly cloudy _____ Cloudy _____ Raining _____ Night _____
Visibility _____ Wind direction _____ Wind speed (if possible) _____

BOAT/VESSEL DATA: Registration or Doc. Number _____ Name _____
Make _____ Year _____ Hull I.D. Number _____
Model _____ Type of Boat: Pleasure _____ Commercial _____
Hull Material _____ Length _____ Width of Beam _____ Side Free Board _____
Transome Free Board _____ Transome Width _____ Depth Amidship _____ Weight _____
General Stability _____ Max Persons Allowed _____ Persons on Board _____

ENGINE: Propulsion Type _____ Mfg. Name _____ Year _____
Max. Horse Power _____ Horse Power on Boat/Vessel _____

OTHER INFORMATION: Drain Plug: In _____ Out _____ Light switches: On _____ Off _____
If on, which lights were on? _____
Ignition switch: On _____ Off _____ Battery switch: On _____ Off _____ Marine or CB radio: On _____
Off _____ Channel (if possible) _____ Fire Extinguisher: Yes _____ No _____ If yes, type _____
Qty _____ Where found _____
Were any other items found in the immediate surrounding area? Yes _____ No _____ If yes, type of items: _____ Amount of items _____

Additional Comments:

Was any contraband found in the boat or around the boat? _____ Yes _____ No _____ If yes, what kind of contraband and the total amount

You should always sketch the area completely before anything is moved. Photos should be taken whenever possible. The following statement should always be made and noted in a police report also for court.
"That all measurements are approximate, because not all measuring devices are exact. Also objects viewed by a diver under water appear to be nearer and larger than they appear on land."
© 1988 A.I.R. SPECIALTIES, INC.

Slates copyrighted © and available from A.I.R. Specialties, Inc.

BODY REFLOAT

Body refloat time is a grossly misunderstood phenomenon, often asked by the press and bystanders and seldom accurately predicted. It would be convenient if all bodies popped back up in an hour or two — this would save the dive team having to spend many hours in dirty water, looking for someone they can't save anyway.

Once a body sinks it will go to the bottom, contrary to theories extolled by "experts." Refloat is the result of expanding gases trapped in the body, primarily a product of decomposition. Calculating refloat time is not an exact science and dive team members should refrain from attempting predictions or discussing the possibilities with press or spectators. The following are just some of the factors involved in refloat:

Water temperature — Colder waters will delay the decomposition process and ice cold waters could hold their victims indefinitely. Water temperatures below 38 degrees F. will inhibit bacterial action to the point that the gas formation is insufficient to cause refloat. On the other side of the coin, warm waters may surrender the body in 24-48 hours.

Depth — Since depth places a greater amount of pressure on the victim, the initial small amounts of gas produced in the digestive tract may be insufficient to create positive buoyancy. Deeper waters are also generally cooler.

Clothing — Heavy boots, tool belts, gun belts, loaded back-packs, thick clothing and camera equipment have all contributed to drownings and have held their owners on the bottom.

Type of water —Dirty, murky waters are often more conducive to bacterial action than clean, clear waters.

Food recently eaten — A person who has eaten a meal a few hours before drowning will have increased gas production in the digestive system. Beer, chili and other high carbohydrate foods can have a significant impact on an early refloat.

Marine life — If animals or marine life begin feeding on the victim's body immediately, this could reduce or eliminate the chance of a refloat. Some have been consumed to the bone with no time for decomposition and the accompanying gas production.

Cause of death — Traumatic injuries could accelerate the decomposition process but large open gashes and puncture wounds may serve to vent off the gases as they develop. Another unpredictable variable.

When a body does refloat the gases that lifted the body from the bottom will expand as the body ascends through the water column. This expansion will cause the body to accelerate and possibly break the surface in a dramatic manner. If the body holds the gases it may float high in the water and be carried by the wind.

The body may also sink immediately only to refloat at a later time. Another unpredictable phenomenon. Whatever the case the body should be recovered and bagged as soon as possible. In air it will decompose even faster.

When diving operations are suspended for the evening, night patrols should check the site frequently, and down-currrent, on the off chance the body may refloat during the hours of darkness.

When bodies finally float to the surface they will ride very high on the water and can be moved considerable distances by the wind.

EVIDENCE COLLECTION

The evidence most commonly recovered by police dive teams is weapons used in the commission of a felony, e.g., homicide, armed robbery, assault, etc. Secondarily it may be stolen property that was too hot to fence or controlled substances thrown overboard during a drug search.

All techniques of topside crime scene containment and preservation of evidence must be applied to the underwater crime scene. Mark, sketch, measure, photograph, bag, tag and secure all evidence. The diver may wish to surface and discuss the situation with the senior investigator before proceeding with the recovery.

A fingerprint can be lifted from a weapon that has been submerged for several months, if it is handled correctly. Water and mud can act as a preservative for many firearms and objects. It is the exposure to air that will cause rapid oxidization, rust and deterioration.

It is important that firearms and evidence be recovered in the same medium in which they have been lying. This generally means plastic containers, custom-made PVC containers, plastic zip-lock bags or buckets. The evidence should be kept in water until the time for processing at the crime lab.

One word of warning: Loaded firearms can still fire after several months under water, and modern ammunition is usually quite water resistant. Handle firearms with the utmost care, especially if the safety is off and the hammer is cocked.

Even wet papers and documents can yield their secrets if handled correctly. Keep them in a container with water and when ready, unfold them in water, holding them by the edges, and lay them out on a sheet of clean, dry paper to dry. Do not expose them to direct sunlight, wind or blow-dryers. Do not lay them on newsprint, as this will bleed through and hinder the efforts to distinguish the writing on the recovered documents. Consult your crime lab technicians for further tips in this area.

Wet clothing and papers should not be left in plastic bags after recovery as they will begin to rot and mildew. They must be dried and preserved as soon as practical.

PVC evidence container developed by Mike Van Alvensleben of the Marine Technologies Department, Santa Barbara City College.

As one diver brushes the sand away from the weapon the other can record information for future reference.

Plastic bags are an expedient method of handling evidence and weapons underwater.

CHAIN OF CUSTODY

Inadequate documentation, sloppy investigative procedures and contamination of the crime scene can all result in the loss of an important bust. Similarly, a screw-up in the chain of custody of evidence can lose a case just as easily.

The diver must be able to identify the evidence that he finds, especially two years later when it finally gets to court. This may mean marking or inscribing his initials on the weapon or evidence to help his future efforts at identification.

The number of persons handling the evidence must be kept to a minimum: diver — investigator — lab technician. This movement must be documented on a standard "chain of custody" form and then ultimately, the evidence must be correctly preserved, tagged and stored.

The correct handling of evidence may be one more demonstration of a dive team's professionalism. Crime labs will need to stay up to date on the latest techniques for the handling of submerged evidence.

Mike Gast of Metro Dade Police Department recovers a weapon from a man-made quarry.

Diver recovers suspicious case thrown into the water.

A suppressed UZI is recovered from Miami's waterways.

Some access points are so steep divers require a knotted rope to enter and exit the water.

Assorted weapons and suppressors recovered by Metro Dade Police divers.

Weapons recovered from New York Harbor during a routine search in front of a pier.

VEHICLE RECOVERY

Based on the physical evidence, skid marks, oil slick, a broken barrier and a last-seen point, the dive team has found the car and is ready to commence the recovery.

Some considerations are:

- Are there still bodies in the car? How many?
- Is it rescue or recover?
- Are there suspicious circumstances?
- Has documentation, photography and sketching been completed?
- What is the Risk/Benefit factor to the team?
- Do the wreckers have sufficient cable and power?
- Should the bodies be removed under water or on land?

Before the vehicle is pulled from the water, there are some investigative procedures to be followed, to ascertain some of the circumstances leading up to the incident:

- Note the position of light switches, emergency brake, wiper switch, ignition switch and gear stick.
- Check windows, doors, door locks and trunk for signs of forced entry
- Check to see if any accessories, stereos, speakers, hubcaps, cellular telephones, T-tops or license plates are missing
- Check the ignition for signs of tampering or hot wiring
- Check the gas pedal and steering wheel to see if they have been tied or blocked in position
- Check to see if driver and passengers are in their seat belts

218

Any of the above details could lead to suspicion of car theft, "midnight auto supply" stripping, homicide or suicide.

Now to the unfortunate occupants of the submerged vehicle.

The trauma that a victim receives in an auto accident, that results in the vehicle going into the water, greatly reduces the victim's chances of survival, even if cold-water near-drowning is a consideration. The myth about air pockets in the passenger compartment should not be a consideration when the team is deciding whether to go in Rescue Mode or Recovery Mode.

Leaving the bodies in the car during recovery has its pros and cons. The pros are that doors and windows do not need to be opened, evidence is preserved and the recovery can proceed immediately. In rescue mode the victims will most definitely be recovered immediately and given medical attention.

The reasons not to leave the bodies in the vehicle during recovery are also valid. The bodies may sustain more contusions and damage banging around inside the car, or the rear window or windshield may pop out during recovery and spill the contents of the car back into the river or lake. When a vehicle is being winched up an incline, the water remaining in the passenger compartment has sufficient weight and force to blow the downhill window. For this reason divers should be prepared to go after any bodies or contents.

If the bodies are left in the vehicle, possibly still in their seat-belts, the vehicle should be pulled from the water very slowly, giving ample time for the water to drain and not build up. This is also good procedure to follow even with empty vehicles.

Powered extraction tools (Hurst Jaws of Life) can be used to free bodies from damaged vehicles, but this is best left until the vehicle is out of the water. The problems of limited visibility, currents and cold water only compound the potential hazards to the divers.

The size of the wrecker(s) called will depend on the size and depth of the vehicle to be recovered. Large trucks can be a real bear if the right recovery equipment is not on hand. It is good policy to select a tow operator to train with the recovery team and learn what is required of him during an actual operation. A dive team member should still be assigned to the tow operator during any winch operations when divers are in or under the water.

The divers will find it easier to handle strong nylon web straps under water rather than chains or cables. Experience, training and the tow operator will dictate the best attachment points for the straps or chains. Two winch cables have many advantages over just one, e.g., safety, power, control and balance.

219

U.S. Border Patrol Blazer being pulled from an irrigation canal. Driver failed to place the vehicle in "park" when exiting the truck to pursue an illegal alien.

Often times it is easier to recover the vehicle with the victim still in it. Especially if the victim is in the advanced stages of decomposition.

Dive recovery teams should find local towing companies that have trucks capable of pulling vehicles from under the water.

On occasions two heavy wreckers will be required to pull a vehicle up a steep bank.

Police divers prepare video for underwater investigation.

Vehicles won't always come out on their wheels, although it is easier if they do.

VEHICLE CHECK LIST AND PHOTOGRAPHY
TAKE PHOTOGRAPHS AND MEASUREMENTS OF SCENE

Investigating Officer _____ Department _____

Phone _____ Date _____ Time Start _____ Finish _____ Case Number _____

WINDOWS:

Are all windows intact? Yes _____ No _____ If not, which ones are broken or missing? _____

_____

ALL DOORS:

Doors: Closed _____ Open _____ If open, note which ones and where _____

_____

CHECK VEHICLE FOR VICTIMS

INSIDE:

How Many? _____ Front Seat _____ Right _____ Left _____ Center _____

Back Seat _____ Right _____ Left _____ Center _____

Third Seat _____ Right _____ Left _____ Center _____

OUTSIDE:

How Many? _____ What Depth? _____

Front _____ Right Side _____ Rear _____ Left Side _____

R _____ L _____ F _____ R _____ R _____ L _____ F _____ R _____

Direction from vehicle: N _____ E _____ S _____ W _____

Distance from vehicle: Feet _____ Inches _____

Under vehicle: Front _____ Rear _____ Right Side _____ Left Side _____

Describe location of body under vehicle: _____

POSITION OF VICTIM

Face Up _____ Face Down _____ Right Side _____ Left Side _____

Sitting Position _____

If any parts of the body dismembered, describe location on body and to what degree. _____

_____

BODY REMOVAL

Is extraction going to be easily accomplished? Yes _____ No _____

If not, explain why? _____

_____

Note anything that is out of place on the victim _____

_____

KEY IN IGNITION: How many keys found? _____

Yes _____ No _____ Not found _____ What Position _____

VEHICLE TRANSMISSION IN GEAR: Yes _____ No _____ If yes, what gear? _____

STICK SHIFT: First _____ Second _____ Third _____ Fourth _____ Fifth _____ Neutral _____ Reverse _____

AUTOMATIC: First _____ Second _____ Drive _____ Reverse _____

Parking break on? Yes _____ No _____ Was a trunk key found? If so, where? _____

Trunk open? _____ Closed? _____ What was found in trunk? _____

Headlights On _____ Off _____ Parking Lights _____ Low Beam _____ High Beam _____

Windshield wipers On _____ Off _____ Delayed _____ Low _____ High _____

VEHICLE INFORMATION:

Registration Found: Yes _____ No _____ If yes, complete the following information:

Owner's Name _____ Address _____

City _____ State _____ Zip _____

VEHICLE DESCRIPTION:

Year _____ Make _____ Model _____ Type _____

COLOR: Top _____ Bottom _____

Tag No. _____ Decal No. _____ State _____ Year _____

Vin Number _____

If Vehicle is stolen, Local Case Number _____

Out of Town Case Number _____ Authority _____

FOREIGN OBJECTS:

Gas in water? Yes _____ No _____ Was gas pedal depressed? Yes _____ No _____

If yes, what kind of object? _____

FINAL RESTING POSITION OF VEHICLE:

Right _____ Left _____ Top _____ Front _____ Rear _____ Sides _____ On Wheels _____

Glove compartment locked? Yes _____ No _____ What was found inside? _____

_____ Any more personal items found inside vehicle? Yes _____ No _____

If so, what and where located? _____

Was contraband found in vehicle? Yes _____ No _____ If so, what and where found. _____

Photographs should be taken inside of the vehicle and outside. Items found outside vehicle should be measured from the point central of the steering wheel.

Depth and direction the vehicle was facing in its final resting place.

Comments: _____

You should always sketch the area completely before anything is moved. Photos should be taken whenever possible. The following statement should always be made and noted in a police report also for court.

"That all measurements are approximate, because not all measuring devices are exact. Also objects viewed by a diver under water appear to be nearer and larger than they appear on land."

© 1988 A.I.R. SPECIALTIES, INC.

Slates copyrighted © and available from A.I.R. Specialties, Inc.

223

Investigators check identification numbers when checking for stolen vehicles.

A broken ignition is a good indicator of a stolen vehicle.

The brick on the gas pedal is a classic example of a vehicle intentionally run into the water.

It can be seen that the light switch is still on, so this vehicle probably went into the canal during the hours of darkness. Decomposition of the driver indicates that the vehicle has been underwater for some time.

225

Routine vehicle recovery changed into a homicide investigation when bones were noticed behind the driver's seat.

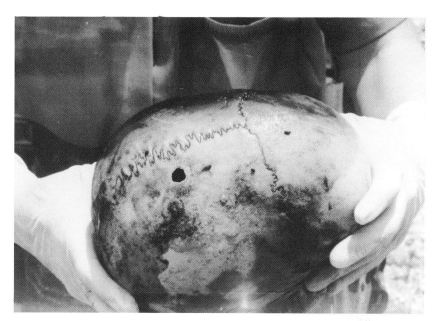

Suspicion increased when one bullet hole was found in the skull of the vehicle's occupant.

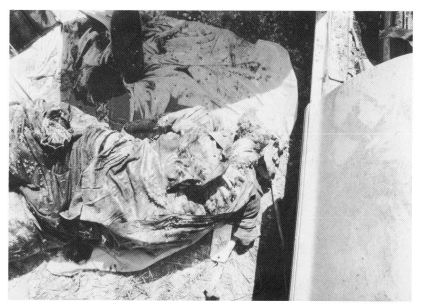

The clothing of heavily decomposed victims must be searched for any possible identification.

LIFT BAGS FOR VEHICLES

There are three ways to rig lift bags to a car: on the sides, front and rear or inside the vehicle. Pillow bags rigged front and rear work well but pontoon bags on both sides give the best balance and control. The bag inside the vehicle is generally only a secondary system.

Keep a line and buoy attached to the vehicle during lifts in case a bag bursts and the car rolls or sinks. Deep lifts will require a staged lift with extra bags. Tow lines should be long enough for the vehicle to sink without pulling the boat down and the tow should be over shallow water and away from mid-channel in case of a resink.

WARNINGS TO THE DIVER

There are several hazards involved in vehicle recovery, even though most cases may be of a simple, routine nature. A car is a 2,000-pound-plus object that had considerable mass and momentum before it came to rest in the water. Some safety considerations and practices are:

- Do a complete site survey before diving, with special attention to strong currents and debris in the water
- Fix a Risk/Benefit factor to the operation
- Learn as much as possible about the vehicle and its contents before committing to the dive
- Stay on the uphill side of the vehicle in case it should move or roll into deeper water
- Be aware of jagged metal and broken glass
- Do not extend more than half your body into the vehicle when searching
- Secure cables or straps to the vehicle as soon as possible
- Do not let strong currents push you into jagged metal
- Do not remain near the vehicle or downhill during the recovery
- Be especially wary when working with complex rigging and lift bags
- The tow cables or lift lines could break at any time and steel cables can whip violently when stressed
- Study tanker trucks for haz-mat placards or toxic leaks
- Try to stay up-current of oil or chemical spills
- Do not approach haz-mat containers without full contaminated-diving gear and a decontamination team
- Be sure that your rigging can handle the weights and strains involved in the recovery

AIRCRAFT

It must be understood from the start that an SRT diver is not a salvage operator, nor is the team responsible for complex, heavy lift operations. When a plane goes down in the water the local county dive team is only

Steve Linton of Dive Rescue International trains San Diego Water Utilities divers in the art of vehicle recovery.

expected to locate the wreckage and recover the bodies. But with federal control over aircraft operations, the FAA, NTSB or even the FBI may request the team's assistance in collecting evidence, photographing the wreckage and recovering the airframe and debris.

The Diving Supervisor will need to work in close cooperation with the topside experts in air crashes, investigations and aircraft construction. Once the crash site has been located, either by the surface debris, under-water search, dragging a hook or witness interview, the team leader will need to consult with the aviation experts to determine the number of passengers, type of aircraft and cargo manifest.

Jet fuel and av-gas are not as easy to see as a crude oil slick, but these fuels can cause severe skin irritation to the divers. If these fuels are present on the surface, divers should avoid contact with them, not use snorkels and preferably use a full-face mask (AGA or EXO-26) to prevent accidental ingestion or contact with the eyes.

Although explosive cargos are uncommon on aircraft, it is not impossible that they could be present. More commonly, one might find herbicides or pesticides as used in farming communities and dropped from crop dusters. Military aircraft may be carrying explosive ordnance or be armed with missiles, bombs and machine guns. Ammunition for any weapon above 50 caliber (20mm, 30mm, etc.) will usually have explosive projectiles. Military weapons specialists and EOD personnel must be consulted before approaching any downed fighter, bomber or transporter.

An additional problem with military aircraft, that will require expert guidance, is dealing with ejector seats. The pilot ejection seats are armed with small explosive charges to blow both the canopy and pilot clear of the jet. Any careless movement or effort to free a trapped pilot could trigger the mechanism and injure or kill the diver, either by the concussion from the charge or impact with the seat itself.

The forces in play during an air crash are tremendous. They can twist, stretch, rip and shear the skin of the fuselage and wings as if it were putty. These torn edges will be razor sharp and a very real hazard to the divers. In addition the fine stainless steel control cables that normally run from cockpit to wings and tail will be strung throughout the wreckage. A dive knife will not cut these and they can be difficult to see under water.

So the first order of business will be the body recovery. If it is a large airliner, many body bags will be needed. If the fuselage has broken up, bodies could be spread over a large area, normally along the path of the crash. If the plane has been down for a few days the bodies will be found floating grotesquely against the overhead or still in their seat-belts. In warmer, deeper waters the bodies should be bagged on the bottom so that if the bodies rupture from the expanding gases it will happen in the body-bag.

Because of the severity of passenger injuries (burns and dismemberments), wallets, jewelry and clothing should not be removed from the bodies. Clothing, jewelry and teeth may be the only means to identify the victims.

AIRCRAFT INVESTIGATION

Once the team has done its job, located the crash and removed the bodies, the local and federal investigation begins. In this day of mass air travel, crashes are not unusual, so the FAA and NTSB have set investigative procedures and specific information that they will require.

Once the major wreckage and fuselage has been located and marked, the search will continue for wings, engines, tail sections, landing gear, instrumentation and bodies that may have been flung from the wreckage. Each piece will either be sketched, photographed, plotted and recovered or labelled and marked with a buoy for future recovery.

The Aircraft Dive Checklist will fill in all the blanks with regard to additional information to be collected. Photograph the entire scene from the eight points of the compass, overhead, near and far, and then try to show other wreckage in relationship to the primary crash site. Close-up photographs can be shot of all doors, instruments, damage, propellers and engines. These will be invaluable to the investigators, especially if the aircraft sustains additional damage during the recovery.

AIRCRAFT DIVE CHECK LIST AND PHOTOGRAPHY
TAKE PHOTOGRAPHS AND MEASUREMENTS OF SCENE

Investigating Officer

Phone _____ Date _____ Time Start _____ Finish _____ Case Number _____

Location of Aircraft _____ Department _____ Home Port _____

If known - where aircraft was coming from _____

Type of Aircraft - (if known) _____ Tail Number _____

Military: _____ Private: _____ Commercial: _____

Crash location identified Yes _____ ; No _____ ;

Aircraft located yes _____ : No _____ ;

DIVER'S REPORT: FIRST DIVER - GENERAL INFORMATION

Time at which aircraft was sighted underwater _____

Depth at which aircraft rest on ocean floor: Top _____ Bottom _____ Tail _____

Nose _____ Right Wing _____ Left Wing _____

Reef _____ Sand floor _____ Uneven _____ Coral Shelf _____

Aircraft resting on: Even _____

Does aircraft appear to be stable? Yes _____ No _____ If no, describe situation on ocean floor: _____

Is area damaged by the aircraft, describe situation: _____

Is aircraft intact Yes _____ No _____ If no, answer the following questions:

Wreckage strewn over scene: Yes _____ No _____ If Yes, deepest depth. _____

Shallowest depth _____ Total distance _____

Bodies visible from external Yes _____ No _____ How many _____

Internal Yes _____ No _____ How Many _____

Temperature of water — surface: _____ Bottom: _____

Current strength Swift: _____ Moderate: _____ Slow: _____

Visibility Excellent _____ Good _____ Poor _____ Distance _____

SECOND DIVER: OBSERVATIONS OF AIRCRAFT EXTERIOR:

If retractable gear, are wheels extended Yes _____ No _____

Nose wheel collapsed: Yes _____ No _____ N/A _____ Describe _____

Right main collapsed: Yes _____ No _____ N/A _____ Describe _____

Left main collapsed: Yes _____ No _____ N/A _____ Describe _____

If fitted gear describe _____

How many access points: Windows _____ Doors _____ Are all doors intact: Yes _____ No _____

Closed _____ Open _____ Are all windows intact: Yes _____ No _____

Closed _____ Open _____ If no, which ones are broken or damaged, describe where, number,

which side, windscreen, etc.: Doors: _____ Windows: _____

Is debris floating out and about from where: Windows: _____

_____ Doors: _____

Divers come to the surface after finishing all the above information to let appropriate personnel know what you have found.

PHOTOGRAPHING OF THE AIRCRAFT: Taken by: _____

Time: _____ Camera type & lens: _____

ASA: _____ Number shots: _____ Strobe used: Yes _____ No _____

OUTSIDE PHOTOGRAPHS OF AIRCRAFT will be done in a clockwise direction starting at nose of aircraft. A total of 12 external pictures will be taken of the total aircraft. This will be done at a distance where the total aircraft can be seen. Two pictures of tail number; one overall, two from overhead of aircraft (top). Four pictures of the aircraft will be taken at a distance of 5 feet or less, from four different angles. Pictures will be taken of all strewn aircraft parts and wreckages.

INSIDE PHOTOGRAPHS OF AIRCRAFT - THIRD DIVER OBSERVATION OF AIRCRAFT INTERIOR:

Is there cargo aboard aircraft Yes _____ No _____ Outside the aircraft Yes _____ No _____

Can cargo be identified as:

Suspected contraband	Yes ___ No ___	Kind ___
Explosive	Yes ___ No ___	Kind ___
Chemical	Yes ___ No ___	Kind ___
Radiation material	Yes ___ No ___	Kind ___
General Cargo	Yes ___ No ___	Kind ___

Will special equipment and personnel be needed to remove all cargo Yes _____ No _____

If yes, describe equipment or personnel: _____

Photographs of cargo inside aircraft (several closeups and a few back off photographs — if you are not in any danger) before removing cargo out of the aircraft.

Photographing of deceased persons in aircraft. Photograph interior of aircraft with respect to deceased persons aboard. Two (2) facial close-ups for identification. All persons. Two (2) showing overview of body position of deceased persons and anything which the observer thinks might have contributed to actual cause of death.

Body removal:

Is extraction going to be easily accomplished? Yes _____ No _____

If not, explain why? _____

If dismemberment has to be done then stop. Let the team leader, Sgt. of unit or Lt. of unit know. It is recommended that the nearest hospital be contacted and a physician be enlisted to advise and or assist in dismemberment.

It is always the rule to destroy the aircraft in lieu of body mutalization. Take a minimum of two (2) photographs of the body part that will have to be dismembered. Then record each body as it is found in its position with body bag, and whether or not seat restraints are intact. Remove body to surface vessel, let the surface team do identification duties and all other duties.

FINAL INTERIOR AIRCRAFT SEARCH & PROPERTY RECOVERY

Search aircraft as shown in diagram. You start your search from left to right every seat pocket, underseat, side pockets. All items found are brought aboard the surface vessel by finder and given to team captain who logs it in the following manner. All items are then sealed in plastic bags marked with appropriate case number.

FIREWALL

		Item		Personal property
1	2			of deceased
3	4	Found by		Aircraft effects
5	6	Time		Item photographed
CARGO A		Where found		
CARGO B		Case number		

PHOTOGRAPHING THE COCKPIT

Photograph each instrument or device starting with top left and working across to the right. Each device should be photographed and overlapped.

"Explain", work down to the power console quadrant. ADF _____ Transponder _____

Fuel selector valve positions _____ Show each radio frequency and Nav. frequency

Flap handle positions _____ Photograph all equipment attached to cockpit, i.e., stereo tape player.

You should always sketch the area completely before anything is moved. Photos should be taken whenever possible. The following statement should always be made and noted in a police report also for court.

"That all measurements are approximate, because not all measuring devices are exact. Also objects viewed by a diver under water appear to be nearer and larger than they appear on land." • 1988 A.I.R. SPECIALTIES, INC.

Slates copyrighted © and available from A.I.R. Specialties, Inc.

Passenger who failed to escape from this light aircraft is still retained by the seat belt.

The Corona Beer carton led investigators to believe that alcohol contributed to the air crash.

Divers attach ropes to the engine mounts for recovery.

Although this rope was slung around the tail section, the hard point on the tail could also have been utilized.

233

AIRCRAFT RECOVERY

Where a car will usually go into the water at the shoreline, an aircraft can go down anywhere, often in deeper mid-water. The lift may be made with cranes, barges, lift bags or by helicopter.

Whichever method is utilized, it is the harnessing and rigging of the airframe or engines that will be critical. Not all parts of the airframe are structurally firm or strong enough to bear the weight of the wreckage. Engine mounts, the junction point between wings and fuselage or supplied lift points are all good locations to position slings. It is also a lot safer if the load is balanced and stable during the lift.

Be careful not to position nylon slings over areas with torn metal. The sharp edges could cut the slings and cause the load to drop. The aviation investigators and experts will be the best source of advice with regard to lift points and load slinging.

One of the simplest methods of recovering a submerged aircraft is to harness the load, bring the lift slings to the surface, and then have a helicopter with a good lift capability come in and pick up the whole package. The lift will have to be done slowly to give water time to drain from the cabin areas. (The pilot may choose to release the load if it overtaxes his machine.) Divers must be well clear during helo lifts but they will be required to swim in and make the initial hookup to the slings.

The crash site must be marked with lines and buoys when the airframe is removed, in case the investigators or dive team need to return to search for more debris or bodies.

Munson aluminum boat towing float plane to shallower water.

BOATS

As with aircraft, the dive team is not responsible for the salvage of large ships that sink in their jurisdiction. Such jobs are best turned over to professional salvage companies and commercial divers. Nevertheless, a dive rescue team should be able to lift a small boat if it is blocking waterways, a navigational hazard or just as a community service.

The object of the exercise will be to lift the boat off the bottom, get it to shaliower water, maybe rerig and lift again, and eventually get it to a ramp or dock where it can be pulled from the water for repair.

A boat with a hole in the hull will need to be beached and repaired, whereas a capsized boat may neet only to be righted, floated and pumped out. Gale force winds and heavy seas can be responsible for many capsizings and sinkings within a marina, especially if the owners had not secured their mooring lines and hatch covers.

Pontoon lift bags have proven ideal for boat recovers since they can be slung low on the hull and float the super-structure clear out of the water. Pillow bags and the more common parachute-type bags tend to leave much of the decks still under water and require towing the boat to shallower water for a rerig.

Transom and stern hooks are excellent attachment points for lift lines, but the diver should not confuse these with the deck cleats which are not strong enough and may tear out under load.

In towing sinking or refloated boats there are a few precautions to follow:

- Keep a marker buoy on the boat during the tow
- Make sure the tow line is longer than the water depth
- Have a man ready to cut the tow line if necessary
- Try to stay over shallow water and avoid mid-channel crossings
- Avoid active waterways and harbor entrances
- Alert other traffic to the fact you are towing
- Keep speed to a minimum and monitor the depth

VESSEL/BOAT DIVE CHECKLIST AND PHOTOGRAPHY
TAKE PHOTOGRAPHS AND MEASUREMENTS OF SCENE

Investigating Officer _____ Department _____
Phone _____ Date _____ Time Start _____ Finish _____ Case Number _____

TYPE OF BOAT/VESSEL ACCIDENT:
Boat to Boat _____ Boat to Shore _____ Boat to Skier _____ Boat to Diver: Scuba _____ Snorkel _____
Boat to Swimmer _____ Boat Explosion _____ Boat Fire _____ Boat Sinking _____
Additional Comments: _____

PERSONS ABOARD BOAT/VESSEL:
How Many: Adults _____ Children _____
Location on Boat/Vessel: Front _____ Back _____ Inside Cabin _____
Right _____ Left _____ Deck _____ Tower _____
Once location has been determined, how many persons in the area: _____
Additional comments: _____

PERSONAL FLOTATION DEVICES: (USCG Approved)
Available: Yes _____ No _____ If yes, type _____
Color _____ Size _____ Total Number _____ Adults _____ Children _____
Who had them on? Adults (number) _____ Children (number) _____
Additional Comments: _____

BOAT/VESSEL LOCATION UNDER WATER:
Depth: Front _____ Rear _____ Right Side _____ Left Side _____
Direction Facing: North _____ South _____ East _____ West _____ What Degrees _____
How many parts is the boat/vessel broken into: Intact _____ Two _____ Three _____
Anymore than three parts, describe, photography and drawing should be made with official report.
Additional Comments: _____

TEMPERATURE: Air _____ Surface Water _____ Water Bottom _____

LOCATION OF ACCIDENT: Intercoastal _____ Nearest channel marker distance (feet or miles) _____
Number _____ Open ocean _____ Nearest channel opening name _____ Distance from
opening in feet or miles _____ Distance from shore line in feet or miles _____ Direction from shore
line: North _____ South _____ East _____ West _____ What degrees _____
River Name _____ Quarry Name _____ Reservoir Name _____
Direction from shore line: North _____ South _____ East _____ West _____ What degrees _____
Nearest boat ramp (feet or miles) _____ Name _____
Additional Comments: _____

DIVING ON SCUBA:
Mask on face: Yes _____ No _____ If no, explain where found from body in feet: _____

REGULATOR:
In mouth: Yes _____ No _____ If no, explain where regulator was found: _____

Second regulator, where was it located: _____

AIR IN TANK:
Pressure per square inch _____ (turn off valve after reading is taken)

DEPTH BODY FOUND:
Victim(s) depth gauge reading (if possible) _____ your depth gauge _____
Bottom time reading (if possible): time _____ Dive Number _____
Additional Comments: _____

COMPASS HEADING: (if victim(s) has a compass and is easily readable)
Degrees _____ North _____ South _____ East _____ West _____
Your compass reading from head of victim(s):
Degrees _____ North _____ South _____ East _____ West _____

WEIGHT BELT:
On _____ Off _____ If off, explain where found from body in feet: _____
Could the weight belt quick release be used? Yes _____ No _____ If no, explain why? _____

Was all equipment worn properly and in place? If no, explain why? _____

DISTANCE OF PHYSICAL EVIDENCE FROM VICTIM(S) HEAD:
What items: _____
Distance in feet:
Degrees from head: North _____ South _____ East _____ West _____
Depth in feet: _____

ACCIDENT CLASSIFICATION: Before _____ Report: _____
Swimming _____ Skin diving _____ Scuba diving _____ Pool _____
Commercial _____ Training _____ Fatality _____ Body injury _____ Near miss _____
Other: _____

VICTIM(S) EXPERIENCE:
Swimmer: Begin _____ Novice _____ Professional _____ Pleasure _____ Training _____

DIVING EXPERIENCE:
No experience _____ Receiving instruction _____ Professional _____
Certified Novice _____ Occasional Diver _____ Experienced _____

DIVING LEVEL CERTIFICATION:
Level _____ Month(s) or year(s) diving _____ Number of dive(s): Non-log _____
Log _____ Additional information or comments: _____

You should always sketch the area completely before anything is moved. Photos should be taken whenever possible. The following statement should always be made and noted in a police report also for court.
"That all measurements are approximate, because not all measuring devices are exact. Also objects viewed by a diver under water appear to be nearer and larger than they appear on land."
© 1988 A.I.R. SPECIALTIES, INC.

Slates copyrighted © and available from A.I.R. Specialties, Inc.

Simple slates are very useful for underwater investigation but the slates marketed by Julius Wiggins (Miami PD) of A.I.R. Specialties, Inc., are considerably better. (See pages 210, 223, 231, 236.)

U.S. Navy magnetic mine

238

PART IV
TACTICAL OPERATIONS

Assorted patches from assault swim teams.

U.S. Navy counter terrorist/hostage rescue team.

INTRODUCTION

It is not the intention of this book, or the author, to suggest that law enforcement personnel and in particular SRT dive teams should be trained up to the level of U.S. Navy SEAL teams. Apart from the constraints of time, budget and raw talent, a police diver could not be expected to handle the complexities and risks involved in military assault swim operations. But, without contradiction, there are several areas in conventional law enforcement where a tactical dive capability could be an asset to an agency.

Any time high risk warrant service, surveillance, diplomatic security, or SWAT/HRT operations must be performed in, near or over water, the officers or agents involved will require special training and should have a dive team on hand.

Even if a county dive team is not routinely involved in some of the following types of operations, they could be called on for an assist by a State or Federal agency:

- Surveillance of suspect locations around docks or marinas
- Disabling suspected drug boats
- Recovery of evidence thrown overboard during maritime drug raids
- Support of DEA, FBI, U.S. Customs or Coast Guard search and seizure operations
- Support of State Fish and Game or U.S. Fish and Wildlife operations
- Support of Secret Service or State Department protective details
- EOD/bomb searches of docks, boats, bridges, dams or sea front hotels and restaurants
- Rescue of surface tactical team members who may fall from boats, helicopters or wharves
- Provide diversionary fire for a surface or air assault onto a ship
- Assault/rescue from the water, if the only possible approach

Since the SRT divers are generally of the same cut as the officers who will apply for the SWAT team, both units can be combined. Some agencies draw their divers from their tactical teams so as to centralize their resources. L.A. Sheriff's divers are all members of the Emergency Services Detail which is in turn part of Special Enforcement Bureau. All ESD personnel go through the SEB SWAT school before they go on to the more advanced Paramedic, mountain rescue and dive training.

On a Presidential visit to any municipality the Secret Service advance team and attached EOD personnel do not have time to check under every bridge, wharf, manhole cover or boat that the motorcade or delegation may cross. The underwater searches will be left to the local dive team who will then have the support and expertise of the EOD team, should they find a suspicious object.

241

Few SWAT teams are equipped or experienced in maritime operations, or have even considered the consequences of falling into deep water with 50 pounds of equipment, e.g., entry vest, radio, handgun, SMG, ammunition, boots, knife, stun grenades, flashlight, et al. Team members should be trained for such eventualities or have dive rescue personnel ready for an immediate rescue of the man and recovery of his equipment. Losing submachine guns can prove very embarrassing and quite costly.

SEALS prepare to enter the water on closed-circuit rebreathers.

17
BASIC TRAINING

Whether the tactical diver trainee is coming from SWAT or SAR, there should be a set program of conditioning and basic training he must complete before being deployed on an actual operation.

The training will not compare to the hell that SEALs and Special Forces must endure but it should equip the diver with the skills and confidence to complete his assigned task. The training should also show him the limitations of his equipment, conditioning and training.

SWIMMING & FITNESS

Nothing conditions a diver better than many hours of diving, swimming and working in the water. The legs must be conditioned to handle long swims with fins, and alternate exercises like running or cycling will not develop the correct muscles.

The training can be varied and interesting by including:

- Confined water and ocean swimming
- Surf lifesaving drills
- White-water sports
- Night and navigational swims
- Water polo, octo-push (underwater hockey) and relay races
- Drown proofing training

Leg and upper body strength can be improved in the gym with free weights or machines, but it must be balanced with aerobic exercise, stretching, good diet and adequate rest. Prolonged periods in cold water can be very fatiguing, not just from physical exertion but also from heat loss (22-25 times faster in water), even with thermal protection.

When a diver starts adding equipment to his body, he increases his drag factor in the water, thus increasing his energy output considerably. (The drag increases by the square of the surface area of the equipment added, but the energy output and effort required from the diver increases by the cube.)

When one considers the physical and thermal demands placed on the assault swimmer, and then adds the stresses and psychological demands of working under water, in confined areas, at night and with the real or not-so-real fears of marine life, one begins to appreciate the need for peak physical and mental condition.

A basic swim test would be:

Confined water, no equipment —
25 yards under water on one breath
440 yards nonstop, any stroke, in 10 minutes

Survival swimming for 20 minutes (treading water, drown proofing)
Tow another swimmer 100 yards

Confined or open water, mask, fins and snorkel —
Swim 880 yards nonstop in 18 minutes (no use of hands)
Ditch and recovery of mask, fins and snorkel in 12+ feet of water

Open water, mask, fins and snorkel —
(wet suit optional)
Timed open water swims
Full entry and rescue of another skin diver
Surf entry, exit and rescue if applicable

DIVING

All potential candidates for a diving team should have a minimum of Advanced SCUBA certification before their application is accepted. Or they may be trained to Advanced level in a pre-selection process. Command personnel and team leaders should be certified and qualified as Divemasters, assistant instructors or instructors.

The additional training should include:

- Advanced diver rescue and self rescue
- Advanced navigational exercises
- Night operations
- Covert swimming techniques
- Long distance underwater swimming
- Equipment loading and water proofing
- Rapid ditch and recovery exercises
- Stress and problem-solving exercises
- Introduction to Closed-Circuit Breathing Apparatus
- Boat and helo casting in full equipment
- Underwater survey and sketching
- Rocky shore entry and exits

DIVER RESCUE

Since tactical dive operations can leave a diver and his buddy a long way from rescue or support, all divers should get advanced in-water rescue training. The other role of the diver, to rescue agents or officers overboard, will also necessitate a certain degree of confidence and ability in rapid rescue swimming.

Areas to concentrate on are:

- Handling stress, cramp, fatigue and panic
- Unconscious diver rescue
- Long distance tows with unconscious victim
- Surf, current and rip-tide techniques
- Advanced first aid and CPR
- Removing an injured or unconscious diver from the water
- Oxygen management and administration
- Rescue of SWAT members in water with a full load
- Use of signal flares, strobes and safety equipment
- Boat handling and victim transportation
- Helicopter deployment and litter extraction

Long swims and surf entries require peak physical conditioning and intestinal fortitude.

SPECIAL WEAPONS TRAINING

If divers are to be deployed in support of tactical operations, they must be equipped with both the weapons and training to defend themselves. High risk warrant service, raids, assaults and hostage rescues are all dynamic operations that require speed and tactical flexibility. The criminal response to an assault is unpredictable so all law enforcement personnel must train and prepare for a worst-case scenario. This includes the dive team.

Divers should go through a minimum two-week SWAT school with additional training and exercises on a regular basis. The program must extend past just weapons training to tactics and team drills. One of the author's other books, "ADVANCED WEAPONS TRAINING for Hostage Rescue Teams" goes into considerable detail about special weapons and tactics and is strongly recommended reading for the SRT diver.

When designing a special weapons program, the following areas must be covered:

- Intro to specialized weapons and their application
- Live-fire training on all agency weapons systems
- Close proximity, shoot/no-shoot scenarios
- Fire discipline and zones of responsibility
- Swimming with weapons
- Exit from water and engaging multiple targets
- Cleaning and maintenance of weapons after swim ops.
- Basic tactics, cover and concealment, diversion
- Team drills and tactical communications
- Scouting and briefing procedures
- Containment and negotiation
- Night operations
- Noise and light discipline in covert operations
- Prisoner/hostage handling
- Explosive search, identification and handling
- Explosive entry and stun munitions
- Helicopter deployment
- Building, boat and bus assault
- Introduction to sniper tactics
- Post-assault scene mangement

RAPPELLING, FAST ROPING & CLIMBING

All three of these specialties are an integral part of modern search and rescue and tactical operations. Fast roping in particular, is ideally suited to deploying assault teams onto the deck of a moving ship, oil tanker or oil rig. It allows several team members to hit the decks almost simultaneously without having to hook-in or unhook from a rappel rope.

SRT personnel practicing rappel entry and live fire shooting.

Hostage Rescue drills are an important part of SRT training.

Approaching a ship, wharf or shore-based installation from the sea will require some form of climbing, whether it be a rocky cliff, a steep embankment, a dock piling, ladder, or the side of a tanker. Most rescue teams will have had some experience in mountain rescue, free climbing and rope assisted climbs. This knowledge and experience can now be applied to the tactical theatre of operations with extra emphasis on route selection, noise discipline and available cover fire when needed.

All climbs, rappels or long swims can be covered by well positioned snipers with night vision equipment and long-range rifles. Divers should not be required to operate in the open without available effective cover fire (snipers) and a support assault team. The worst-case scenario is always considered in the planning stages.

Author demonstrates explosive entry/door cutting charge.

Skilled snipers can add considerable security to assault swim operations.

Realistic targets must be used for realistic training.

Live fire entry and team house clearing drills must be practiced to perfection for the safety of both hostages and team members.

HELICOPTER OPERATIONS

As with rescue work, the helicopter has become a valuable tool to the tactical team as well. Unfortunately, the helicopter can be an easy target for hostile ground fire so the pilot will want to spend as little time on location as possible. This means that the assault team must be proficient in rappelling, fast roping, helo-jumping and helo-extraction.

Some helicopters are rigged with hard-points on the outside so that the tac team can skid ride in and out. Others will have sufficient room to carry the team on the inside, under the control of the crew chief or pilot. Whatever the configuration, the team must work closely with the local Aero Bureau or Air Sea Rescue and establish procedures that are safe and effective for both parties.

In smaller helicopters the dive team leader may have to be trained to double as a Crew Chief.

SURVEY RECONNAISSANCE

The dive team may not be required to make assaults from the water, but they could well be required to assist in surveillance operations around marinas and docks, or help plan an operation from the seaward side. The assault element may come in by boat but they will need an advanced survey and update on what they are going into. This can be done by the divers.

The SRT diver should be conversant with all the correct terminology and techniques to complete a survey of a beach, dock structure or ship. Working around these areas, gaining familiarity, seeking assistance from the Navy or Coast Guard, studying Marine Recon and Navy SEAL manuals will all prove invaluable to the dive team.

The height of a ship's decks above the water line, the steepness of an embankment, the lack of ladders on a dock or the distance of a building from the shore could all have significant impact on the assault plan. Excessive boat traffic, too many innocent bystanders, high ambient lighting or lack of suspect activity may be visible to a dive team concealed under a dock, helping coordinate a drug seizure.

BOAT DEPLOYMENT & EXTRACTION

Long swims can be very tiring, so it is important that assault swim teams develop techniques for boat delivery and pickup that can be done without alerting the suspects. Dropping from the seaward side of the boat as it cruises by, faked reasons for stopping, diversionary tactics and high-speed casting at night are all methods that a team may wish to experiment with.

If an operation is compromised, the boat may have to come in fast, supplying cover fire, to effect an extraction of the divers. Extra ballistic vests, aluminum plating or bomb blankets can be added to the sides of the boat to supply cover for the shooters and crew. Bright spotlights can be turned on the suspects to temporarily blind them and protect the divers in the water.

Tactical training must be done under realistic local conditions with full equipment.

Diver in D.U.I. AAOPS dry suit with waterproof drag bag

18
EQUIPMENT SELECTION

Few agencies have the budget to indulge their fantasies with spending sprees into the exotic, and a tactical team that becomes "equipment dependent" is doomed to failure when their "toys" fail to perform to expectation or manufacturers' claims. Successful operations are a result of highly trained personnel, sound tactics and simple, proven equipment.

Most law enforcement agencies must play with the hand they are dealt, and try to get the job done with what's available or can be obtained within their budget. However, there are limits to what can be expected with minimal equipment and, to a rational team leader, these limits will dictate whether an operation can be handled safely, with a good chance of success, or passed over.

The key to equipment selection is **task loading.** Even though an agency may have a large inventory of gear to choose from, the diver should select only that which will help his mission and is essential for success. Excess gear hinders movement, increases drag and results in fatigue and exhaustion.

DIVE GEAR

With tactical diving in mind, dive gear falls into four categories:

- Surface swim operations
- SCUBA
- Surface tended EOD searches
- Closed-circuit rebreathers (CCBA)

Rebreathers are covered in Chapter 19 and EOD operations are covered in Chapter 22 so we will confine our study to swim ops and SCUBA in this chapter.

Surface swim operations are a common part of waterborne warfare as well as having several applications for law enforcement. The advantages to wearing no dive gear are ease of movement, speed, silence and the freedom to carry more tactical supplies. There is also less stress on a diver who is uncomfortable with long, under-water navigational swims in the inky blackness of a port or marina.

The disadvantage of swim ops is the inability to slide beneath the surface and disappear, the chance of being run over by boat traffic and the stress of working in seemingly plain view.

The equipment load of a surface swimmer will depend on his assigned task, the water temperature and his anticipated time/distance away from a support team. The least would be his standard SWAT uniform and load in conjunction with a flotation collar, fins and mask. Any tactical officer working around water should wear a flotation device capable of supporting the weight of all his hardware in water. The fins are essential if he wants to dominate the water and cover distance. These can be pulled on over his boots and carried on his belt when not in use.

Colder waters and longer swims will require an exposure suit suitable to the local climatic conditions. Wet suits are acceptable in moderate temperature and dry suits in the colder north or for prolonged inactive exposures. Whichever is selected they must give freedom of movement for both swimming and fighting without sacrificing comfort and warmth. Moving inland with an exposure suit may result in overheating, so this must also be taken into consideration.

Wet suit booties are not the ideal for fighting or walking, so should be substituted for lightweight tactical boots with a better sole and ankle support for climbing and running.

SCUBA has its advantages and disadvantages in tactical operations. Bubbles are the first problem that comes to mind. SCUBA is not a covert swim system like an oxygen rebreather or closed-circuit mixed-gas unit, but there are several instances when the bubbles do not create a problem.

Any time that the divers are deployed in a support role on DEA, Customs or Coast Guard operations, they will generally be present to search the bottom of a boat for drug pods or to recover evidence thrown from a ship or wharf. On SWAT operations the divers will be responsible for rescuing suspects or officers overboard, the recovery of evidence or the recovery of dropped weapons. Whichever instance, the element of surprise is lost, the divers have cover fire from the topside assault element and the bubbles will not be a problem.

There are surveillance and assault operations where SCUBA could be used, but only in waterways that cannot be observed from the suspect location. All diving equipment should be purchased with color, construction and function in mind: black equipment with blackened metal, non-reflective surfaces, no unnecessary protrusions or gadgets and simple design. Hard surfaces can be taped and padded to prevent noise and power inflators, hoses, gauges and regulators must be checked for leaks or accidental free-flows. Tanks should be selected for air duration and weight. Twin 80s may be needed for long swims in and out, but a single 72 or twin 30s will be lighter and possibly still adequate for the mission.

Seatec horse collar type vests are ideally suited to surface swim and tactical diving operations.

Viking special forces dry suit for colder operations.

Wet suits can be used for most operations.

For short swims SRT personnel will only require fatigues, masks, fins, flotation vests and weapons.

DUI dry suits and EXO-26 full face masks used for cold or lightly contaminated waters

WEAPONS

Most modern military and police weapons can be taken in and under water with no ill effect or loss of dependability. Similarly, some commercial and most military ammunition can survive a long swim without contamination or misfiring. Now that we have made that bold statement, there are a few qualifications to make.

Different bodies of water and conditions can adversely affect the weapons system. Obviously fresh water is less corrosive than salt water, but corrosion is a long-term effect and few swim ops will put the divers in the water long enough to see rust and pitting. This will only be evident if the team members do not clean, dry and oil their weapons immediately after a swim.

As for the ammunition, different factories manufacture to different standards. The military sets standards and procures ammunition that will survive the harshest conditions (submersion to 200 fsw), but commercial ammunition may not be as dependable. It is recommended that divers take a sampling of their agency's ammunition, immerse it in water for two to three hours and then test fire it. Misfires, a sign of powder contamination or primer pocket leaks should indicate a need for a more waterproofed brand.

Operations in deep water, mid-ocean, mid-channel or across lakes and rivers will seldom have an adverse effect on the guns or ammunition, and should be ready to fire as soon as the water is voided from the barrel. Movement across beaches, through surf zones, in silty canals and deltas, or anywhere sand is present can jam a weapon and render it inoperable.

It is not the water that seizes the action but the particles of sand that accumulate around the bolt, slide, locking lugs, charging handle and trigger group, that create a problem. Some weapons are more prone to sand and grit contamination than others but even the best will cease to function if left unprotected in the surf zone long enough. Weapons used on one or two passages through the surf functioned flawlessly, but with enough build-up of sand it was eventually impossible to cycle the action, even manually.

A general rule would be to bag the weapons for swim ops unless working in the face of imminent danger, and then the team security should be in the hands of the sniper element. For work in silty or sandy waters the weapons should most definitely be bagged, either in custom carrying cases, wrap cloths or plastic bags. Several companies manufacture weapons cases from neoprene or vulcanized rubber, complete with buoyancy purge valves and waterproof zippers (KME, DUI, Viking, etc.).

Improvised waterproof bags can be made from heavy plastic bags, heat sealed with an iron along the open edges. A small hole should be left in the seam to push or suck out all the excess air and reduce buoyancy problems. After the bag is voided, the hole can be heat-sealed as well. Without a hot iron the weapons may have to be double bagged and the openings individually twisted and tied.

When exiting the water with a wet weapon and preparing to fire, the barrel should be tilted down and voided of any remaining water. In some weapons it is best to chamber the first round on surfacing so that the cartridge does not form a seal in the chamber and prevent water from flowing freely out of the muzzle. Weapons that fire from an open bolt (Uzis, Macs) should be carried bolt closed, to prevent dirt getting into the action, and only cocked on surfacing.

Most of the current family of 9mm handguns are suitable for use around water. The H&K P7-M8, P7-M13, the Beretta 92F, the Sig 226 and the Glock have all been tested underwater and on swim ops. Some weapons have factory or custom finishes that make them impervious to salt water corrosion. The SEALs are constantly testing new finishes to find the ones most suitable for the harsh environments in which they must operate. Electro nickel, industrial hard chrome, Polymax, Teflon, Chromalloy, Nitex, Z-coat, Electrofilm, NP-3 and Black "T" are a few of the many finishes offered to improve the life and reduce the cleaning of combat weapons. The better processes are dull, no-glare finishes that reduce friction in the action and seal the pores of the metal.

Sniper rifles that are to be transported on or under the water should have the barrel and action plugged or protected from contamination, and a scope must be selected that will take a swim without flooding, fogging or seizing. The Leupold ULTRA scopes are well suited to waterborne operations and are factory tested to 30 feet under water. The 10X-M3 is the scope currently being issued with the Army's M24 sniper rifle and the SEALS have had the M1 and M3 for some time on their McMillans.

Stun grenades can also be taken on assault swims, as long as they are kept in heat-sealed plastic containers, and only opened when ready for immediate deployment (for assault or diversion).

A primary assault, by law enforcement personnel, will almost never come from the water, so the team should not weigh themselves down with excessive ammunition and ordnance. Assaults by boat, land or helicopter will be faster and more effective.

The Robar SR60D with synthetic stock and non-corrosive finish is well suited to SRT sniper operations.

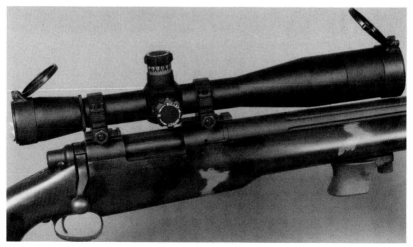

The Leupold ULTRA 10X-M1 & M3 scopes are rugged, waterproof units that can be taken underwater.

Beretta 92F, current issue of the U.S. military.

H&K P7-M13 in use by the German GSG9.

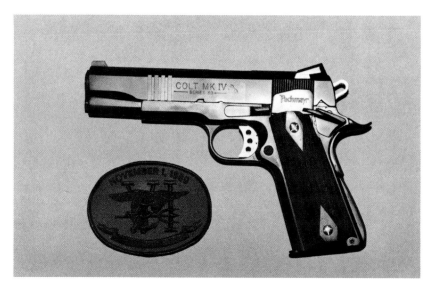

Customized Colt 45ACP Government Models are still favored by many U.S. counter terrorist teams including Delta and SEALS. This example is a D&L custom with Robar polymax finish.

The 9mm Browning Hi-Power is the standard issue weapon of the British SAS and SBS and can be often found in use by several U.S. teams.

H&K G3-SG1 semi- or full-automatic sniper rifle.

5.56mm Steyr AUG is constructed mostly from high density plastics and is well suited for waterborne operations.

The H&K MP5 is still the first choice for most SRT teams but the UZI, MAC10 and S&W 76 have also proven their reliability in assault swim operations.

The third generation S&W 5904 is a descendant of the suppressed Model 39 "Hush Puppy" developed for the U.S. Navy during the Vietnam conflict.

NP3 is just one of the many modern protective coatings that can be applied to weapons for use around salt water.

Suppressed H&K P9S intended for special operations.

H&K PSG1 is probably one of the finest semi-automatic sniper rifles available to SRT teams in the U.S.

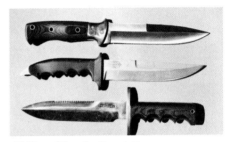

Al Mar, Albach, Randall.

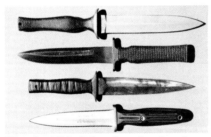

Albach, ARA, Princelou, Applegate.

USN MK2 combat knife.

Knives are an important part of the tactical diver's kit.

264

WEAPONS MAINTENANCE

Weapons with custom finishes, suited to salt water exposure, will be far easier to clean and maintain than those with conventional bluing or painted finishes. The finishes that are self lubricating will also require less oil or Breakfree in the action to maintain reliable function.

When a weapon is heavily oiled, the oil serves as a retainer for sand and dirt particles. Where sand will pass right through a weapon that has a dry-lubricant finish, it will stick to oil, collect, build up and eventually clog the weapon. An oiled bore will also collect grit and on discharge could damage the barrel or at least throw the first shots off target.

However, some teams heavily oil their weapons before wrapping. As they clear the water, the wrappings or cases are removed and the weapons are ready to fire. Some individuals pre-set a pull-through bore cleaner in the bore so that as it is drawn from the muzzle end of the barrel, any remaining water or grit is wiped out.

Experimentation with various finishes and lubrication procedures is essential if a team is to develop a system best suited to their needs and conditions. Most weapons can take a short dip in the ocean with no special preparation or adverse effect.

WEAPONS CLEANING

As soon as the training session or operation is over, the weapons should be immersed in and rinsed with **fresh water.** A bucket on deck is all that is necessary for the initial rinse. Remove the magazine, lock the slide back and give the weapon a vigorous shake in the fresh water to dislodge any large sand particles. Next, remove the rounds from the magazines and do likewise with both ammunition and magazines.

Dry the weapons as much as practicable on site, blow out with air from a SCUBA cylinder if possible, run a patch or two through the barrel, then reload for the trip back to base. As soon as possible, completely field strip the weapon, remove stocks and fore-end, blow out any visible sand and dirt with compressed air, then heavily spray with Gun Scrubber or solvent.

Blow out all solvent with compressed air (being careful not to get it in the eyes), swab the barrel with Shooter's Choice Bore Cleaner and run patches through until clean and dry.

When no visible carbon, sand or dirt deposits are left and the weapon has dried, lightly oil and reassemble. Check the function and smoothness of all working parts and then test fire the weapon on the range. If all works well and the weapon is still zeroed, run a patch through the barrel and store. If the weapon is to be carried, only lightly oil moving parts. If it is to be stored or not used for some time, thoroughly reclean, heavily oil and store in a dry armory. If cased, weapons should be checked periodically for rust, salt deposits or moisture.

Ammunition will also oxidize and deteriorate if not cleaned and dried after a swim or dive. Remove from mags and pouches, rinse in fresh water, air dry and wipe clean. Keep this lot separated from operational ammunition supplies, and shoot it up in the next range training session. No point in pushing your luck by carrying ammunition that has been under water more than once.

LOAD BEARING EQUIPMENT

There are several companies that manufacture load bearing equipment for conventional SWAT operations and HRT teams (Eagle, Seatec, Assault Systems, etc.). Since many of these vests and belts are constructed from nylon and cordura with plastic fasteners, they can also be used for assault swim ops and U/W spec. warfare.

The vest should be impervious to salt water, fit closely to the body, have secure pockets and pouches, no non-essential accessories and be comfortable to swim in. Keep in mind that these vests and pockets were designed for running and vertical carry, and may not be suited to horizontal movement and swimming.

The vest must not interfere with the diver's ability to doff and don his diving equipment. Fasteners should allow the diver to ditch all equipment in an emergency or at least make himself positively buoyant. Where velcro works well in water it wears out with use and is quite noisy to tear open on dry land. Steel snaps can also seize-up in sandy waters, or rust to a point that knives cannot be pulled and pouches cannot be opened.

One vest designed specifically for the SpecWarfare market, and in use by U.S. Navy SEAL teams, is Eagle's **SOMAVS** (Special Operations Modular Assault Vest System). The vest is constructed from 840 Denier ballistic nylon with twist lock fasteners on interchangeable modules. The individual pouches are placed for ease of access and close with slip-lock buckles that can be operated silently and without jams.

One unique feature of this vest is retrofittable buoyancy modules that can be fastened to the inside of the vest to supply 18 pounds of positive lift to offset the weight of ammunition, etc. The buoyancy panels are equipped with dual oral inflator valves that are secured onto the front of each shoulder for ease of access and hands-free operation.

The **SOMAVS** vest system can be expanded to include leg holsters, leg pouches for magazines, a rappel belt, chest mounted emergency extraction harness, radio packs, E&E kit or day pack.

The final word on load vests is "task load." Keep it light, quiet, comfortable and accessible.

For heavier loads, seldom required in police work but common to military operations, there is the **SOWB** (Special Operations Waterproof Bag) manufactured by **Viking.** The **SOWB** is designed for clothing, communications and surveillance equipment, weapons or any electronics or support gear that must be kept dry.

266

With an internal capacity of 40 pounds and nine external pockets that can handle an additional 20 pounds, the SOWB can be taken to depths of 50 fsw and towed as a bag or worn as a pack (fitted for standard Alice frame).

The **Viking SOWB** is also equipped with an oral inflator, power inflator valve, pressure relief valve and a 3,000 psi, half liter integrated air bottle for total buoyancy control. The waterproof zipper is rated to 50 fsw but has been successfully tested to 150 fsw. Additionally, each bag has three carrying straps, fifteen tie-down D-rings and internal straps to prevent load shift.

U.S. Special Forces diver with Viking dry suit, SOWB, M16, Draeger closed-circuit breathing apparatus and compass attack board.

SEALS with PRC-77 in Bruno Bag

Motorola MX300 mounted on front left of SOMAVS.

Optional twin radio pack requested by the U.S. Navy for special operations.

Drager LAR-5, and Military compass attack board

SEALS in full combat swimmer equipment: LAR-5, MP-5, etc.

SUPPORT EQUIPMENT

Tactical operations will often require the use of equipment that is not standard to U.S. law enforcement. The divers will need familiarization and training with any vehicles, vessels, machinery, heavy weapons, communication gear, navigational aids, rescue equipment and tools that they may be required to operate.

The most common items will be the patrol boats, IBSs, tactical radios and signalling systems. If the team has surveillance, night vision or photographic equipment that can be taken in or under the water, training with those must also be on the agenda.

SAS Boat Troop load go-boxes and diving equipment onto Navy support ships.

Night operations, camouflage and concealment are important facets of spec. warfare.

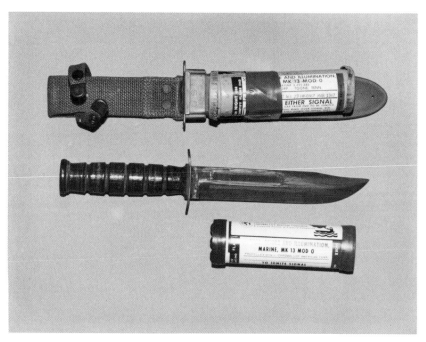

Navy MK2 combat knife and MK13 day/night smoke/illumination flare.

271

19
CLOSED-CIRCUIT BREATHING APPARATUS

A discussion of tactical diving would not be complete without addressing closed-circuit oxygen under-water breathing apparatus (UBA), as it is known to the U.S. Navy; CCBA to the British frogmen and oxygen re-breather to the masses.

There are in fact two types of closed-circuit breathing apparatus in use by the military: deep water, mixed-gas units and the shallow-water oxygen units that have the most application to law enforcement and SRT. The advantages are obvious: no telltale bubbles on covert swims, silent operation, extended bottom time and lightweight, compact units. There are limitations and dangers with oxygen rebreathers that will be covered in due course.

Closed-circuit oxygen UBAs require special training that no book can supply, and it is not this author's intention to try to change that situation. This chapter will deal with closed-circuit diving only in the most general terms to give team leaders and administrators some insight into what is involved in terms of equipment, training, liabilities and limitations. The actual training will be left in the hands of the professionals — U.S. Navy and Special Forces diving instructors.

DEFINITION

Closed-circuit oxygen rebreathers are highly specialized under-water breathing apparatus in which the exhaled breath is retained without the release of bubbles, as in conventional open-circuit SCUBA.

The exhaled breath is carried to an absorbant canister containing a carbon dioxide scrubber that removes the carbon dioxide produced by the diver. From the canister, the gas is returned to a breathing bag where

273

it is again available to the diver. The small amount of oxygen metabolized by the diver is made up from a small cylinder of compressed oxygen that is part of the apparatus.

Only pure oxygen is used in these units so as to prevent inert gas build-up and to allow all the gas carried by the diver to be used for metabolic needs. A third advantage is that since there is no inert gas (nitrogen) present in the breathing system, the diver is not subject to decompression sickness or nitrogen narcosis (which isn't a real problem considering the depth limitations of CCBA).

The **closed-circuit mixed-gas** units are designed to give the diver the option of deeper dives while maintaining the advantages of a silent, bubble-free system and eliminating the dangers of oxygen toxicity. The Carleton MK16, in use by hundreds of military and governmental agencies worldwide, is a good example of one of these more complex and expensive systems.

The MK15/MK16 is an expensive mixed gas rebreather that utilizes complex sensors to maintain the correct breathing mix, drawing on both oxygen and diluent gas (usually helium) cylinders within the pack. As the diver descends (down to 1,000 feet) or ascends, the breathing mixture is adjusted to suit, and small bubbles are released only during ascent.

The mixed-gas MK16 can support life for up to six hours while the shallow-depth oxygen rebreather, the Cobra, allows up to three hours of bottom time at less than 25 fsw. The Cobra weighs 33 pounds in air and is neutral in sea water, while the MK16 tips the scales at 64 pounds.

Carleton Cobra

HISTORY

The first closed-circuit oxygen UBA was developed by Henry Fleuss in 1876 and successfully tested in 1879. Little was done with CCBA until World War II when the British, Italian and Japanese combat swimmers showed considerable success in demolition and sabotage operations.

The U.S. efforts were pioneered by divers of the Office of Strategic Studies (OSS) during the same time period, using the Lambertson Amphibious Respiratory Unit (LARU).

With increased use and apparent problems with central nervous system (CNS) oxygen toxicity, recommendations were made that the units not be dived deeper than 25 fsw.

After WWII the Underwater Demolition Teams (UDT) and SEALs were the prime users of this technology. The LARU, Pirelli 901 and 701 and the Draeger LT LUND II were replaced in 1963 by the Emerson (actually Lambertson-Emerson UBA) which served the teams well until the late seventies. The Emerson had a dry weight of approximately 35 pounds, including the six pounds of baralyme contained in the absorbent canister, and was near neutral in the water. A 12.7 cubic foot oxygen bottle charged to 2,000 psi gave a useful duration of about 120 minutes under water.

About the same time that the Emerson was introduced, a **semi-closed-circuit** diving system was also being adopted, the Mk VI (replacing the deficient Mk V, tested in 1959). The Mk VI utilized a nitrogen/oxygen mixture that allowed dives to 180 feet and was ideally suited to long duration SDV (Swimmer Delivery Vehicle) operations. The small amount of bubbles released by a semi-closed-circuit system were at first a concern to UDT/SEALs, but proved otherwise with a high percentage of successful hits on enemy targets.

The Emerson was gradually replaced by the German-made **Drager LAR V** which is still in use by the U.S. and the special forces of several foreign nations. The LAR V is a ruggedly simple closed-circuit breathing apparatus that is eminently well suited to unconventional warfare/SpecOps and those government agencies in need of an oxygen rebreather.

The Drager (also spelled Draeger) LAR V has a fully charged dry weight of 24.2 pounds, is 16.9 inches long, has a 1.5 liter oxygen bottle that is charged to 2,900 psi (300 liters) and a first stage regulator that reduces bottle pressure to 50 psi. The duration of the unit can vary with metabolic consumption rate (work load), gas loss and water temperature. A fast swimming diver, consuming two liters of oxygen per minute, may get 150 minutes out of the rig while one swimming at a relaxed pace, one liter/min., could get as much as 300 minutes. Cold water can greatly reduce these times. See "Diving Procedure" in this chapter.

The Navy Experimental Diving Unit (NEDU) in Panama City, Florida is credited with developing the modern oxygen training and diving procedures for military combat swimmers, in so doing, greatly reducing the dangers of oxygen toxicity and the other problems that can be associated with closed-circuit UBA.

U.S. law enforcement has dabbled with rebreathers for counter-terrorist application, covert surveillance and, more unusually, for the capture and relocation of the sea otter. State Fish and Game have found the bubble-less oxygen units well suited to approaching the wily otters for capture and relocation.

There may well be several other agencies that have the rebreather in their bag of tricks, but choose to maintain operational security for the day that it may be needed.

Japanese SF diver second from right with closed circuit breathing apparatus.

Interspiro Oxydive Unit.

*NZSAS diver with British 1942
breathing apparatus (1983).
Now replaced by
Drager LAR-5.*

Cobra Closed Circuit Oxygen Rebreather

277

U.S. Special Forces out of Ft. Lewis, Washington utilizing the Draeger LAR V in cold water operations.

MEDICAL ASPECTS OF CCBA

CCBA divers are subject to many of the same physiological/medical problems as the air breathing SCUBA diver, e.g., embolisms, barotrauma, cramps and squeezes, but those can be left to the standard diving manuals. For now we will study the disorders more closely associated with closed-circuit oxygen divers.

Oxygen Toxicity — Oxygen breathed at high partial pressures (above 1.6 ata) may have toxic effects on systems in the human body. The exact cause of CNS oxygen toxicity is not known but it is associated with biochemical changes in the brain brought on by the high oxygen partial pressures.

The symptoms are better known: primarily convulsions. This is the most serious symptom of oxygen toxicity and is manifested as a fit or seizure. There is often no pre-indication of a convulsion, so the fact that this may occur under water makes the buddy lines essential.

Factors which increase the chance of oxygen toxicity are:

- Increased PP of oxygen, as at depths of 30+ fsw
- Increased exposure time
- Immersion
- Exercise
- Carbon dioxide build-up, which may go undetected
- Cold stress
- Systemic diseases such as certain thyroid or adrenal disorders

There are also non-convulsive symptoms of CNS O_2 toxicity, remembered by the acronym **"VENTID"**:

V — visual symptoms such as tunnel or blurred vision
E — ear symptoms manifested by ringing, roaring or pulsing sounds
N — nausea or vomiting
T — twitching of small facial muscles or extremities
I — irritability, confusion or agitation
D — dizziness

The treatment for oxygen toxicity will depend on whether the diver is convulsive or non-convulsive. If **convulsive** the diver must be brought safely to the surface with a controlled ascent. The victim may suffer a gas embolism but he must be prevented from drowning or aspirating water which could cause long damage. Upon surfacing the diver may require mouth-to-mouth resuscitation and should be rushed to a recompression chamber and treated for a possible embolism.

Non-convulsive divers should signal their buddy to make a controlled ascent to the surface at the first sign of oxygen toxicity. Upon surfacing the affected diver should come off oxygen. His buddy should watch him closely and possibly inflate his life-jacket, since the severity of the symptoms can increase up to two or three minutes after going off oxygen.

Since either occurence could compromise a covert operation or cost a life, only divers with a proven oxygen tolerance should be on the closed-circuit team.

The risk of oxygen toxicity can be reduced by following these suggestions:

- Understand and observe oxygen exposure limits
- Swim at 15-20 fsw
- Swim at a comfortable pace
- Maintain depth and buoyancy control through constant training
- Prep equipment carefully
- Do not exceed canister duration times
- Avoid skip breathing
- Do not swim with a reduced volume in the breathing bag
- Wear adequate thermal protection
- Use an accurate depth gauge
- The buddy with the depth gauge should always be the deeper partner on a swim

Hypoxia — Insufficient oxygen to meet the metabolic needs of the body can also occur with closed-circuit UBA. This is caused by too much inert gas (nitrogen) left in the breathing loop after the pre-dive purging procedure. It can also be caused by the accidental filling of the oxygen bottle with air.

Unconsciousness is often the first symptom of hypoxia but others may be dizziness, convulsions, lack of coordination or confusion.

The treatment is to remove the UBA mouthpiece, follow the ABCs of first aid if unconscious and administer 100% oxygen (not from the UBA).

Carbon Dioxide Build-up — This can be caused by failure of the CO_2 absorbant or poor breathing by the diver. Symptoms are: increased breathing rate, headache, labored breathing, confusion and unconsciousness. The symptoms are dependent on the partial pressure of carbon dioxide and will worsen with depth.

Treatment is to abort the dive, return to the surface and breathe fresh air. The diver should ascend vertically in case the CO_2 build-up was a result of a flooded canister. Staying vertical may prevent a "caustic cocktail."

Caustic Cocktail — This unpleasant term refers to the introduction of a caustic solution from the CCBA into the diver's upper airway. It is caused by water leaking into the absorbent canister and combining with the Sodasorb to form an alkaline solution. This solution is irritating to the mouth, esophagus and upper airway.

Choking, gagging and burning will make a caustic cocktail hard to miss. Immediately assume an upright position, use the manual bypass on the UBA, exhale through the nose and make a controlled ascent.

If fresh water is available, rinse several times and swallow water. If only sea water is available, rinse but do not swallow.

The victim should seek immediate medical attention and if the ascent was uncontrolled, possibly recompression.

DIVING PROCEDURE

Before any individual or agency anticipates diving a closed-circuit rebreather they must first study the operations manual of the particular rebreather (LAR V, CCR 25, AGA Oxydive, Emerson, etc.), then study the U.S. Navy guideline to Closed-circuit Oxygen Diving and finally, and most importantly, get **professional instruction** from the factory or the Navy.

Submerged swim time with a CCBA is dictated by several factors apart from the diver's physical condition and resistance to cold. There is the oxygen partial pressure exposure limits, the Sodasorb canister duration time (affected by temperature) and the capacity of the oxygen bottle.

Even though the Navy allows **single** excursions below the recommended 20 fsw, these are not recommended for police divers and should only be used in extreme situations. The U.S. Navy single depth oxygen exposure limits are:

25 fsw — 240 minutes
30 fsw — 80 minutes
35 fsw — 25 minutes
40 fsw — 15 minutes
50 fsw — 10 minutes

A **Successive Oxygen Dive** is considered any dive within two hours of the previous oxygen dive. After more than two hours **off O₂** the dive can be considered the same as an **Initial Oxygen Exposure.**

Divers may fly immediately after oxygen diving, unless the oxygen dives were part of a multiple-UBA profile in which the divers also used air or nitrox.

As stated earlier, the carbon dioxide absorbent has a limited operational use time that will vary with canister size and water temperature. Warmer waters are more conducive to longer dives. The Drager LAR V canister duration times for various temperatures can vary as follows (based on a diver oxygen consumption rate of 1.3 liters/min.):

Degrees (F)	Time (min.)
40	115
50	135
60	155
70	200

SAS divers prepare for a training dive with closed-circuit breathing apparatus   (CCBA).

Because of the risk of oxygen toxicity the buddy system is extremely important when diving oxygen rebreathers.

Since civilian and police divers are not required to go to the extremes of time, distance or depth required of military combat swimmers, **NOAA** recommends that oxygen dives should be limited to 75 minutes at 25 fsw and that the maximum depth should be 40 fsw for 10 minutes.

For complete pre-dive, dive and post-dive procedures with the Drager LAR V the reader is directed to the Navy Experimental Diving Unit, Report No. 7-85, Closed-Circuit Oxygen Diving by F. K. Butler Jr. LCDR, MC, USN.

CLEANING & STORAGE

As with any equipment subjected to salt water, the rebreather must be rinsed and dried after use. Refer to the Operator's Manual for each individual type of rebreather, but in general it will go as follows:

- Secure system, close valves and rinse in fresh water
- Record oxygen bottle pressure
- Close supply valves, vent system, remove bottle, replace protective cap and plug regulator
- Fill oxygen bottle
- Remove hoses, canister and breathing bag. Clean and dry.
- Reassemble with dive/surface valve in the open position
- Record dive duration in rig log
- Check all of the above on Draeger Post-dive Checklist, sign and date

Carleton MK-16 UBA

284

20
TACTICAL DIVING PRINCIPLES

Even though the police diver may aspire to be a pseudo-SEAL, he will probably never be in good enough physical condition to even qualify for BUD/S (Basic Underwater Demolition/SEAL) training, let alone complete a SEAL mission. Secondly, and more to the point, no law enforcement agency will have the time, budget or inclination to train a dive team to that level of expertise. This does not mean that an agency could not put together a very effective tactical diving team to handle most tasks on a **limited scale.**

As long as the SRT divers are in above average physical condition, are willing to train and learn, don't mind getting wet and have adequate equipment, a tactical capability is well within their grasp.

Whether it be Navy Spec Warfare, maritime counter-terrorism, water-front hostage rescue or shipboard drug interdiction, the basic tactical principles are very similar. The following guideline can be modified to suit most agencies involved in SRT diving and covert swimming.

PREPARATION

An operation can only be a success if the preparation is complete and meticulous. The team must have:

- Adequate training and physical conditioning
- A high standard of individual skills
- Rugged, proven equipment
- Good intelligence
- Adequate rehearsal time
- A thorough briefing
- Escape and evasion plan
- Pre-op individual equipment check

APPROACH CONSIDERATIONS

Before a team tries to cover open water, either on the surface or below, there must be available cover-fire in place. Snipers are ideal for this task but there should also be a vehicle, helicopter or boat mobile rescue team ready to come in fighting. Other considerations are:

- Time limitation of CCBA or SCUBA
- Distance
- Water temperature, sea-state, weather forecast, boat traffic
- Ambient light level and available shade/shadows
- Ambient noise level from ships, machinery or aircraft
- Covered routes under pilings, docks, bridges, etc.
- Ship or building blind spots
- Alertness and spacing of sentries
- Security support equipment; night vision, spotlights, flares, etc.
- Deception plans and location of diversion

All of the above will come from good intelligence, surveillance and logged observations.

The next order of business is an in-depth understanding of the principles of camouflage, concealment and movement. There are many ways that an inexperienced or careless diver can blow a covert operation. Detection may occur as a result of a noise, a movement, a reflection or just poor judgment in selecting a route in. Whatever the cause the results are the same — failure. Only practice and experience can make a truly good combat swimmer out of a police diver, but there must also be a working knowledge of fundamental tactics.

The buddy system is an important part of Spec Ops diving, especially when using closed-circuit breathing apparatus, as seen in use by these French combat swimmers.

MOVEMENT

The human eye has a natural attraction to movement, as any hunter can testify to as he looked directly at game but did not see it until it bolted. Careless movement by a diver/swimmer can have a disastrous result. Avoid the following:

- Excessively fast surface swimming
- Kicking or splashing on the surface
- Creating any ripples or waves
- Carelessly breaking the surface from a dive
- Making bubbles in calm, open water

NOISE

Noise, like movement, can be a dead give-away, especially since noise travels well over water. Quiet nights are potentially more hazardous than periods of rain, heavy wave action, frequent boat traffic or high ambient noise levels from dock cranes, machinery, wildlife or wind. Some sources of unwanted noise from the team are:

- Voice communication
- Unexpected radio transmissions
- Weapons hitting against hard dive gear
- Accidental discharge of firearms
- Metallic noises from weapons or equipment
- Water related splashes during entry
- Climbing on wood or steel ships/structures
- Positioning ladders or climbing ropes
- Bubbles against the underside of the hull
- Positioning magnetic mines or demo charges

LIGHT

Less critical during daylight hours, the careless use of a flashlight, match or cigarette at night could compromise the whole operation. The diver must also study the light he is moving in or through. Avoid:

- Accidental or careless use of lights
- Wharf or ship floodlights
- Muzzle flashes
- Indiscriminate or accidental use of flares
- Swimming out of shadows or dark patches
- Smoking
- Illuminating gauges

REFLECTION

Reflection refers to light catching any shiny or reflective surface on the diver. The faceplate of the diving mask must be shielded from reflection when on the surface. It can be removed or turned to the back of the neck upon surfacing. Flashlight lenses, binoculars, camera or night vision lenses must be carefully hooded. Shiny metal parts on the regulator, mask retaining ring, backpack or weapons systems may need to be painted or taped.

The diver must also be cognizant of the fact that as he leaves the water he will be wet and somewhat reflective. This is especially so in smooth-skin wet suits or vulcanized-rubber dry suits.

SHAPE

The human outline is uniform in shape and very recognizable at a distance. To disrupt this smooth outline, jungle fighters and snipers will hang branches, leaves and pieces of material from their fatigues. A diver also has a distinct outline, especially when surface swimming or leaving the water to move inland. As a diver:

- Make maximum use of rocks and shadows to confuse outlines
- Avoid skylining yourself on high ground or open areas
- Keep a low profile in the water
- Use cloth and weed to disrupt humanoid shape
- Avoid grouping on team operations
- Maintain spacing in the water
- Make maximum use of available cover
- Select next cover/concealment before moving out

This diver should make maximum use of the rocks for concealment and avoid standing in open water.

288

COLOR

The diver must be aware of not only the color of his suit and equipment but also the color of the background he is moving over or in front of. A black wet-suit on white sand is far from the ideal, just as light or bright colors on a dark background are quite visible.

Light facial skin tones must be covered with camouflage, blond hair must be covered by a hood or ski mask and hands should be gloved or blackened. Camouflage uniforms can be worn over swim trunks in warmer regions, and over exposure suits in cooler waters. All equipment must be taped or painted in dull, matte colors to match the terrain or structures.

TRACKS

Sandy beaches and soft ground are just two mediums that will hold a footprint long after the infiltrator has passed. This may be all that is needed for an observant guard to sound an alarm. Wet footprints on decks, docks or concrete will also show the divers' passing, unless it is a hot, dry night and the prints have had time to dry. But even if they dry there may still be sand deposits to cause concern and further investigation.

Any equipment used to infiltrate, and abandoned on the way out, such as ladders, ropes, or inflatable boats, will alert the suspects to the operation. If the mission was one of intelligence gathering, the information that was collected will be compromised and of little future value.

This assault swimmer risks exposing himself as he moves from a darker background in front of the light colored concrete.

Conclusion: study your targets and approach routes carefully. Plan your moves for maximum concealability. Allow ample time to get in and get out silently. Carry only essential equipment and weapons. Stay close to your buddy; he may be your only source of rescue in cases of exhaustion, cramps, hypothermia or hypoxia.

Dark cold water is the home of the combat swimmer. This French diver receives a final brief before the swim in.

The bubble-free CCBA is the optimum system for covert approaches. Note compass attack board and buddy-line.

BASIC ARMED TACTICS

Operational tactics must be as flexible as possible to meet the unpredictable reactions of an adversary. However, all plans are based on some basic tactical principles:

Know your enemy — Know his numbers, location, armament, prior record, probable reaction, the stakes involved and his mental stability.

Fire and movement — Whenever covering open ground, a support team must be capable of laying down cover-fire in the dive team's defense.

Maximum use of cover — Concealment hides the diver but cover stops bullets. Always know the nearest available cover during a tactical operation or approach.

Firepower superiority — Never engage an enemy that outnumbers you or has greater firepower. Wait for support, use coordinated assaults, make effective use of automatic weapons and always have a reserve force.

Surprise — The element of surprise will reduce casualties, increase chances of success, allow a smaller force to defeat a larger one and stun the enemy. Stealth, imagination and silence are all paramount to surprise. Attack when least expected and from the less than obvious direction.

Speed — Like surprise, speed and the aggressive use of force will reduce the chances of sustaining casualties or of the suspects destroying the evidence. Speed also reduces exposure time to hostile fire and confuses the enemy.

Accuracy — An attack that is fast but lacks effect, causes casualties and reduces a potential success to failure. Target selection and the **discriminate** use of deadly force are the hallmarks of a professional SRT team.

Diversion — Loud noises, flash-bangs, stun grenades, intense light or simulated fire can all draw the suspects' attention and give the team precious seconds of advantage to gain entry.

For a more complete study of special weapons and tactics the reader should obtain a copy of **"ADVANCED WEAPONS TRAINING FOR HOSTAGE RESCUE"** by Mark V. Lonsdale, from STTU or a local police book supplier.

Assault swimmers should stay low in the water for maximum concealment and be sure to camouflage exposed skin, face and hands. Note water-proofed radio in Bruno bag.

As one swimmer climbs the wall the other covers with an SMG. Note the climber's weapon slung out of the way on a TEAM sling.

Divers must practice shooting immediately upon surfacing. Suppressors are used to eliminate sentries.

SEALS coming ashore as combat divers cover their movement.

Law enforcement divers with narcotics recovered during interdiction hull search

21
INTELLIGENCE OPERATIONS

One of the primary tasks of combat swimmers in wartime is to collect data on enemy beaches, port facilities, coastal defenses, shipping schedules and troop movements. The law enforcement diver can be used in a similar role, but with the apprehension of felons in mind. Government intelligence agencies, like the CIA, may have use for fully trained combat swimmers, but this is far beyond the scope of the SRT dive team.

More realistically, SRT intelligence operations will involve the surveillance of suspect locations and the mapping of possible assault routes for a drug bust or SWAT operation. Additionally, since the military cannot be utilized in a counter-terrorist role, within the continental U.S., a shipboard assault or rescue would fall at the feet of the FBI Hostage Rescue Team.

Ships moving in and out of U.S. ports may be suspected of smuggling drugs, either in pods under the hull, or by dropping them overboard at discreet locations. Divers may be able to spot the pods or record the drops for future action by the DEA, U.S. Customs or local police.

State and Federal wildlife agencies can utilize divers to collect information on commercial fishermen, fishing nets, lobster pots, traps, poachers and hunters. Many USFWS confrontations occur at sea or on rivers where fish and game regulations are being violated.

COLLECTION TECHNIQUES

The method of intelligence collection will be dictated by the nature of the operation. Some operations will carry a high risk factor to the divers while others will be relatively safe and free from danger. One consideration is whether the suspects are considered armed and dangerous and would attempt to shoot at the divers if detected.

The approach and tactical aspects of intelligence gathering are almost the same as those outlined in Chapter 20. It is imperative that the divers not compromise their own safety, or the success of the operation, by accidentally exposing themselves to the suspect location. Divers should only be used in situations where other intelligence gathering techniques are ineffective.

Suspect Surveillance: When a marina or boat is being used to conduct some form of illegal business, e.g., drug distribution, exotic wildlife smuggling, gun running, stolen boat brokering, etc., divers can be pre-positioned to try to observe the transactions. Information to record could be:

- Time and nature of transaction
- Number and description of persons involved
- Boat's name, nationality and registration
- Size and design of boat, estimated performance
- Berth number and location
- Vehicles observed
- Weapons carried by suspects
- Number of security guards observed

A diver may be able to slip right under the planking, below the actual transactions and overhear parts of the conversation. This could supply the agency with information about future suspect movements, and possibly a name or piece of intelligence of value.

Another ruse that an undercover agent can use in a marina is to pose as a marina diver actively involved in cleaning boat bottoms, replacing zincs and doing minor maintenance. This gives an agent an excellent opportunity to be in close proximity to the suspect's boat or office.

Boat or Ship Surveillance: In situations where there is no specific suspect, it may be a ship or boat that is suspected of illegal activities. The drug lanes from Colombia and the Caribbean are wide open to the boat captain who is willing to carry drugs and contraband. U.S. Customs are quite thorough in their searching of the holds and cabins of arriving ships but there is seldom time for a complete search below the waterline.

Ships should not be approached from underwater while in motion, but the hulls can be searched once they have moored or anchored. Even the short time involved in a Coast Guard stop may give the diver an opportunity to check for pods.

When a ship or boat has a known berth, divers can be pre-positioned under the docks to search the hull, before the suspects can remove any packages that were smuggled in. If packages are found, the divers may choose to wait and apprehend the perpetrators in the act of removing them.

Shipboard Raid Planning: There are much faster and safer ways to assault a boat than from under water, but the intelligence gathered by divers may greatly assist in the raid planning. If no other route is feasible, the assault may have to come from the seaward side, in which case the divers will play a more active role.

Some information worth gathering would be:

- Size and description of boat or ship
- Name and country of registration
- Estimated range and speed
- Construction of hull and superstructure
- Number and location of open hatches
- Height of deck from waterline
- Proximity of dock or other boats
- Number of anchors set, if applicable
- Activity observed on deck
- Guards on deck or dock and weapons seen
- Ropes, fenders or ladders over the sides
- Degree of difficulty to approach and scale
- Ambient light and noise level on deck
- Security cameras or security system if evident
- Engines or generators running
- Timetable of guest/owner movement and crew shift changes
- Additional power boats tied to the mother ship
- Helicopter or heli-pad

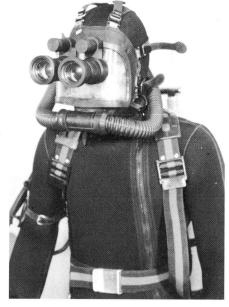

Israeli night vision goggles designed for underwater operations.

Wharf or Dock Assault: Intelligence should be collected on the following:

- Materials used in construction
- Design
- Height from water level
- Tidal range
- Ladders, bumpers, ramps or hand-holds
- Ambient lighting and noise level
- Boat traffic
- Marine growth on piles and braces
- Pedestrian and vehicular traffic
- Proximity of power boats, fuel docks and buildings
- Suspect location and distance from water
- Distance from available cover
- Locations for sniper/cover team

Beach or Shoreline Assault: Collect intelligence on the following:

- Nature of objective
- Sand, rock or cliffs
- Shape of shoreline
- Wave action, wave height, currents, rip-tides and swells
- Marine growth, kelp and marine life
- Ambient light and noise level
- Proximity to roads or structures
- Nearest available cover-concealment
- Bottom contour
- Natural or man-made obstacles
- Distance from waterline to objective
- Distance to hinterland and vegetation
- Vehicular or pedestrian traffic
- Possible escape routes
- Possible locations for sniper/cover team

For all forms of intelligence gathering, the divers will require a waterproof slate to record details, a watch to record times, a compass for bearings and possibly binoculars and night-vision equipment. Underwater cameras with high-speed film can be used to photograph anything of interest. Be sure to use lenses that are suitable for photography in air (the Nikonos V with a 35mm or 80mm lens works well). When swimming with slates, the divers must take care not to erase the penciled notes accidentally.

The divers should be debriefed immediately after an operation, while the information is fresh in their minds. They will need to take their notes and slates and transfer all the recorded data to paper while they can still read their own scrawl.

Hypothermia will be a major limiting factor, even in warmer waters. Select wet suits or dry suits that will keep the divers warm enough for the long, slow swims and the lack of activity while observing.

Divers should carry personal weapons for self defense, in case the operation is compromised and they draw hostile fire. If the divers have SCUBA or CCBA they can probably just dive to escape, but surface swimmers will need to utilize available cover and concealment.

Divers should only be deployed for intelligence gathering in conjunction with a larger support operation. In a worst-case scenario, the rest of the narcotics enforcement or SWAT team must be prepared to come to the divers' assistance. The divers can alert the rescue team to their predicament by the use of flashlights, radios, strobes or flares. The Mk 13 day/night flare or a strobe should be carried on all night swims.

EFCOM pinger locator.

Visual and audible signal.

Pinger transmitter components.

Surface tracking option.

French CINC divers using closed-circuit breathing apparatus were responsible for the mining and sinking of the Green Peace flagship "Rainbow Warrior" in Auckland Harbor, New Zealand.

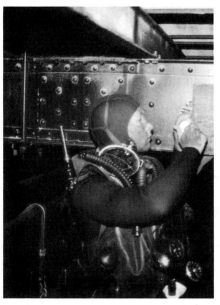

French DINOPS diver positions explosive device and sets time delay mechanism under a steel bridge.

22
UNDERWATER EOD SEARCH

There are literally hundreds of places for a criminal, extortionist or terrorist to conceal a bomb, that are a lot more convenient than under water. But, after careful consideration, one will realize that explosive devices placed below the water-line are the hardest to find, the most difficult to identify and a curse to disarm.

Military combat swimmers are trained to infiltrate enemy installations underwater, position demolition charges for maximum effect and exfiltrate before their deadly packages explode. The total tonnage of military and merchant shipping that has been sunk at the hands of UDT/SEALs, or enemy sapper divers is staggering, and a tribute to the frogman's determination, skill and ingenuity.

Any time a military tactic, like underwater demolitions, is honed to a science, it is only a matter of time before a crazed or misguided individual applies this art to some form of criminal activity.

When the bad guys adopt a tactic, law enforcement must develop a counter-tactic. In this case, underwater Explosive Ordnance Disposal, abbreviated to EOD. EOD specialists are usually attached to the military, while most law enforcement agencies refer to their resident experts as Bomb Technicians. Most bomb techs receive their basic training at the military EOD schools, and then continue it through membership to organizations like IABTI (International Association of Bomb Technicians and Investigators).

The job of actual identification, handling or disarming of explosive devices is exclusively reserved for highly trained EOD personnel, with the proverbial "nerves of steel." But since these gentlemen, and ladies, are in short supply, law enforcement officers and agents can be trained to handle the initial search and evacuation. This holds true for the SRT dive team that may be required to check ships, docks or bridges for suspicious packages, hoax or real.

The following are just some of the situations that may require underwater EOD search:

- Secret Service Advance Detail site surveys
- Cruise line extortions
- Dock, wharf or marina extortions
- Union strong-arm/intimidation tactics on the waterfront
- Threats against ships of specific nationality
- Terrorism directed against oil loading facilities
- Extortion of oil companies
- Protests of nuclear powered ships or submarines
- Attempted assassination of a Saudi prince on his private yacht
- Homicide attempt of a wealthy/private boat owner
- Explosive munitions accidentally dropped overboard during loading
- Diplomatic security in a maritime environment
- An attempted take-over of a drug running operation
- Investigation of boats sunk under suspicious circumstances
- Investigation of planes that suspiciously crashed into the water
- Hoaxes associated with all of the above

EXPLOSIVE IDENTIFICATION

Explosive identification classes have become a common feature of tactical conferences, and a regular part of many police academy programs. Basic and advanced classes can usually be arranged through the local bomb squad or military EOD unit. All law enforcement personnel, especially patrol officers and tactical teams, should be familiar with the more common forms of explosives and their local distribution.

The nature, construction and placement of an explosive device can tell the investigators a lot about the background and level of sophistication of

Corroded and encrusted unexploded shell lies on the sea bed. These hazards should be handled with considerable care and only by experienced EOD personnel.

302

the bomber. Experts in world terrorism and bombings are able to tell which political or religious group is responsible for a bombing, or attempted bombing, by the type of explosive used and the manner in which it was rigged. Often all the bombs used by a terrorist faction will be manufactured by one bomb maker. The construction and effect of each bomb identifies the bomber as clearly as a fingerprint or known MO (modus operandi/method of operation).

For training purposes we can divide explosives into six categories:

Military Ordnance — Grenades, shells, rockets, mortar rounds, anti-tank weapons, explosive projectiles, mines, claymores, aerial bombs, basic explosives, satchel charges, bangalores, etc.

Improvised Military Munitions – Booby-traps, rerigged shells or rockets, altered mines and grenades, raw C4 with simple initiators, devices made with TNT or det-cord, etc.

Underwater Military Ordnance — Limpet mines, Mk133 & 135 u/w demo packs, specially made shaped charges for cable and chain cutting, magnetic mines, floating mines, bottom anchored mines, torpedos, etc.

Commercial Explosives — Construction charges, mining explosives, primer cord/det-cord, time/safety fuse, blasting caps, binary two-part explosive compounds, tri-mix, quadra-mix, shaped cutting charges, canister charges, boosters, etc.

Homemade Explosive Devices — Booby-traps, flares, fireworks, pipe bombs, mortars, rockets and anything that may be found in the Anarchist Cookbook or survivalist literature.

Improvised Underwater Devices — Homemade floating mines, magnetic mines, demolition charges or hoax devices.

Explosive devices can also be categorized by the nature in which they are initiated. That is to say, what exactly triggers the explosion. It will usually be one of the following:

- Mechanical time delay/viscosity
- Electrical time delay/watch
- Movement/anti disturbance switch
- Temperature change/thermal sensor
- Proximity to metal/magnetic switch
- Chemical reaction/electrical current
- Movement through water/venturi/impeller
- Altitude/barometric pressure
- Mechanical pressure switch/plunger
- Radio controlled/acoustical/ultra sound
- Electrical switch/booby-trap
- Command detonated by hard wire
- Command detonated by suicidal bomber

As it should now be coming evident, explosive devices can come in any shape, size, color or form. The nature of the device is only limited by the imagination and ingenuity of its creator. Anything that appears to be out of place, suspiciously located or attached, must be treated as a device until EOD says otherwise.

SEARCH PRINCIPLES

Since the underside of a ship or structure is the hardest place for a criminal to locate a bomb, the obvious must be searched first: topside. If the search is a routine check requested by a protective detail, then topside and underwater searches will continue together. If the search is being conducted in response to a specific underwater threat, the ship and dock must be evacuated first.

Searches fall into three categories:

- Response to specific threats
- Routine underwater security checks
- Investigation of an explosion

Investigation of an explosion is basic police work that will be directed by the bomb squad. The investigators will be primarily interested in any pieces of the device that may remain, the amount of damage and witness observations. The divers will have to do a thorough grid search of the surrounding sea bed for any small pieces of wire, timer, batteries, casing or debris that may be even remotely connected to the incident.

Damage will need to be sketched, photographed and measured before the ship or structure is disturbed. Each piece of the device found will need to be logged, to assist in estimating the blast radius and size of device.

Routine underwater security checks can be long, boring tasks if the threat level is low. The obvious places are searched first, followed by the less obvious. A plan must be established and adhered to, to be sure of covering every square inch of the job site. The diving supervisor will sketch out the location, assign areas of responsibility, brief the divers and supervise their progress. As areas are declared "clear," the supervisor will log the time and location and reassign the divers to a new search site.

Clear water will greatly speed and facilitate an EOD search, but will be seldom found in metropolitan harbors where most work is done. Bomb searches should be avoided at night or in rough weather. The chance of missing a device is too great, and the danger to the divers is unwarranted.

In low visibility the diver must mentally picture his assignment, be it a hull, piling, sea wall or bridge support, and then systematically search it by feel. If he is tethered to the surface, he can signal when he finds something out of the ordinary. Surface monitored video is an excellent aid on this type of operation, since the camera can "see" better than the human eye.

Under a hull, the divers will swim linear patterns, starting at the waterline and working down, or at the keel and working up. To speed the procedure, several divers can be connected with buddy-lines, and then swimming in a line across/under the hull, sweep the whole ship in one pass. Pay special attention to engine intakes, sonar and electronic equipment, the screws and rudder, zinc anodes, thruster tunnels, bilge keels, pad eyes, outlets and recesses.

The seabed under a dock or ship should be searched in the same manner as any other bottom search; circular patterns, linear patterns, grid searches, etc.

Diver receives briefing before EOD search from Diplomatic Security advanced team.

Police divers performing EOD hull searches must be familiar with all the hardware and fittings found underneath a ship. The round object in this photo is a sacrificial zinc anode, not an explosive device.

Inert limpet mine manufactured by British Aerospace-Naval and Electronics division for EOD diver training.

Setting controls for magnetic Exercise Limpet Mine show 2-120 minute firing timer and anti-lift switches to prevent removal.

PROCEDURE

When responding to a specific threat, the divers may not be the first on the scene. If an explosive device is involved, or a hoax device, the bomb squad will be the first responders. They will take control and supervise the evacuation of the surrounding area, ships and docks. A command post will have been established, which the Diving Supervisor will report to upon arrival.

The team can begin preparing their equipment, setting up the dive site and awaiting a briefing. The dive site should be within the outer perimeter, but a safe distance from the suspected device. The size of the perimeter and dive site location will be dictated by the size, location and nature of the device.

Hard-wire communications are very useful for EOD searches, either the lightweight Mk 5 Buddyline or full surface-supplied gear. Through-water communication, wireless single-side band and diver recall systems should generally not be used on EOD operations. The radio signals and emanations could trigger devices that are operating on similar frequencies. EOD divers will even go to the extent of diving specially manufactured, non-magnetic diving gear. This is to offset the chance of triggering a mine that is sensitive to metals or magnetic fields.

Consult with the EOD team before using any underwater or topside communications or electronic equipment.

If the device has already been identified and located, the average SRT dive team should not be committed to the water. This is now the responsibility of EOD divers. The rescue and recovery team may be kept on site to assist the EOD divers with equipment and in the case of an explosion. If the device does detonate it will become a rescue or recovery operation.

Where the device has not been located, the SRT divers may be called upon to help the EOD divers search for it. In this case the EOD supervisor will handle the briefing, with the SRT team's diving supervisor on hand to handle dive safety and procedure.

Before the divers can be committed to a hull search, the ship's engines, steering gear and intakes must be shut down. The captain must be notified that divers are going under his ship, and his full cooperation is required for their safety. A guard can now be placed on the controls so that no other crew member inadvertently turns anything on that may endanger the divers or detonate a device.

The EOD personnel will lay down the exact procedures to be followed if a suspicious package is discovered. The first part is easy: "DO NOT TOUCH IT." Note the location and immediately notify the EOD supervisor. The SRT diver can then guide an EOD team back to the device, and back off as soon as they have located it. When approaching or working around a device, the divers must be aware of currents, swells, surges and ship movement. An unexpected surge or movement could carry the diver right onto the device that he is trying so hard to treat with caution. As soon as one diver finds something, he should notify his buddy immediately, so that the buddy can also stay clear of the object.

Once EOD is on the job, the SRT divers should leave the water as soon as possible. An accidental detonation in the water, of even a small device, sends out a shock-wave that can cripple or kill a diver if he is too close.

DISPOSAL

What the EOD divers and bomb techs decide to do with the device will depend on where it is located, the apparent difficulties of disarming it on site, or the possibility of simply blowing it in place. Crude, homemade devices may prove no problem to the bomb techs but a sophisticated military magnetic limpet mine may prove too much. They may as well cut out the entire hull section, around the device, and move it to a safer location.

Before any work is done to remove or disarm a device, all the ship's internal compartments and hatches should be sealed. This will minimize the potential damage and lessen the ship's probability of sinking.

In busy ports or commercial waterways the EOD team may choose to tow the vessel to a more secluded site, or shallower water, before attempting to continue with the operation. When the value of the ship is small, and the risk to the EOD divers great, they may choose to blow the device in place and write the ship off.

A device on a high-pressure oil pipe, between a production platform and a refinery, or storage tanks and a loading buoy, could create more complex problems. The pipe will need to be shut down and the line purged with salt water. Only after assurances from the oil company officials, and verification by law enforcement representatives, should EOD work commence.

Warning: Bomb disposal is a very specialized field that requires extensive training and experience. There is no such thing as a "simple bomb." Even the most basic pipe bomb can be booby-trapped with an anti-disturbance device. If an SRT dive team is to be involved in bomb searches, they must receive special training and work under the supervision of the bomb squad.

U.S. magnetic mine

EOD diver on MK16 mixed-gas rebreather

23
ASSAULTS

It must be stressed again that few law enforcement agencies will ever reach the necessary level of training, fitness and experience to be able to successfully assault an objective from under water. But there are many other methods for assaulting maritime or coastal targets other than just with the use of divers/assault swimmers. The following is a broad overview of just some of the techniques that can be used in law enforcement SRT operations.

SHIP ASSAULT

The assaulting of ships is a difficult and specialized task at the best of times. Where a law enforcement team may have gained considerable experience in SWAT operations in residential dwellings, banks and apartment buildings, this will not prepare them for the complexities of shipboard exercises.

Firstly, the team must learn the layout and construction methods used in ship building, and spend many hours of study and rehearsal on several different ship designs. Cruise liners are quite different from oil tankers, just as large private yachts differ in design from cargo or container ships.

Some of the key points to study are:

- Overall design and layout
- Size of passageways, stairwells and doors/hatches
- Materials used in construction of bulkheads
- Operation of hatches and ports
- Location of key areas like the radio room, passenger compartments, engine rooms, bridge, captain's cabin, etc.
- Alternate access routes
- Thickness of windows/ports in bridge and passenger areas
- Location of fire suppression systems
- Nautical nomenclature and signs

Unlike wooden walls in a house, the steel bulkheads of a ship will cause serious ricochet problems during live-fire entries. The glass laminates used in the ports will also create unique deflection problems for the sniper element, which can only be eliminated by frequently shooting through similar mediums on the range and logging the data. Hatches are generally made of steel and cannot be breached as easily as wooden doors, but they are seldom locked. The steel deck surfaces can be extremely slippery when wet, and difficult to move quietly on without soft rubber boots. Expended shell casings can roll around on the deck and cause a fall if stepped on. Add to all this the fact that the ship may be rocking, rolling or pitching, resulting in a challenging assault.

The method used in the assault will depend on whether the ship is at anchor, at sea or tied up alongside a dock; moving at sea being the most difficult and requiring a simultaneous boat-helicopter assault. Tied up to a wharf is the easiest, utilizing a land assault force and a helo attack. At anchor in open water, combat swimmers, boats and helos should be deployed, each serving as a diversion for the other.

SEA TO SHIP

The team's intelligence efforts will dictate the best methods of approaching and boarding a ship from the water. The things to look for and take advantage of are boarding ramps and ladders still in place; ropes, fenders and bumpers near the water line that can be climbed; open service hatches in the hull of the ship that may give direct access to the lower decks; smaller tender boats tied up alongside that can be used as assault platforms; a low stern or transom that will facilitate a boarding.

Without any of these tactical advantages, the divers can still swim in with several long, padded assault ladders that can be prepared under water, pushed up the side of the ship and hooked over the railings or scuppers. The divers can then swarm up and over the sides at multiple locations. This movement can be covered by sniper fire, gunboats, helicopter gunships or fast roping teams.

BOAT TO BOAT

Boat to boat boardings are a common part of the drug interdiction program being run by U.S. Customs, U.S. Coast Guard and DEA. The only use for divers on this type of operation would be to recover evidence thrown into the water or personnel who have fallen overboard.

The actual assault team would function very similarly to a shore-based entry team except that they would need to add a personal flotation device (PFD) to their kit. The amount of equipment that they carry should also be reduced to a minimum to facilitate climbing, crossing and boarding. The amount of ammunition and support equipment carried will be dictated by the size of the ship to be searched, the number of suspects and the level of threat. Primary weapons should be on slings so that they are not accidentally dropped overboard when both hands are needed for boarding drills.

The suspect boat should be stopped and engines cut before any boarding is attempted. Although boats can be boarded at speed it is an unnecessarily dangerous practice and best left to "Hollywood." One injury that is common to boarding drills is crushed fingers. This can occur when boarders accidentally get their hands between the railings of the two boats or when suspects try to repel boarders by using clubs, gaffs or boat-hooks. The actual crossing must be carefully timed to coincide with the boats' movements, available cover-fire and the suspects' location.

Boat-hooks, grappling hooks and lines can be used to hold the two boats together while the boarding team is making the assault. If possible, the entire crew of the suspect boat should be ordered onto the decks before the crossing is attempted. The boarding party's movement should be covered by a deck-mounted machine gun, a static cover team or even a helicopter-mounted automatic weapon. In the absence of these, the team should be split into two halves, one covering while the other moves.

In selecting an assault boat one must consider speed, performance, maneuverability, resistance to gunfire and height above the other boat. It is always better to fight down than to have to fight up. An assault boat that has a higher deck and wheelhouse than the suspect boat commands a considerable tactical advantage over the lower vessel. At night the deck-mounted spotlights can also be used to blind the occupants of the target ship.

Assault swimmers relax before a parachute deployment at sea. Faces and hands will be camoed closer to the objective.

313

HELICOPTER TO BOAT

The technique of fast roping was developed specifically for assaulting maritime targets. It allows an entire team to be deployed onto the deck of a ship in the minimum amount of time, without the hassles associated with conventional rappelling. The alternative to fast roping would be helo-jumping but often a helicopter cannot get close enough to the ship's decks because of radio/radar antennas, deck cranes, davits and the raised superstructure.

Oil tankers, large container or cargo ships and ships with helo-pads could be boarded by helo-jumping but it is still very hard for the helicopter pilot to anticipate the rise and fall of the decks. One team member may jump from four feet and the next find that he has to drop 12 feet. With rough seas the ship may well strike the skids of the helicopter with disastrous effects. Fast roping gives the pilot a good margin of error but still allows several team members to be landed in a few seconds.

All helo-ops and fast roping must have some form of cover fire available — either from land, another helicopter or a friendly ship.

SEALS fast rope from UH60 Blackhawk.

Even with fast roping, the landing on a steel deck can be very hard, especially in full kit. Assault team members should wear lightweight boots with ankle support, gloves, lightweight helmets and be prepared to move away from under the helicopter as soon as their feet hit the deck. Several injuries have been sustained by team members landing on top of one another or getting kicked in the head during descent.

If an assault team member falls into the water during the assault, the rest of the team must maintain their momentum and leave his rescue to the support team. This will be the divers and surface swimmers on hand specifically for this occurrence.

SEB team fast ropes onto a drug boat during a maritime interdiction exercise.

SEB shooter supplies cover to ESD diver as he rescues a suspect that attempted to escape by jumping ship.

SEB deputy inspects drug package recovered by ESD diver. The suspects had attempted to ditch the evidence overboard.

SEA TO LAND

There are several land-based targets that may require an assault to come from the sea. These would be extortion targets like oil loading facilities and power stations; terrorist targets like military installations and ports; or the coastal dwellings of wealthy drug lords. In most cases an assault from the land side will prove faster and more effective but an assault from the sea may be less expected.

Houses and installations that are built on the coast, often have substantial amounts of security equipment and fences on the land side but very little on the seaward side. In fact most houses have large open patios and picture windows so that they can enjoy the view.

There are two methods commonly used for beach assault: small, fast boats or assault swimmers. Swimmers and divers are used where a covert approach is critical and the team members can get quite close to the objective without exposing themselves. Rigid Raiders and inflatables are best suited to high-speed surprise attacks where several fully equipped men can be landed simultaneously. The UM series Sillinger boats are particularly well suited to this application and can also be mounted with heavy machine guns and mortars.

These assaults should be in conjunction with a land-side attack so that one serves as the diversion for the other. The search and handling team will need to come in from the land-side to complete the operation and transport the prisoners.

SEAL drops from UH60 Blackhawk.

If the assault objective is an island or has no land approaches, then helicopters should be used to deploy the second team and extract the suspects.

When assaulting from inflatable boats the members straddle the sides of the craft and maintain a low profile. One shooter supplies suppressing fire from the bow, if needed, while the motor-man handles all the controls. As the boat hits the beach or shallow water the team leaves the sides of the boat simultaneously and runs forward, being careful not to cross in front of the bow gunner.

There is a big tendency to jump too early and end up in deep water, so the team leader must initiate the assault only when he knows that the boat is on the beach. If the intent is to actually beach the boat by running it into the sand, the team members must brace for the impact so as not to be thrown forward.

If the choice is to use combat swimmers, ample time must be allowed for the swimmers to get into position before initiating the diversion or other elements of the assault. See Chapter 20 for other tips on tactical approach and assault.

Personnel must be carefully positioned in the assault boat to balance the load.

Marine commandos utilizing the Sillinger TRS 500 UM for high speed boat assaults.

U.S. Special Forces divers establish communications link with land forces. Equipment includes Viking dry suit, LAR5 rebreathers, M16s and compass attack boards. Radios are transported in Viking Special Operations Waterproof Bag (SOWB).

OIL RIGS AND PRODUCTION PLATFORMS

It has often been debated as to which agency is responsible for criminal/terrorist acts against oil rigs within the coastal waters of the U.S. The Navy SEALS are obviously the best equipped and trained for such a task but the military cannot be used for civilian law enforcement within the continental United States. In the North Sea, Europe and the Pacific, teams like the SAS and SBS take full responsibility for the recapture of offshore installations occupied by criminal or terrorist extortionists.

An oil production platform, towering some two or three hundred feet above the water line could prove a real challenge to all but the most experienced teams. As with ships, there must be a period of intense study of the construction, layout and operation of these facilities. Any team members with experience as oil-field divers will be a great asset to a team that is anticipating an assault on a rig.

All rigs are serviced by helicopter and supply boat so there will be both a heli-pad on top, and stairs coming down to the water level, or very close to it. This immediately gives the options of covert swim approach, high-speed boat attack and fast roping from helicopters.

The idea would be to get the combat swim team at least under the rig, but preferably onto it; create a massive diversion and launch a simultaneous helicopter/boat assault with cover fire from other surface vessels and helicopter gun-ships.

SEAL fast attack/intercept boat in action

Like ships, oil platforms are virtually all steel and can create richochet problems when the lead starts flying. There is also the added danger of fire since oil rigs are considered high risk zones and even smoking is forbidden on deck.

The greatest risk to the helicopters is the crane booms, antennas and flare booms that may be all but impossible to see at night if the barricaded suspects have cut the power to the external lights.

Assault teams on boats coming alongside the platforms should be aware of the fact that the suspects will be shooting almost straight down onto the decks, denying anyone cover behind the gunwales or wheelhouse. The villains will also be shooting from a stable platform while the return fire will be less effective since it is coming from a pitching deck.

With all the risks involved in an open assault, the covert swim approach may well be the most effective. Considering the high ambient noise level of a rig and their considerable size, it would be very difficult for a small team of terrorists to cover all access points 24 hours a day. Those that do expose themselves as guards on the lower levels can be eliminated with suppressed weapons before the divers leave the water and make the final assault.

French combat swimmers negotiate an underwater obstacle in the form of an anti-submarine fence.

CONCLUSION

Tactical operations will always be the smallest part of any law enforcement dive team's responsibilities, compared to rescue, recovery and investigative operations. But if an agency anticipates any deployment of their divers in a tactical role, special weapons training will take the lion's share of allocated training time.

Any time SRT personnel may be put into a life-threatening situation, they must be thoroughly trained in all aspects of individual and team tactics, covert approach, hostage rescue, advanced clos-quarter shooting techniques, shooting policy, shoot/no-shoot procedures, prisoner handling and preservation of evidence.

Conventional dive skills like search patterns, diver rescue, low visibility and night diving, light salvage, surface-supplied diving, etc., can be easily maintained with periodic practice. But advanced special weapons operations require intense and frequent training sessions to hone skills, learn new ones and perfect team drills. Scenarios must be created to replicate future problems, fitness must be maintained and procedures modified to counter the criminals' innovative methods for evading the law.

If a tactical dive team is to have a high probability of success, then considerable time, money and manpower will have to go into preparation. There is no value in just "playing SWAT" so that everyone can have a good time and do fun things. Teams confronted with a high probability of tactical deployment in or around water can often get technical assistance from the U.S. Navy, Coast Guard or Special Forces.

SEAL method for swimmer recovery

322

Note the night vision device (NVD) attached to an Aga mask.

A shore-based sniper can cover the approach of the conventional assault teams and SRT divers.

323

APPENDIX "A"

GLOSSARY

ASAP — Arctic, sub-arctic, aquatic, para-rescue

BAIL-OUT — A small emergency air supply used for surface-supplied operations

BAND-MASK — A commercial diving mask that consists of a fiberglass frame banded to a rubber hood, e.g., DSI-18

BELL — Pressurized capsule used in deep diving operations

BELL WIRE — Bell lift cable

BIBS — Oxygen masks used in recompression chambers / Built In Breathing System

BLEED-OFF — To slowly reduce pressure

BLOW-DOWN — Pressurize a chamber or bell

CCBA — Closed-circuit breathing apparatus

CHAIN STOPS — Used to anchor a steel cable during recovery operations

CLUMP WEIGHT — A bottom weight used as an anchor for a search line

COMMO — Communications

CONTROL VAN — Diving control center

DCS — Diving control system

DCS — Decompression sickness

DDC — Deck Decompression Chamber

DEA — Drug Enforcement Administration

DECON — Decontamination

DMC-7 — Aquadyne helmet

DIR – Doing it Right

DRI — Dive Rescue International

DRAIN VALVE — A valve used to bleed excess moisture from a volume tank

DRY BAG — Slang for a dry suit

DRY HABITAT — An underwater chamber for living or welding

DS — Diving Supervisor

DSI — Diving Systems International

ECU — Environmental control unit

EDU — Experimental Diving Unit

EOD — Explosive ordnance disposal

ESD — Emergency Services Detail / LASD

ESU — Emergency Services Unit / NYPD

FLUSH — An exchange of gas in a chamber to reduce carbon dioxide levels or change percentages

FSW — Feet of sea water

GAS — Generic term for all breathing mixtures including air

GAS RACK — Control panel of breathing mixtures

HABITAT — Underwater living chamber

HARNESS — Strong chest or full body harness used as an attachment point for the diver's umbilical
HAT — Slang for a helmet
HATCH — Door in a ship, chamber or bell
HAZ-MAT — Hazardous Materials
HELLE — Brand of surface to diver radio
HOSE — Slang for umbilical or tether
HOT — Slang for electrical current "on"
HP — High pressure
HRT — Hostage Rescue Team
ICSURT — Imperial County Sheriff's Underwater Recovery Team
KMB — Kirby Morgan Bandmask
LASD — Los Angeles Sheriff's Department
LP — Low pressure
MEDICAL LOCK — Small transfer lock in a recompression chamber
NITROX — Nitrogen/oxygen gas mixture
NTSB — National Transportation Safety Board
PLATFORM — Oil rig
PNEUMO — Pneumofathometer type depth gauge taped into the diver's umbilical
PONY BOTTLE — Small SCUBA cylinder used as a bail-out system
PORT — Window in a ship or chamber
PORT — Left side of a ship
PSI — Pounds per square inch
QUADS — Large gas supply cylinders arranged in special handling frames
RCV — Remote control vehicle/video
RIG — Oil platform
ROV — Remote operated vehicle/video
SAS — Special Air Service
SAT — Saturation diving
SAT SHACK — Saturation system control room
SBS — Special Boat Service, Royal Marines
SCRUBBERS — Carbon dioxide filters filled with Soda-sorb
SEAL — Sea, air and land — U.S. Navy combat divers
SEB — Special Enforcement Bureau/LASD
SF — Special Forces
SLACK — Letting out the diver's umbilical
SPECOPS — Special operations
SPECWAR — Special warfare
SRT — Special Response Team
SSD — Surface-supplied diving
STAGE — A steel cage used to lower the diver into the water or recover him
STARBOARD — Right side of a ship

STRONG-BACK — Support beam on a pressurized hatch
SUBMERSIBLE — Small commercial mini-submarine
SUR-D-O_2 — Surface decompression using oxygen
SUPERLITE — DSI helmet
SURFACE PACKAGE — Surface-supplied diving system as opposed to a bell/sat system
SWAT — Special weapons and tactics
TELEDYNE — Gas analyzer
TRANSFER CHAMBER — A small chamber that allows divers to move from the storage chamber to the bell under pressure
TRANSFER LOCK — A division in a chamber that allows personnel to enter and leave without changing the pressure in the primary chamber
TREATMENT TABLE — Recompression schedule used to treat the bends or embolisms
UMBILICAL — Divers' gas, communication and safety line all in one bundle
UW — Underwater
VOLUME TANK — A pressure tank attached to an LP compressor to prevent fluctuations in the divers' supply pressure
WHIP — High pressure line

ADDITIONAL TITLES
AVAILABLE FROM S.T.T.U.

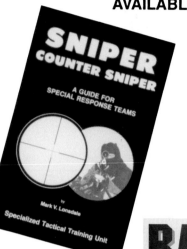

APPENDIX "B"

RECOMMENDED READING

U.S. Navy Diving Manual
U.S. Navy Diving Technical Manual
NASAR Guideline for Public Safety Diving
NOAA Diving Manual
Stress and Performance in Diving — by Arthur J. Bachrach and Glen H. Egstrom
Advanced Diving Technology and Techniques — NAUI
Cave Diving Manual — NSS-CDS
Manual of Cave Rescue Techniques — NSS
On Rope — NSS
U.S. Navy Salvors Handbook
Handbook for Riggers
Dive Rescue Specialist Training Manual — by Linton, Rust and Gilliam
The Underwater Investigator — by Corporal R. G. Teather, C.V.
Adventures in Underwater Rescue — by Liam F. Rooney
The Dry Suit Diving Manual — by Steven M. Barsky
The Nikonos Handbook — by Jim and Cathy Church
Special Forces Waterborne Operations — FM 31-25
U.S. Navy SEAL Combat Manual
Advanced Weapons Training for Hostage Rescue Teams — by Mark V. Lonsdale/STTU
Sniper Counter Sniper — by Mark V. Lonsdale/STTU
CQB — by Mark V. Lonsdale/STTU
Raids — by Mark V. Lonsdale/STTU
Sniper II — by Mark V. Lonsdale/STTU
Bodyguard – by Mark V. Lonsdale/STTU
Alpine Operations – by Mark V. Lonsdale/STTU

Additional periodicals:
    Response — NASAR
    Emergency
    Rescue
    Air Beat — ALEA
    Sources — NAUI
    Searchlines — IADRS

www.STTU.com

EXTREME
EXPOSURE

APPENDIX "C"

DIVING EQUIPMENT:
EXTREME EXPOSURE - Equipment made by Explorers for Explorers
www.extreme-exposure.com
800/378-7820; 352/377-2547; Fax 352/378-1862
HALCYON DIR EQUIPMENT
940 NW 1st Street, Fort Lauderdale, FL 33311
954/462-5570 Ex208; Fax 954/462-6115; www.halcyon.net
DIVE RITE MANUFACTURING, INC
117 West Washington Street, Lake City, FL 32055
904/752-1087; Fax 904/755-0613; www.dive-rite.com
OCEANIC
2002 Davis Street, San Leandro, CA 94577-1211
510/562-0500; Fax 510/569-5404
OMS – OCEAN MANAGEMENT SYSYTEMS
PO Box 146, 23 Factory Street, Montgomery, NY 12549
914/457-1617; Fax 914/457-9497; www.omsdive.com
SCUBAPRO
1166-A Fesler St, El Cajon, CA 92020
619/402-1023; Fax 619/402-1523; www.jwa.com
ZEAGLE SYSTEMS
813/782-5568; Fax 813/782-5569; www.zeagle.com

COMMERCIAL DIVING EQUIPMENT:
DECA DIVING
333 E. Haley St, Santa Barbara, CA 93101
805/564-1923; Fax 805/962-3120
DSI – DIVING SYSTEMS INTERNATIONAL
425 Garden St, Santa Barbara, CA 93101
805/965-8538; Fax 805/966-5761
AMRON INTERNATIONAL
759 West 4th Ave, Escondido, CA 92025
760/746-3834, Fax 760/746-1508; www.amronintl.com
EXTREME EXPOSURE
7607 NW 29th Place, Gainseville, FL 32606
800/378-7820; 352/377-2547; Fax 352/378-1862
www.extreme-exposure.com
GLOBAL MFG - Gas flow systems, fittings and analyzing.
800/558-1811; 414/774-1616
www.gmcscuba.com   Sales@gmcscuba.com
BROWNIES THIRD LUNG
954/462-5570; www.browniedive.com; www.halcyon.net

COMMUNICATIONS:
OTS - 2950 Airway Ave, D-3, Costa Mesa, CA 92626
714/754-7848, Fax 714/966-1639
www.oceantechnology systems.com
TEA Inc.
2022 Route 22, PO Box 404, Brewster, NY 10509
310/457-7401; Fax 310/457-0023; Fax 914/278-0964

LIGHTS:
EXTREME EXPOSURE
800/378-7820; 352/377-2547; Fax 352/378-1862
PELICAN PRODUCTS – Lights and Cases
23215 Early Ave, Torrance, CA 90505
800/473-5422, 310/326-4700, Fax 310/326-3311
PRINCETON TEC - 800/257-9080; 609/298-9331; Fax 609/298-9601

CAMERAS & VIDEO:
GATES UNDERWATER PRODUCTS
5111 Santa Fe, Suite H, San Diego, CA 92109
619/272-2501; Fax 619/272-1208; www.gateshousings.com
LIGHT & MOTION INDUSTRIES
831/645-1525; Fax 831/375-2517; www.lmindustries.com
AMPHIBICO – www.amphibico.com

INSTRUMENTATION:
UWATEC / SCUBAPRO
1166-A Fesler St, El Cajon, CA 92020
619/402-1023; Fax 619/402-1523; www.jwa.com
BEUCHAT USA Inc
305/548-3483; beuchatusa@worldnet.att.net
OCEANIC
14275 Catalina Street, San Leandro, CA 94577-5589
415/352-5001; Fax 415/352-4803
OCEAN REEF - Digital Depth/Bottom Timer
760/744-9430; Fax 760/744-9525; www.oceanreefgroup.com
RJE INTERNATIONAL
949/833-8423; Fax 949/833-8557; www.rjeint.com

DIVING SUITS:
AEROSKIN – 415/551-2400; www.aeroskin.com
BODYGLOVE – www.bodyglove.com
DUI - 1148 Delevan Drive, San Diego, CA 92102-2499
800/325-8439; 619/236-1203; Fax 619/237-0378;
www.DUI-Online.com
TRELLEBORG VIKING
800/344-4458; 603/463-1236, Fax 603/436-1392

USIA UNDERWATER EQUIPMENT
800/247-8070; 503/366-0212; www.usia.com

DECOMPRESSION PROGRAMS:
ABYSMAL DIVING INC - Advanced Dive Planning Software
    6595 Odell Place, Suite G, Boulder, CO 80301
800/55 ABYSS; 303/530-7248, Fax 303/530-2808;
WWW.ABYSMAL.COM

REBREATHERS:
HALCYON DIR EQUIPMENT
    940 NW 1st Street, Fort Lauderdale, FL 33311
    954/462-5570 Ex208; Fax 954/462-6115; www.halcyon.net
CARLETON TECHNOLOGIES
    3910 Riga Blvd, Tampa, FL 33619
    813/623-3711; Fax 813/693-5373
DRAEGER SAFETY
    412/787-8383; www.draeger.com
STEAM MACHINES Inc
    310/937-5200; Fax 310/937-7555

TACTICAL EQUIPMENT:
BIANCHI INTERNATIONAL
    800/477-8545; Fax 909/676-6777
    www.bianchiinternational.com
BLACKHAWK INDUSTRIES
    1133 Executive Blvd, Chesapeake, VA 23320
    800/694-5263; 757/436-3101; Fax 757/436-3088;
    www.blackhawkindustries.com
EAGLE INDUSTRIES
    400 Biltmore Dr, Suite 530, Fenton, MO 63026,
    314/343-7547; Fax 314/349-0321
SAFARILAND
    3120 E. Mission Blvd, Ontario, CA 91761
    909/923-7300, Fax 909/923-7400
SHOMER-TEC
    P.O. Box 28078, Bellingham, WA 98228
    360/733-6214; Fax 360/676-5248
TAC-ORD – Tactical Ordnance and Equipment Corp
    PO Box 428, Meridian, ID 83680
    208/288-1450; Fax 208/288-1451; www.tac-ord.com

WEAPONS:
ROBAR (Handguns, Rifles, Coatings)
     21438 N. 7th Avenue, Suite B, Phoenix, AZ 85027
     623/581-2648, Fax 623/582-0059
WILSON COMBAT
     2234 CR 719, PO Box 578, Berryville, AR 72616-0578
     800/955-4856, 870/545-3310
NOVAK'S - P.O. Box 4045, Parkersburg, WV 26104
     304/485-9295, Fax 304/428-6722
D&L SPORTS - P.O. Box 651, Gillette, WY 82716 - 307/686-4008

SCOPES & MOUNTS:
LEUPOLD & STEVENS
     P.O.Box 688, Beaverton, OR 97075 – 503/646-9171
PREMIER RETICLE – 703/722-0601
     920 Breckinridge Lane, Winchester, VA 22601 - 703/722-0601

ROPE RESCUE GEAR:
CMC – CALIFORNIA MOUNTAIN COMPANY
     800/235-5741; 805/562-9860; Fax 805/562-8260
     PO Drawer 6870, Santa Barbara, CA 93160-6870
     www.cmcrescue.com

BOOKS & TRAINING MANUALS:
STTU - P.O.Box 491261, Los Angeles, CA 90049
     Fax 310/829-0868; www.sttu.com
BEST PUBLISHING
     2355 North Steves Blvd, PO Box 30100, Flagstaff, AZ 86003
     520/527-1055; Fax 520/526-0370

SPECIALIZED TRAINING:
S.T.T.U. - SPECIALIZED TACTICAL TRAINING UNIT
     P.O. Box 491261, Los Angeles, CA 90049
     Fax 310/829-0868; Web: WWW.STTU.COM
TEES – Tactical Explosive Entry School
     800/970-8337; www.tees-training.com
GLOBAL UNDERWATER EXPLORERS – www.gue.com

Author training with LASD-ESD Air 5 rescue crew

APPENDIX "D"

NASAR
National Association for Search and Rescue
Diving and Water Rescue Committee
P.O. Box 3709, Fairfax VA, 22038

DAN
Divers' Alert Network
www.dan.ycg.org
919/684-2948

IABTI
International Association of Bomb Technicians and Investigations
P.O. Box 6609, Colorado Springs, CO 80934

IADRS
International Association of Dive Rescue Specialist
201 N. Link Lane, Ft. Collins, CO 80524-2712
1-800-IADRS-911, 303/224-9101

NAUI
National Association of Underwater Instructors
813/628-6284; FAX 813/628-8253

PADI
Professional Association of Diving Instructors
1251 East Dyer Rd., Santa Ana, CA 92705

THE COUSTEAU SOCIETY
www.cousteau.org

NSS-CDS
National Speleological Society – Cave Diving Section
www.caves.org

NACD
National Association of Cave Diving
P.O. Box 14492, Gainsville, FL 32604
www.AFN.org/~NACD

NTOA
www.NTOA.org

NOTES

COMING IN 2000

SRT 2

EXTENDED RANGE

DIVER

DEEP RECOVERY OPERATIONS
NITROX & MIXED GAS DIVING
DECOMPRESSION DIVING
CAVE & WRECK PENETRATION
REBREATHERS
SUPERVISION OF DIVING OPERATIONS
POLICIES & PROCEDURES

By
Mark V. Lonsdale
Specialized Tactical Training Unit

SRT DIVER 2

LONSDALE

S.T.T.U.

www.sttu.com
For a full list of current titles